HOW TO
cheat IN
Unity 5

Bound to Create

You are a creator.

Whatever your form of expression — photography, filmmaking, animation, games, audio, media communication, web design, or theatre — you simply want to create without limitation. Bound by nothing except your own creativity and determination.

Focal Press can help.

For over 75 years Focal has published books that support your creative goals. Our founder, Andor Kraszna-Krausz, established Focal in 1938 so you could have access to leading-edge expert knowledge, techniques, and tools that allow you to create without constraint. We strive to create exceptional, engaging, and practical content that helps you master your passion.

Focal Press and you.

Bound to create.

We'd love to hear how we've helped you create. Share your experience: **www.focalpress.com/boundtocreate**

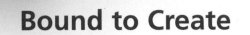

HOW TO cheat IN Unity 5

Tips and Tricks for Game Development

Alan Thorn

Focal Press
Taylor & Francis Group

NEW YORK AND LONDON

First published 2016
by Focal Press
70 Blanchard Road, Suite 402, Burlington, MA 01803

and by Focal Press
2 Park Square, Milton Park, Abingdon, Oxon OX14 4RN

Focal Press is an imprint of the Taylor & Francis Group, an informa business

Library of Congress Cataloging in Publication Data
  Thorn, Alan.
  How to cheat in Unity 5 : tips and tricks for game development/
  Alan Thorn.
  pages cm
  Includes index.
  1. Computer games—Programming. 2. Unity (Electronic
  resource) I. Title.
  QA76.76.C672T4965 2015
  794.8′1526—dc23
  2015000628

ISBN: 978-1-138-80294-0 (pbk)
ISBN: 978-1-315-75397-3 (ebk)

Typeset in Minion Pro and Myriad Pro
by Florence Production Ltd, Stoodleigh, Devon, UK

Printed and bound in the United States of America by Sheridan Books, Inc. (a Sheridan Group Company).

Contents

v

Introduction

Cheating is traditionally regarded as a "bad thing"—as something to be avoided and criticized. But, cheating shouldn't be understood in that narrow way for *this* book. The word "cheating," when used here, conveys only one aspect or feeling from the traditional idea. This book is a catalogue of easy-to-follow, but lesser known, tips and tricks that speed up and enhance your productivity in Unity, giving you more from less—plain and simple. This makes the tips *seem* or *feel* like a kind-of *cheating*. It's in *this* more *positive* sense that cheating is meant. Cheating to be recommended rather than avoided.

By reading this book, you'll see how to achieve *better* results in Unity by doing *less* work. There's an inverse proportion here. And that'll make you a more powerful game developer. Game development is largely an exercise in project management, generally speaking of course. It's about bringing together many aspects, including people, ideas, time, resources, and skills, and about mixing those together in an ideal balance for creating a quality product that gamers will *want* to play for a long time to come. To help you achieve that, this book lists practical tips and techniques in bite-sized chunks, and these are specifically targeted to optimize your workflow in virtually all aspects of Unity. These are the kinds of chunks you can pick up and read anywhere, either altogether in a concerted sitting or randomly while traveling on a train or an airplane. In sum, they'll make the familiar Unity software seem strange, because you'll see Unity in new ways and potentials you may never have seen before.

The aim of the tips is to help you get things done with *fewer* people, in *less* time, and from *less* money and resources. The tips are mostly obscure or "lesser-known," and they'll sometimes seem so simple or trivial that their benefit may be difficult to spot, at least initially. That's why, along with the tips and tricks themselves, I also detail ways the tips can be *applied* practically. This will help you appreciate their true relevance in an everyday context. Some tips, taken alone and used sparingly, might save you only a few "bucks or pence," or only a few minutes of time. But, taken in combination with other tips and applied both consistently and appropriately throughout your projects, the total savings and optimizations you'll make will be significant. Right now, you've only got my word for that, but once you put the tips into practice they'll speak for themselves.

Introduction

As it stands, Unity can already save you lots of time when making games. That's one reason developers choose the engine in the first place, as opposed to making their own. But, even within Unity, there's still lots more we can do to save *even more* time and money. And that's exactly what we'll see everywhere in this book. So let's get started at being cheaters.

What Is This Book About?

This book reads like a semi-ordered collection of field-tested and powerful tips for working with Unity. Want to see quick and powerful ways to use Empty GameObjects? Want to know an easy method for creating split-screen games? Or want to know simple steps for improving your game's performance on mobile devices? This book can help. These are just some of the tips we'll be covering. The tips can essentially be read in any order you like as they all "stand alone" in an important sense. But, in terms of their presentation here, they are collected together by subject matter and usage value across 10 in-depth chapters. For almost every tip, there are two broad sections: **The Main Tip** and **Alternative Applications**. Let's see what these do:

The Main Tip

Each tip usually begins with a clear statement of a practical problem or obstacle that you may encounter when making games in Unity. For example, you may feel your code always performs poorly on mobile devices, though you can't really explain why, or perhaps your textures aren't looking as good as you wanted in-game, even though they're looking great in Photoshop or GIMP. These are examples of problematic symptoms. With them, you always get the intuition you're either doing something wrong or could be doing something better. This book outlines problems in this way, and then confronts them head-on.

It's been said that understanding a problem clearly is half the solution. So after stating the problem, there's a solution. This shows you a solid tip, workaround or technique for overcoming the problem directly. It outlines not simply *any* solution, of course (for there may be many), but a generally relevant and strong solution that you'll probably want to use on all your other Unity projects to come. The solution will be detailed in a step-by-step way, with accompanying screenshots. In many tips, the screenshots alone will probably tell the whole tale, and the written text will act more like a supplement to clarify and detail further should you be interested. But, for some tips (those involving code especially), more text and reading will be required to fully understand them. So my recommendation to you in general is to always read the text, even if you think the screenshots say it all. That way, you'll get the most from the book and not risk losing out on any useful tips.

Alternative Applications

For many tips, there'll also be an Alternative Applications section, which will directly follow the main tip section. In this section, I consider possibly unforeseen and alternative ways in which the same solution can be applied differently to solve other problems. The idea with this section is to help highlight the versatility and power of seemingly specific and focused solutions, to show how those solutions can be removed from their narrower context and recycled elsewhere with a minimum of fuss. Reading and absorbing the information contained here can give you enormous power when making games, because from it comes a developing ability and "way of thinking" that lets you reuse the solutions you have already to do so much more with almost no extra work.

Target Audience

Every book has a target audience, and this book is no different. The target audience simply represents the imaginary people that I keep in mind when writing. I write *as though* I'm talking to *those* people. This helps you get the book you expected, written in clear and concise language that's accessible for you and delivers what you wanted to know. Inevitably, however, to write effectively for the audience and to keep focused, I must make educated assumptions about the knowledge and skills you have already when picking up this book. In short: this book is aimed at people who already know the fundamentals or basics of Unity. You may have taken a university degree in game development, or you may have used Unity for creating sample projects or small games. The point is: I'm assuming you have a basic degree of fluency in the Unity software, though it really doesn't matter how you got that know-how. It matters only that you have it. I'm assuming you know about concepts like *Projects*, *Scenes*, *GameObjects*, *transformations*, the *Object Inspector*, *viewports*, and other GUI features. I also assume you can write and read basic script files in any one of the three supported languages, *JavaScript*, *C#*, or *Boo*. The script samples presented in this book are all written in C#, so it's expected that you can at least understand and adapt C# code, if required. Beyond this, however, the book requires no additional or specialized knowledge. If you know the basics of Unity, then you should be ready to go!

But, what if you don't feel like you have the required knowledge? Then, my recommendation is to first study the basics of Unity and C# before continuing with this

Introduction

title. Of course, it's certainly no part of my purpose to discourage or push away anybody who is keen to learn and willing to succeed. No doubt there're people who could discover Unity for the first time through this book and feel much benefited by it. But, with structured and sequential learning in mind, I'd recommend *beginning* with a fundamentals course. You can learn the basics of Unity through my *Unity Fundamentals* book, published by Focal Press, ISBN: 978-0-415-82383-8. And you can develop your coding skills with C# through both my online video course *Introduction to C# Scripting in Unity*, published by 3DMotive, and further through my book *Pro C# Game Development with Unity*, published by Apress, ISBN: 978-1-430-26746-1. These courses together encompass more than the full range of knowledge I'm assuming you're bringing to this book.

Why Is This Book Necessary?

I believe this book holds a special and unique place among the Unity game development literature. As far as I'm aware, it's the only book around to focus specifically on Unity tips and tricks. There're plenty of books covering the Unity basics, and also books on more "advanced" and specialized subjects, such as networking and shaders. But, this is the only book to take a more general and wide-ranging tips and tricks approach, an approach with relevance for almost all Unity users, whatever your specialization and intentions. However, the value of the book may still be questioned by the skeptical. Their challenge runs as follows: "Game development is a technical and open discipline. As such, there's no secret or arcane wisdom to be gained here. This means everything you have to say has probably been said already, and can already be learned independently online for free from forums, articles and videos. And so, there's no value at all in this book." Now, what can be said in reply to this?

It must be admitted that there's probably no secret or magical knowledge about Unity revealed only in this book. Indeed, all the tips, techniques, and workflows covered here have probably been discussed collectively by many others elsewhere, or have been used by the sum total of professionals making games on an everyday basis. There's nothing secret about the information here. And indeed, most of the information can probably be learned online through dedicated searching and crawling, given enough time. But, none of this is a legitimate criticism of the book, because its chief value is not derived from the secret-ness or unknown-ness of its contents. Rather, it's from the power and versatility of the tips, and from the convenience of their presentation. This book collects together *lesser-known* and *useful* tips gained from hard research, dedicated testing, and varied experience. And it presents those tips in easily *digestible* and *bite-sized* chunks. This helps you take away the *core knowledge* necessary, allowing you to *apply* the tips *quickly* in your own projects, saving you considerable time and effort from independent research and experimentation. And that can be a significant saving when you want to make games for a living.

Does This Book Teach Everything about Unity?

No. This book doesn't teach everything there is to know about Unity. The reason is because no book or video, or even the Internet, could do that. Unity is not like a book that can be read entirely from beginning to end. It's not a thing that, once known, has nothing else to offer. Rather, it's a tool (and one that changes!). It has a potentially infinite number of uses and applications, limited only by your imagination and skill as a developer. What this book inevitably lacks, then, in comprehensiveness, it more than makes up for in usefulness and focus. It gives you *quick* and *easy* tips for achieving *tough* and *laborious* tasks that might otherwise take a long time. This is an important benefit because game development, taken as a whole, involves lots of time and work. Time in this sense is a wasting resource: once it's spent, you can't get it back. So it makes commercial and practical sense for all developers to use their time as efficiently and wisely as possible when going about their everyday work. By being careful about time and avoiding its wastage, you get the most from it. You get to do more than you ever could previously. This benefit is known as productivity! And it's exactly this kind of "logistical" and "time-efficient" empowerment that comes from every tip in this book.

How Should the Book Be Read?

One of the things I love about this book is that, for the most part, it can be read however you like! You can read it in the traditional way; that is, sequentially, chapter by chapter and tip by tip. Or, you can flick through the pages, picking up tips at random to see what you get. Or, you can use the chapter headings as guides to search for *specific* tips that are relevant for the work currently at the front of your mind. This book is amenable to all these approaches and more because almost every tip is written to be a stand-alone entity. This means you can read the book from the comfort of your chair at your home or office, or from a train or airplane, or lying in bed or electronically on your tablet or e-book device—almost anywhere, really. However, to get the most from this book, I'd recommend reading it through *first* in the traditional way, chapter by chapter, to get an overview of everything on offer. And then *later* to read it in a reference way, as and when

Introduction

required, to make sure you've picked up on all the tips related to your work in the *here and now*. In short, though: it's important that the book "becomes alive" for you, whichever way you choose to read it. An ancient proverb sometimes attributed to Buddha says: "Tell me and I'll forget; show me and I may remember; but *involve me* and I'll understand." That sentiment applies throughout this title: try to make every tip a part of your habit and workflow. At first, it may seem an awkward fit and tedious. But, once it becomes part of your usual regime, the tips will flow naturally into your work and you'll appreciate their benefits in a very short time.

Is This Book Out of Date Already?

Every book has a lifetime. This describes how long a book remains "alive" and relevant to its target audience; not just for today, but for the foreseeable future. It's about investment. When a reader picks up a book that's "alive," they feel *confident* their time and effort in reading it will be worth the *investment*. A book that doesn't inspire such confidence, however, may be considered "dead." One of the chief threats to a book's lifetime is real-world change. The worry is that the book's content may become misaligned with reality sooner rather than later, because reality may have changed significantly from when the book was written. This problem is especially pronounced today in computing and in the games industry more narrowly. In this field of work, it seems you must always be running merely to stay in the same place. The Unity engine changes frequently, with old features being adapted and new features being added, and there seems no end to this upgrade process. Unity is essentially always a work in progress. For this reason, it's understandable to think the lifetime of this book must be short. However, this concern can be taken too far where it leads to a kind of paralysis, becoming an obstacle to learning anything simply because it may change in future. It's probably true that between my writing this book and your reading it, Unity will have changed to some degree. But, that doesn't mean everything contained here will be invalidated, because it probably won't be. After all, some things change, and some things stay the same. Indeed, most tips presented here are long-standing and have had long-term applicability that's remained across even dramatic feature changes. In selecting the tips, I've been especially careful and mindful of software change, picking those tips that I believe are the most useful and which have the greatest life expectancy. That, of course, doesn't *guarantee* every tip will be as useful or relevant to you when reading this book, because I can't know the future with certainty. But, there's strong reason to think nearly all the tips and techniques here will be solid and useful for the foreseeable future. For this reason, you can approach the book with a confidence and steadiness that it's as alive as any other contemporary computing book.

Companion Files

As mentioned, this book is about tips and tricks for Unity. In demonstrating these, I will sometimes use or relate to example projects, simply to make my meaning clearer in a practical sense. The tips themselves, of course, stand apart from the concrete examples and apply more generally to your own projects and games, and understanding that is critical to benefiting most from this book. Here, I want you to see the tips and tricks in the abstract, and to take those away with you, allowing you to reuse them for your own purposes. However, that being said, I do refer to specific examples in the text and I've provided associated course files where I do so, meaning you can open up the project files and follow along exactly with me, if that's what you really want to do. Overall, however, I'd encourage you to only read the tips and then to apply them to your own work, using your own files, to make them a part of your workflow. The course files for this book can be found at the following URL: www.alanthorn.net.

1

Editor Cheats

This chapter is about some of the powerful but simple things you can do with the Unity Editor, in terms of its menus and options and windows. These tips improve usability and they'll enhance your overall workflow, allowing you to make games faster. Actually, editor cheats like these appear throughout every chapter and not only here. But, this chapter groups together many *general* and *widely applicable* tips, tips that attach themselves to no dedicated use or narrow field. They apply for so many different purposes you simply can't pin them down into just one category.

1.1 Working with Components

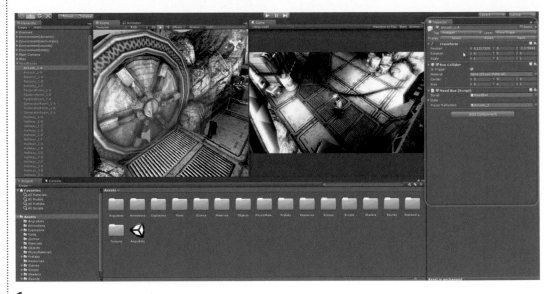

1 The Unity Object Inspector

Components are the essence of GameObjects. They help bring your scenes to life. Because of this, every Unity developer spends lots of time working with Components. The Object Inspector is the main tool in Unity for viewing and editing Component Properties. It's very powerful. ▶1 Let's see more.

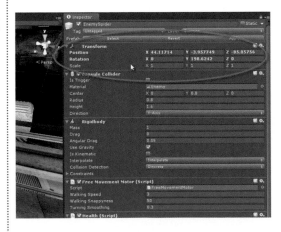

1.1.1 Copy and Paste Component Values

You'll often want to copy and paste *all* values from one component to others, whether in the same scene or not, *without* having to manually copy and paste every property individually, or without having to write initialization code. Doing this is useful when you need all weapons or enemies in a scene to share the same starting values, like health points and ammo. Unity does offer copy and paste functionality, but it's not immediately obvious how it can be accessed. ▶2

To copy and paste all data between a source and destination component from the Object Inspector, first click the *Cog* icon on the source component. ▶3

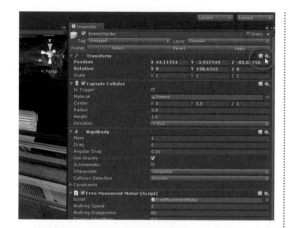

3

Then choose *Copy Component* from the context menu to copy component data to the clipboard. ▶4

4

Then click the *Cog* icon on the destination component, and choose *Paste Component Values* from the context menu. This will overwrite any existing data on the destination with pasted data copied from the source. This technique works with all types of components, just not the native Unity types. ▶5

5

6

You can also choose *Paste Component as New* to instantiate a *completely new* component on the selected game object, initialized with the pasted data. This is especially handy if you're planning to instantiate many components all using the same data across different game objects. ▶6

Alternative Applications: Creating a History Object

Copying and Pasting Component values offers an excellent form of non-destructive editing, when combined with a *History Game Object*. This is a deactivated and improvised object in the scene that serves only to collect a backup of components, from which you can restore data if needed. This creates a kind of "time machine" object, allowing you to revert back to earlier changes by copying and pasting component values. For example, you'll often want to test out enemy characters with specific starting parameters—like health, strength and speed—before settling on final values that work best for your game. This process involves some trial and error, jumping back and forth in Play-Mode between different settings, trying out new values and keeping them if they work, or reverting them back to older settings if they don't. To save you from remembering different values and combinations, you can use *Copy* and *Paste* in combination with a communal History Object in the scene.

7

Create a new game object in the scene by selecting *GameObject > Create Empty* from the application menu (or press *Ctrl + Shift + N* on the keyboard). ▶7

Name this object *History* using either the Hierarchy panel or the Object Inspector. This object will maintain a collection of backup components. ▶8

8

Create an initial state for your enemy character (or other object) and then copy its values using the Cog menu and *Copy Component*. Then *Paste Component as New* on the History object. This creates a *snapshot* of the component in the History object. This can always be pasted back (restored) to the enemy again if we later decide against any new changes we might make. ▶9

9

10

Be sure the History object is *deactivated* in the Object Inspector. It's not supposed to be active in-game. It simply contains an archive of component backups for our own purposes. We don't want its components taking effect at runtime. You can delete the history object when it's no longer needed. In fact, be sure to delete it when compiling your final game. ▶10

11

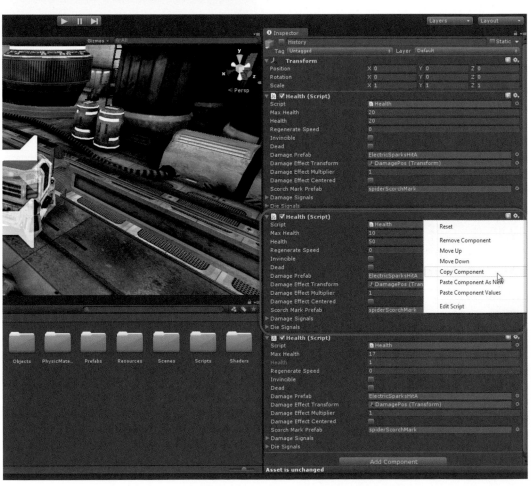

Now go ahead and tweak your component settings as much as you need. Feel free to add more backup components to the history object if you can't decide right away which settings you like. To restore backups, just copy the desired component back from the history object to the original object. ▶11

1.1.2 Resetting and Reordering Components

You'll often want to reset a component back to its starting or default state, *without* manually removing it from the object and then re-adding it to start afresh. Resetting is helpful when you make a mistake entering values in the Object Inspector and can't remember which edit was right or wrong, and so you just want to start over. Additionally, you'll also want to change the stacking order of components in the Inspector, controlling which one appears at the top and which at the bottom. Doing this won't really change how components work on the object at Run-Time, because their stacking order doesn't

matter, technically speaking. But, it's still handy for visual reference and organization, helping you keep track of related components and their purpose. Again, the way to achieve this immediately isn't obvious, but the handy cog menu comes to the rescue once more.

To reset any component back to its default values, click the *Cog* icon for the component and then choose *Reset*. You can also use the shortcut options, *Reset Position*, *Reset Rotation*, and *Reset Scale* if you're working specifically with *Transform* components. Doing this will overwrite all existing values you may have assigned to the component, but you can *Undo* the changes if needed. ▶12

To rearrange the stacking order of components within a single game object, choosing which component should appear higher up in the Object Inspector, you'll need to use the Cog menu. ▶13 Dragging and dropping components won't work—that

12

13

1

method is reserved for *moving* components between different objects. So, simply click the *Cog* icon on the component you need to move, either up or down, and then choose *Move Up* and *Move Down* from the context menu, respectively. This functionality is especially useful for grouping together related components, such as AI components, or for keeping components you edit often toward the top of the Inspector, saving you lots of scrolling time.

Alternative Applications: The Resetting Habit

14 Every time you drag and drop a mesh or game asset from the Project Panel into a scene, it'll be instantiated as a new object. This is standard behavior. Typically, Unity guesses where you want the object positioned based on where you release your mouse in the viewport or on where your viewport is focused. For this reason, a newly added object is hardly ever positioned at the origin. And yet there may be many times when you want automatic origin placement. Your code may depend on origin placement at Run-Time, or you may want to precisely offset objects along a grid, or you may simply be "picky" about precision. For this reason, it can be helpful to cultivate the habit of resetting the *Transform* component of every newly added object, immediately after adding it to the scene. Try it. Using this technique consistently imparts a certain cleanliness to your workflow. ▶14

1.2 Working with the Object Inspector

The Object Inspector is your window for investigating the properties of the currently selected object. It might seem that beyond this, there's not really much else to do. But, that's not the case.

1.2.1 Dual Inspectors

Consider the public C# variable *MyComponent* added to a sample class *FooObject*. Once compiled, this variable will show up as an editable property in the Object Inspector, as expected. This means we can assign it a reference to any component, simply by dragging and dropping one from the object into the *MyComponent* slot. Doing this gives us direct access to the assigned component through the variable *MyComponent*, and we may invoke its functions in script from the *FooObject*. That's convenient because it means we don't need to waste processor time looking up and referencing that component in script at Run-Time. ▶15, 16

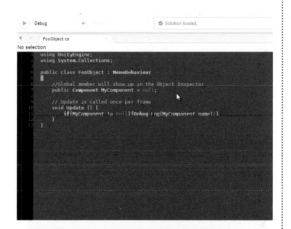

15

16

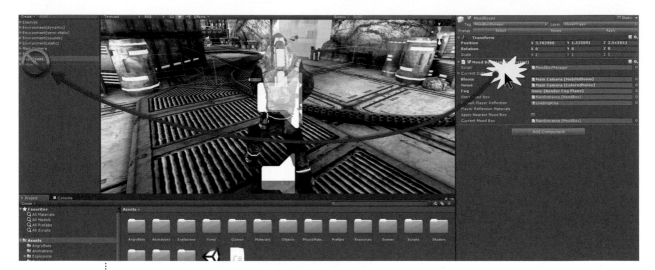

17 But, what happens if we want to drag and drop a component from a *different* object into the *MyComponent* slot of the selected object? How would you do that using the Object Inspector? You *could try* dragging and dropping the component from the source object onto the destination object. However, Unity doesn't understand that you mean to assign a *component reference* to the *MyComponent* slot in the destination. Rather, it assumes you

18

mean to move the *whole component* from one object to another, or it assumes you mean to assign the Transform component. ▶17

Now, at this point, it'd be excellent if we could open up two Object Inspector windows, allowing side-by-side viewing for dragging and dropping components between different objects. But, if you choose *Window > Inspector* from the application menu, nothing will happen if you already have one inspector window open. Let's see how to fix this. ▶18

19

To show two Object Inspectors in the editor, click the Object Inspector *Properties* icon in the top right-hand corner. From the context menu, choose *Add Tab > Inspector*. This adds a new *Inspector* tab. ▶19

You can then undock this tab as a floating window and view both inspectors side by side in the editor. ▶20

20

21

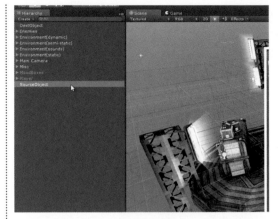

The default behavior of the Inspector is to be context-sensitive, updating to show all properties for the *selected* object. But, we'll need to see two *different* objects, one in each inspector, side by side. To do this, first select the source object in the scene (the object from which we'll be dragging our component). ▶21

22

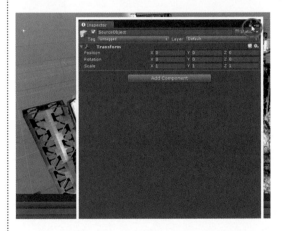

Then lock *one* inspector using the lock icon in the top right-hand corner. It doesn't matter which inspector you lock. This prevents the locked inspector from changing its contents whenever a different selection is made later. ▶22

23

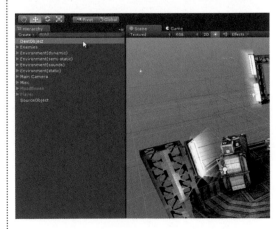

Now select the destination object. This results in two inspectors, one showing the source object properties and the other showing the destination object properties. ▶23

You can now drag *component references* from one object to component slots in the other object. ▶24

24

Alternative Applications: Double Debugging

You can show as many Object Inspectors as you need with this technique. Thus, you can view the properties of many game objects at the same time. This works both in design *and* Play-Mode too. ▶25

25

Consequently, multiple inspectors have debugging benefits. If you need to keep track of multiple objects at Run-Time from the Object Inspector, and you don't want to keep pausing the game to switch your selection between them, then be sure to create multiple inspectors. This technique works even better if you have a multi-monitor setup, viewing multiple inspectors in a secondary monitor!

1.2.2 Array Auto-Generate

Arrays are everywhere in games, usually for keeping together references to many objects in an ordered list, such as GameObjects. One complaint when building arrays in Unity is that it's tedious to drag and drop game objects into each array element individually in the Object Inspector. ▶26

26

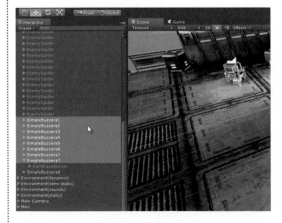

27

But, it turns out you don't have to populate array elements individually! You can actually drag and drop *multiple* objects into an array field. Hold down *Ctrl* or *Shift* while clicking to select multiple. ▶27

Once dropped into the array slot, Unity will automatically generate an array from them. Be sure to drop your objects over the array name field in the Object Inspector. ▶28

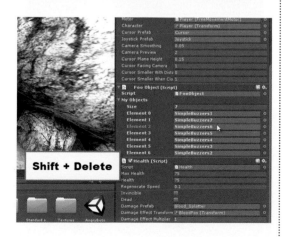

28

Even better, you can easily manage an array from the Object Inspector too. Click an element title in the array to select it, and then press *Delete* on the keyboard to empty the selected element. This doesn't remove the element from the array, but simply *nullifies* it. ▶29

29

To remove the selected element completely, press *Shift + Delete*. ▶30

30

Alternative Applications: The Quick Selector

31

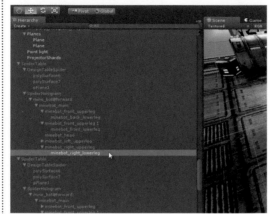

GameObject arrays are especially powerful in the Object Inspector, and in more ways than one. Specifically, they offer a "quick selection" technique. When creating large scenes with many game objects, it can be both tedious and time-consuming searching through complex object hierarchies just to select the object you need—especially if you need to select it many times. ▶31

32

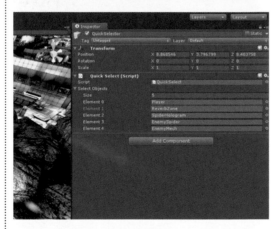

Instead, why not create a new game object named *QuickSelect*, and use a GameObject array to reference all objects you plan on selecting frequently? ▶32

By clicking once on an object in the array, the referenced object will be highlighted in the scene hierarchy, allowing you to locate the object without actually selecting it. Double-clicking the object will select it in the scene. ▶33

▼33

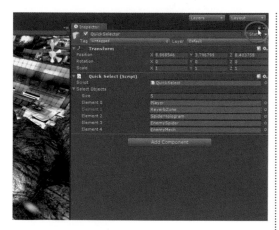

34

When using the Quick Selector, remember to lock the Object Inspector if you don't want its contents changing whenever you select a new object. ▶34

1.3 Working with Viewports

Viewports are your window into the game world. They're a critical feature of the Unity Editor. Navigating around them is easy enough. But it's always helpful to know some extra things you can do too. Let's take a look at these.

1.3.1 GameObjects and View Alignment

Moving the viewport camera around the scene lets you take in the sights and make sure everything is looking good with your layout and design. And sometimes you come across a specific camera angle and shot that really makes your level shine, and you wish you could align your in-game camera to exactly that orientation and position. Well, you can . . . ▶35

35

Editor Cheats

With the perspective viewport positioned where you want it, select your camera object in the scene, probably via the Hierarchy panel if you don't want to move the viewport. And then choose *GameObject > Align with View* from the application menu—or press *Ctrl + Shift + F* on the keyboard. You can also choose *Move to View* instead (*Ctrl + Alt + F*), which only *moves* the game object to the viewport location and its orientation remains unchanged.

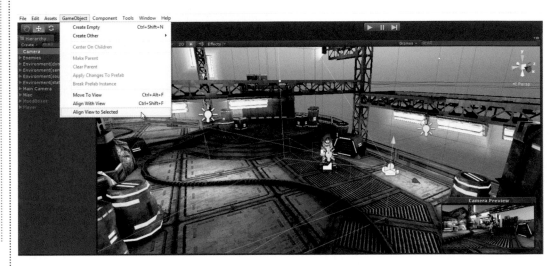

36

In addition, if you ever wondered what the scene looked like from the perspective of a specific object, or if you wondered how the level would look if it were played in first person from a particular character or mesh, then you can do that too. You can align the Scene Viewport with any object by choosing *GameObject > Align View to Selected*. ▶**36**

Alternative Applications: Camera Memory
When level designing and testing large scenes, such as for RPG and RTS games, it's useful to switch between different and fixed camera points, to observe gameplay from vantage points known to offer good views. One way to achieve easy camera switching is by creating empty objects positioned with the *Align with View* command, and then to use the *Align View to Selected* command to switch the viewport camera back to those points.

Create a new, empty GameObject named *CameraViews*. Then create more empty objects, one for each view to save, and Parent them under the *CameraView* object. These will represent all fixed views that we can restore at any time. ▶37

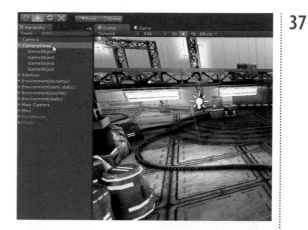

37

For each newly created object, position and orient the Scene Viewport to display the view you want to save. Then select one of your objects, and choose *GameObject > Align with View* from the application menu. ▶38

38

T--I--P

Always give your game objects *unique* and *meaningful* names. If you and others can identify which object is which on the basis of its name alone in the Hierarchy panel, then your naming convention is working!

This saves the current view to the selected object. Be sure also to name the object appropriately to describe the view it represents. This helps you quickly locate the object you need by viewing its name in the Hierarchy panel.

When you've saved all your views to objects, you can restore any of them to the viewport camera. Select the saved view object, and then choose *GameObject > Align View with Selected* from the application menu.

1.3.2 Orthographic Views

39 By default, the Unity Scene Viewport renders in perspective mode, meaning that standard camera and foreshortening effects are applied to the scene. Objects in the distance are drawn smaller and can be seen from many different angles. Most of the time, this is exactly what you want for getting an accurate and useful view of the game world. But sometimes this can get in the way. If you need to precisely position or align objects, or if you're making 2D games, or if you're designing GUIs and other 2D elements, you might want to switch from a perspective view to an orthographic one. An orthographic view is

40 one in which perspective distortion has been removed, meaning parallel lines remain parallel and don't converge at a vanishing point. ▶39

To switch from a 3D view to an orthographic one, you can use the View Cube, positioned in the top right-hand corner of the Scene Viewport. ▶40

Click the center cube to switch from *perspective* mode to *iso* mode (isometric). You can click it again to switch back to perspective mode. ▶41

41

Then click on any of the directional arrows to switch to an orthographic view for that direction: *front*, *side*, *top*, or *bottom*. In this mode, you can worry less about object depth and more about their placement and alignment on a plane. This makes orthographic projection a handy tool for configuring 2D environments and games. ▶42

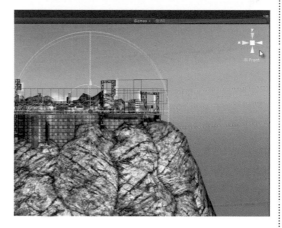

42

NOTE

More information on 2D views and orthographic projection are considered in Chapter 6: Cameras, Rendering, and Lighting.

1.4 Customizing the Editor

The Unity Editor is a powerful tool offering a wide range of features for making game development simpler. But even so, there'll likely be times when the needs of your project will leave you wishing for more. At these times, you could, of course, search the Unity Asset Store for add-ons. But other times, you may prefer to customize the editor for yourself, tweaking it for your specific needs.

Editor Cheats

1.4.1 *ScriptableWizard*

To customize the Editor, you need to create a new class, derived from any of the available types. A full list of acceptable editor classes can be retrieved from the Unity scripting documentation at: http://docs.unity3d.com/Documentation/ScriptReference/index.html. One class to make your friend for quickly and easily adding editor extensions is *ScriptableWizard*. By deriving from this class, you create a new editor window that may be launched as an option from the application menu. All public members of the class will appear in the window as editable fields. Consider the following *ScriptableWizard* class in Code Sample 1.1. Especially important lines are highlighted in bold. This custom tool doesn't really do much—it prints a string to the debug console. But it illustrates the core mechanics of how *ScriptableWizard* works.

Code Sample 1.1: (MyScriptableWizard.cs)—A Class for Extending Editor Behavior

```
01  using UnityEngine;
02  using UnityEditor;
03  using System.Collections;
04
05  public class MyScriptableWizard : ScriptableWizard
06  {
07    //name will display in window
08    public string MyName = null;
09
10    //name of menu option
11    [MenuItem ("Tools/My Custom Tool")]
12    static void CreateWizard ()
13    {
14      //this function is called when the window is created
15      ScriptableWizard.DisplayWizard<MyScriptableWizard>
        ("My Custom Tool");
16    }
17
18    void OnWizardCreate ()
19    {
20      //this function is called when the user presses the
        create button
21      Debug.Log(MyName);
22    }
23  }
```

For this class to work, it must be located inside a folder named *Editor*, in the Unity Project Panel. The *Editor* folder doesn't have to be a root-level folder. It can be nested inside other folders. ▶**43**

43

Line 11 in Code Sample 1.1 determines where in the application menu the extension will be added as a launch-able option. In this case, the extension can be launched by selecting *Tools > My Custom Tool*. For your own editor extension, this path will be different. ▶**44**

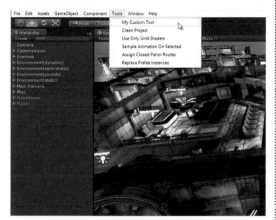

44

The new editor window, when opened, will show all public members of the class as editable properties. When the *Create* button is clicked, the window is closed and function *OnWizardCreate* is executed, allowing you to perform customized behavior. ▶**45**

45

Editor Cheats

Alternative Applications: Batch Rename Tool

One feature that many developers find useful, but which Unity doesn't offer out of the box, is a Batch Rename tool, allowing you to rename multiple game objects in one operation. The *ScriptableWizard* object provides an ideal platform for creating such a tool. Code Sample 1.2 provides the full source code for a Batch Rename tool.

Code Sample 1.2: (BatchRename.cs)—Rename Tool for Multiple Objects

```
01  using UnityEngine;
02  using UnityEditor;
03  using System.Collections;
04
05  public class BatchRename : ScriptableWizard
06  {
07    //Base name
08    public string BaseName = "MyObject_";
09
10    //Start Count
11  public int StartNumber = 0;
12
13    //Increment
14    public int Increment = 1;
15
16    [ MenuItem ("Edit/Batch Rename...")]
17      static void CreateWizard()
18      {
19        ScriptableWizard.DisplayWizard("Batch Rename",
          typeof(BatchRename),"Rename");
20      }
21
22    //Called when the window first appears
23    void OnEnable()
24    {
25      UpdateSelectionHelper();
26    }
27
28    //Function called when selection changes in scene
29    void OnSelectionChange()
30    {
```

```
31        UpdateSelectionHelper();
32    }
33
34    //Update selection counter
35    void UpdateSelectionHelper()
36    {
37      helpString = "";
38
39      if (Selection.objects != null)
40        helpString = "Number of objects selected: " +
          Selection.objects.Length;
41    }
42
43    //Rename
44    void OnWizardCreate()
45    {
46      //If selection empty, then exit
47      if (Selection.objects == null)
48        return;
49
50      //Current Increment
51      int PostFix = StartNumber;
52
53      //Cycle and rename
54      foreach(Object O in Selection.objects)
55      {
56        O.name = BaseName + PostFix;
57        PostFix += Increment;
58      }
59    }
60 }
```

NOTE

The Batch Rename. cs script file is included in the book companion files in the *Chapter01* folder.

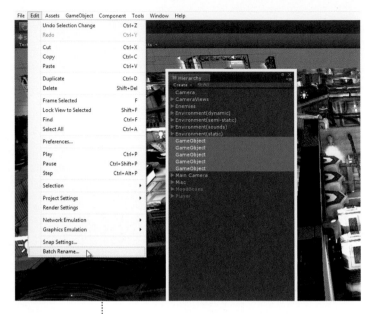

46

To use the Batch Rename tool, select a range of game objects that need renaming, and then choose *Edit > Batch Rename . . .* from the application menu to display the Batch Rename tool window. ▶46

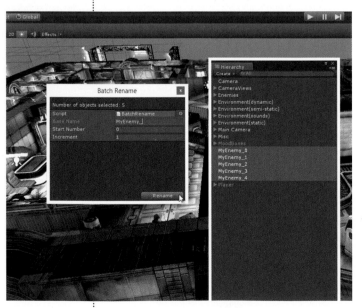

47

Then enter a new base name for all objects, as well as incremental numbering to be appended to the base. Then click the *Rename* button to complete the operation. ▶47

1.4.2 Customizable Editor Keys

Many people feel comfortable with the default Unity keys and shortcuts. But there are times when you may want to change them, especially if you're working across multiple applications (such as Unity and 3D software) and want a consistent control scheme between them.

Though many people think Unity offers no control customization, it turns out that it does offer some. You can access these options first by choosing *Edit > Preferences* from the application menu. ▶48

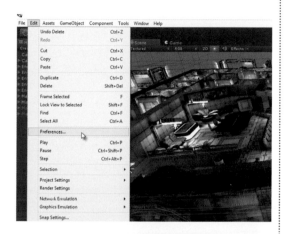

48

Then by selecting the *Keys* tab. From here, you can select some of the most common operations, such as *Window/Maximize*, and assign them new shortcuts within narrow limits. You can also click the *Use Defaults* button to reset the control scheme, if needed. ▶49

49

1.5 Editor Logging

Sometimes you may experience an error or even a crash when working in the Unity Editor. This could be caused by many factors, some of which are attributable to your project rather than to Unity, including "bad" code in script files, such as infinite loops, memory leaks, or other referencing issues. But it could also be caused directly by a Unity bug, or by network latency, or by some kind of incompatibility with other software or hardware. On occasion, it may even prevent you from opening your project files. In these cases and others, you'll want to diagnose the problem and fix it quickly. Even if the problem is the result of a bug that you can't fix personally, there could still be feasible workarounds available until the problem is fixed.

To help you diagnose and assess problems, you can use the Editor Log File, named *Editor.log*. This is a human-readable text file generated every time you run Unity. The file is filled with statements about the running state and initialization steps performed by the editor, and it typically details any problems or errors encountered. It can be a useful file to inspect when troubleshooting, and it can point you in the right direction for resolving an issue. The specific location of the file differs across operating systems, as we'll see. ▶50

50

▶50

NOTE

You'll sometimes find an *Editor-prev.log* file too, alongside the *Editor.log* file. This file represents the log generated on the *previous* run of Unity. This can help you make diagnostic comparisons between different sessions, testing the effects of configuration or hardware changes.

If you can access the Unity Editor, a really quick way to open and view the Editor Log is from the console window. Click on the *Properties* button in the top right-hand corner and choose *Open Editor Log*. ▶51

51

But if you can't access the editor, then you'll need to open and inspect the file manually. For Mac OSX, the Editor Log is located in the folder *~/Library/Logs/Unity/*. ▶52

52

For Windows, the Editor Log is located in the folder *c:\users\username\AppData\ Local\Unity\Editor*. By default, Windows hides this path in Windows Explorer. To show it, you'll need to enable displaying for hidden folders. More information on how to do that can be found online here: http://windows.microsoft.com/en-gb/ windows/show-hidden-files#show-hidden-files. ▶53

53

1 Editor Cheats

Alternative Applications: Text Editor Tools

Accessing and reading Editor Logs touches on the issue of text editor applications. When making games, it's helpful to have a reliable and comfortable text editor to work with for reading and editing configuration files, XML files, JSON files, and other text-based data. MonoDevelop can serve this purpose well. But other text editors can also complement your Unity workflow. Here, I'll introduce two popular and widely used editors.

Notepad++ is a free and popular Windows-only text editor that has many add-ons and features for displaying text files. It offers an extensive range of syntax highlighting schemes for different languages. Notepad++ can be downloaded from: http://notepad-plus-plus.org/. ▶54

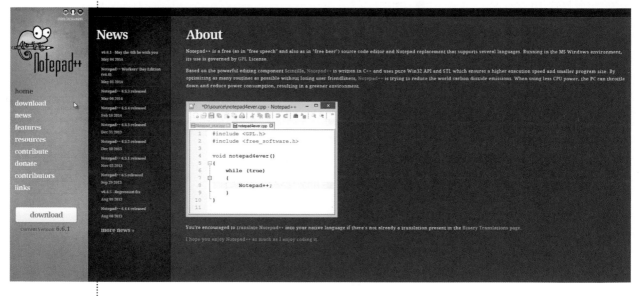

54

Sublime Text is a popular commercial text editor available for Windows, Mac, and Linux. Like Notepad++, it offers syntax highlight for many different languages. Sublime Text can be downloaded from www.sublimetext.com/. ▶55

1.6 Networking Issues

Accessing Unity projects over shared network drives is not recommended, if you want a smooth development experience. But there may be times, if working out of office or at a different location, when your hardware and usability options are very limited. Here, you may have little choice both over how your hardware is configured and how you access Unity projects via a network. One problem that can occur is "getting locked out" of your project. Unity 5 is configured by default to avoid this issue. However, the setting can get changed. When this happens, Unity will automatically open up the last accessed project whenever it starts. This can be problematic because in a networking scenario, it's possible for someone else on the network to have your project open as well on a shared drive. If this happens, Unity will always fail to start on your machine, because the project is already open, and Unity can't have two instances of the same project open at the same time. Unity will not simply cancel opening the project, but will exit entirely—refusing to

56

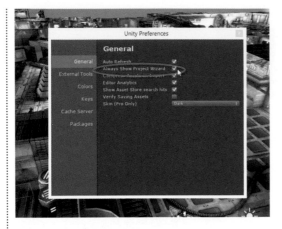

start at all. This means your copy of Unity will always fail to start until the other user closes his or her instance of the project.

You can, however, take steps right from the beginning to prevent this issue ever happening. You can configure Unity to always display the Project Wizard dialog at start-up, as opposed to opening the last accessed project. To do this, select *Edit > Preferences* from the application menu. This displays the Preferences dialog. From here, select the *General* tab and disable the option *Load Previous Project on Start-Up*. ▶56

1.7 External Image Editor

If you're an "indie" developer, the chances are high you use your computer to do lots of other things besides Unity development, like browse the Web, view photos, check email, write documents, create graphics, and more. In these cases, it's convenient to configure image files to open by default in a lightweight image viewing application, such as *Windows Photo Viewer*, allowing quick image viewing whenever you need it. But this doesn't always integrate well with a Unity workflow. Typically, when double-clicking an image file in the Unity Project Panel, you want it to open in your main image editing software, such as Photoshop or GIMP, as opposed to a photo viewer.

You can customize how images open from Unity specifically, using the Preferences dialogue. This lets you leave your default image-opening preferences intact for your operating system, while still allowing you to open images from Unity in your image

57

editing software. To configure this, select *Edit > Preferences* from the application menu. Choose the *External Tools* tab. And then click the *Image Application* drop-down to select your image editing software of choice to use when opening images from the Project Panel. ▶57

2

Asset and Importing Cheats

Every Unity project depends on assets. Assets include textures, script files, meshes, animations, videos, text data, audio, and more. These are the raw materials for games, and they're not typically created in Unity. Rather, they're made by artists in third-party applications, like 3DS Max, Maya, Blender, Photoshop, GIMP, and others. The first step in every Unity project, then, is to import assets from their native files and configure them for optimal use. The process for doing this varies between assets and project types. This chapter considers a range of tips that make general work with assets easier and quicker.

2 Asset and Importing Cheats

2.1 Native versus Exported Mesh Formats

NOTE

More information on supported mesh formats for Unity can be found at the following URL: http://docs.unity3d.com/Documentation/Manual/3D-formats.html.

Meshes (or 3D models) are one of the commonest assets in any Unity game. These are typically modeled in 3D software like Maya, 3DS Max, and Blender, and are then exported to an established interchange format that Unity can read. Unity officially supports many mesh formats, divided into two groups: *Native formats* and *Exported formats*. The Native formats include: *.MAX, .MB, .MA, .BLEND*, and most other kinds of 3D scene files. The Exported formats include: *.3DS, .DXF, .DAE, .FBX*, and many more. The distinction between these two is important for your workflow.

Generally, use *Exported Formats* for your meshes, and *avoid* Native formats. Use Native formats *only* to create and save the master copy of your mesh in your 3D modeling software, allowing you to edit it later, if required. But, otherwise use Exported formats for transferring mesh data into Unity. Native formats come with significant limitations: they result in larger file sizes, they require a copy of the 3D software to be installed on the computer while importing into Unity, they offer less control over the export process, and they are more unreliable generally. Exported formats in contrast are slimmer by featuring only the data you need, they offer the greatest degree of control and tuning over the export process, and they are more portable between Unity versions and systems since they stand alone independently from their original 3D software.

Alternative Applications: Manual Formats

If your game has very specific requirements, or if you simply don't want to use any of the available mesh formats, you can actually create your own. The exact steps on how to do this vary between 3D applications. But most allow for the development of add-ons, plug-ins and customized exporters. 3DS Max offers customization through *MAXScript*, Maya offers *MEL* (Maya Embedded Language), and Blender offers *Python*. Using these, you can write your own exporter to save mesh data into your own format and structure. Unity can also be customized through editor plug-ins to read and import custom meshes, through the *AssetImporter* class. More information on manual mesh generation in Unity can be found here: http://docs.unity3d.com/Documentation/Manual/GeneratingMeshGeometry Procedurally.html.

2.2 FBX Scale Fix

T--I--P

1

Is there an Exported file format to prefer in all cases? In general, it's mostly a matter of preference. Two of the most commonly used in the industry are *FBX* and *DAE*. When creating my own projects, I use one of these two formats. They have a relatively light file size and many different 3D applications can export to them. But choose whichever Exported format works best for you.

The Unity 3D coordinate space officially uses *Generic Units*. This means 1 world unit equals whatever you want it to mean: meters, centimeters, inches, miles, and so on. However, for best performance, 1 unit should be understood as 1 meter. So take time in advance to calibrate your 3D software, to align its coordinate space with Unity's to ensure a 1:1 correspondence. Conveniently, Unity is configured to work out of the box with the default settings in most 3D applications. However, if you're importing meshes with the FBX format, sometimes people find their mesh scale is always initialized to *0.01* on import. Or sometimes they just want to override the default settings, assign the mesh a custom scale automatically. You can see the scale value for a mesh asset by selecting the mesh in the Project Panel and viewing its properties on the *Model* tab in the Object Inspector. ▶1

NOTE

Sometimes a 0.01 scale might be what you want, in which case no change is required. Generally, base your decisions on how the mesh looks and performs *in-game* rather than on whether its mesh scale is what you expected. Even so, having every mesh with a scale of 1 lends a certain neatness and precision to your workflow that can make managing meshes easier.

2

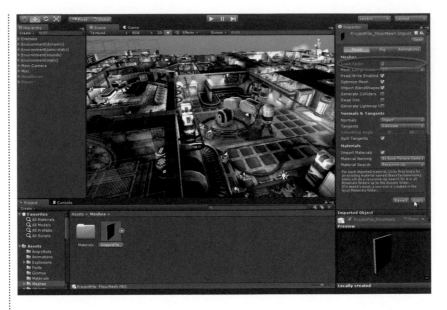

You *can* change the mesh scale manually for every mesh by changing 0.01 to 1, and clicking *Apply* in the Object Inspector to confirm the changes. This process even works when multiple meshes are selected at once, allowing you to batch process meshes. However, rescaling meshes manually is tedious. Additionally, if you reimport or update the mesh, the scale usually reverts back to 0.01. ▶2

Even better, however, is to write a custom C# script that automatically sets the scale on import! This solution is known as the *FBX Scale Fix*. Create the following Editor Script as shown in Code Sample 2.1, making sure it's stored inside a folder named *Editor*. ▶3

3

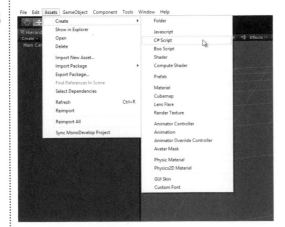

Code Sample 2.1: (FBXFix.cs)—A Class for Resetting Mesh Scale to 1 on Import

```
01  using UnityEngine;
02  using UnityEditor;
03  using System;
04
05  //Sets FBX Mesh Scale Factor to 1
06  public class FBX_Import : AssetPostprocessor
07  {
08    public const float importScale= 1.0f;
09
10    void OnPreprocessModel()
11    {
12      ModelImporter importer = assetImporter as ModelImporter;
13      importer.globalScale = importScale;
14    }
15  }
```

Then finally, import your FBX meshes. Once imported, their scale will automatically be set to 1.

Alternative Applications: Post Processing Assets

Code Sample 2.1 demonstrates how to automatically scale fix an imported FBX mesh. But that code touches only the tip of what you can really do for automating the import process. Lines 12 and 13 of Code Sample 2.1 use the *ModelImporter* class to set the mesh scale via the *globalScale* member. This class offers a wide range of other members too for tweaking mesh settings. In practice, nearly every property you can edit for a mesh via the Object Inspector, you can also edit and automate in code through *ModelImporter*. Other possible applications for automated tasks include: averaging or changing mesh normals, editing material and animation clip assignments, and tweaking mesh UVs. More information on *ModelImporter* can be found in the online Unity documentation at: http://docs.unity3d.com/Documentation/ScriptReference/ModelImporter.html.

Asset and Importing Cheats

2.3 Mesh, Materials, and Importing

One potentially stubborn issue with importing meshes concerns materials. After import, meshes often display in a dull-gray material, both in their thumbnails inside the Project Panel and in the preview pane of the Object Inspector. This is a problem because most developers want meshes to display in-editor using the appropriate materials and textures from the mesh file. This makes it easier and more convenient for browsing meshes. This issue seems difficult to fix, because even if you later import textures and materials into the project and assign them manually onto mesh instances in the scene, the mesh asset itself remains dull and gray in the Project Panel. ▶4

4

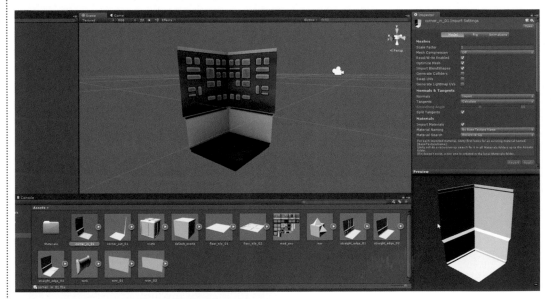

5

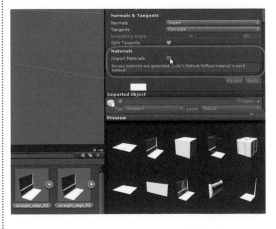

One reason this happens is because you have the mesh setting *Import Materials disabled* for your meshes in the Object Inspector. This setting is especially useful if you don't plan on using any materials, or if you'll be automating or generating materials in script at Run-Time. Normally, though, you'll want texture visualization for meshes, but when this setting is disabled Unity will not import materials from the mesh file. Instead, it'll use a single auto-generated (default) material across all meshes. To fix this problem, simply enable *Import Materials* and then click *Apply*. ▶5

Yet maybe this setting wasn't disabled for you anyway, or maybe you did fix it, but still your meshes won't display textures in the Project Panel as you'd expect them to. To properly resolve this issue with the least fuss: simply import your textures *before* your meshes! First, import all textures into your project, and store them in an appropriately named folder, such as *Textures*. ▶6

Finally, import your meshes into the project. When you import in this order (textures > meshes), Unity will automatically search and detect all related textures, assigning them to the relevant mesh materials. This results in meshes that show textured thumbnails and previews, as expected. If this import workflow didn't work for you, be sure to export meshes from the 3D software with material and texture information included in the file, as well as UV mapping data. Additionally, ensure texture filenames in Unity match those used in the 3D software. ▶7

6

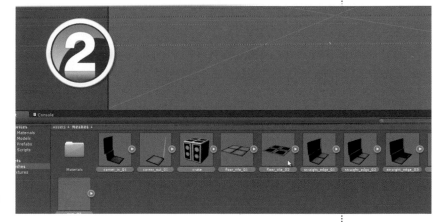

7

NOTE

For further information on how Unity automatically searches for and applies materials to imported meshes, see the online Unity documentation here: http://docs.unity3d.com/Documentation/Components/class-Mesh.html.

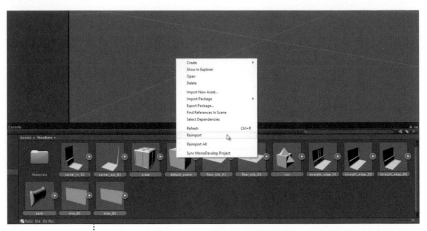

If, however, you've already imported textures *after* meshes and they're looking gray, then don't worry. All is not lost. And you don't even need to remove your meshes and reimport them. You can reimport your meshes automatically from the Unity Project Panel in one operation. First, *delete* any auto-generated materials for the meshes, to clear away any

8 | existing material settings that may be taking effect (these are usually generated when meshes are imported, in a subfolder named *Materials*). Then select all meshes in the Project Panel, and right-click to display the properties context menu. Choose *Re-import*. Or alternatively, choose *Assets > Re-import* from the application main menu. ▶8

Alternative Applications: Meshes and Prefabbing

Mesh assets in Unity don't really have materials, strictly speaking. Materials are not a part of the mesh. Meshes are purely data structures with vertex, edge, polygonal, and mapping information (*MeshData*). Material assignment to a mesh is controlled *on an object* by a *MeshRenderer* component. This is attached not to a mesh asset per se, but to mesh *instances* in the scene. For your convenience, however, Unity generates a temporary and read-only "Imported Object" for each mesh asset, allowing a mesh asset to display its texture and material data in thumbnail images in the Project Panel and Object Inspector,

9 |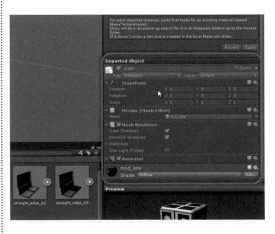

as though it were a complete and whole object. The imported object is also used to generate a properly configured game object in the scene whenever you drag and drop a mesh into the Scene Viewport. However, there may be times when you'd like to change the material assignment *for the imported object*, as opposed to individual mesh instances in the scene. That is, you want to change the material for a mesh asset and have the change propagate to all instances of the mesh in the scene. ▶9

One of the quickest and easiest methods for creating a mesh asset that allows for material changes is to create a prefab object from an instance of the mesh. A prefab is a special asset. It lets you take snapshots of objects (and collections of objects) in the scene, and to instantiate them as an asset in the Project Panel. Doing this allows you to reuse the prefab just like a regular mesh asset. To achieve this, first drag and drop a mesh into any scene—it doesn't matter which scene. ▶10

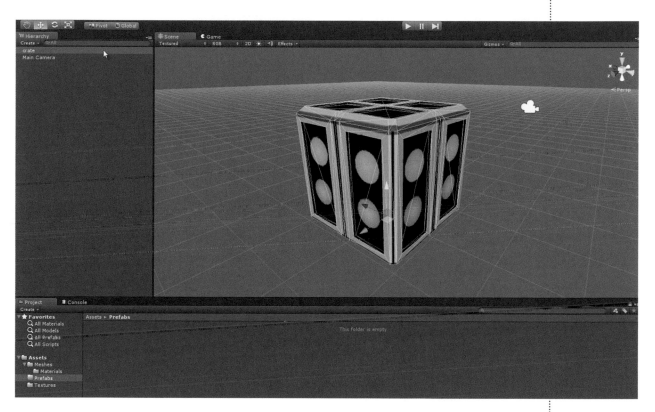

10

2 Asset and Importing Cheats

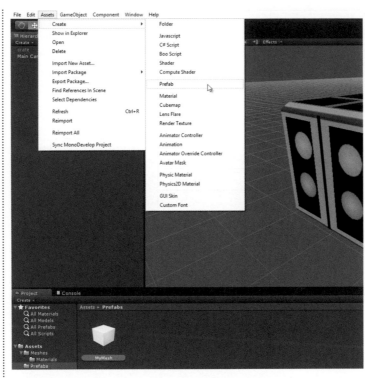

11

Then choose *Assets > Create > Prefab* from the application menu to generate a new, empty prefab object in the project. ▶11

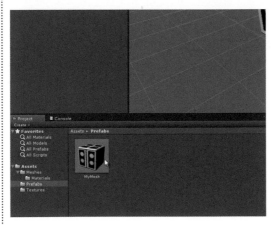

12

Then drag and drop the mesh object in the scene over the Prefab icon in the Project Panel. This instantiates the mesh as a new prefab. The object name may also change color in the Hierarchy panel to indicate that it's no longer an instance of the original mesh asset, but an instance of the prefab. ▶12

Now you can change the material of all prefab instances by accessing the prefab material from the Object Inspector. Open the *MeshRenderer* component, and assign it a new material. All prefab instances will automatically update to reflect the change. ▶13

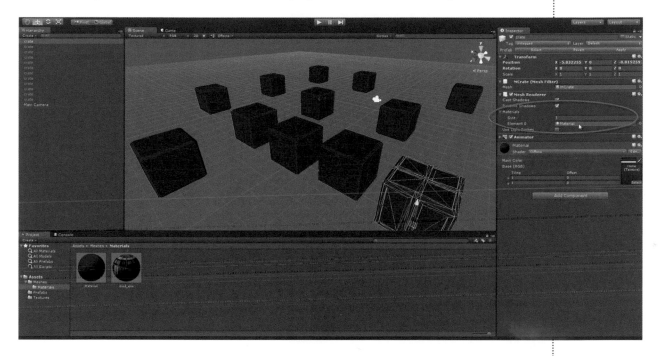

13

2.4 Texture Sizes and Cross-Platform Design

Unity offers many options for configuring and optimizing textures. It's important to optimize textures as far as possible, because they can be a significant factor in causing performance problems, especially on mobile devices. By default, the full set of options and features for configuring textures are not shown in the Object Inspector. To display them, switch the *Texture Type* to *Advanced*. ▶14

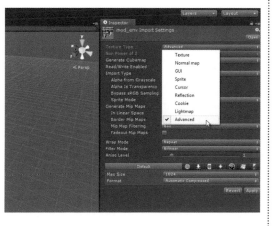

14

15

16

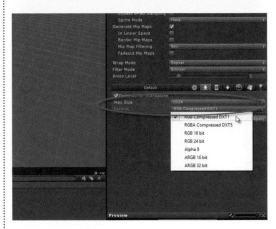

Two properties are especially important for texture performance across platforms. These are: *Max Size* and *Format*. Thankfully, Unity allows you to tailor these fields for specific platforms and build targets using the *Platform Selection* tab. Simply click a platform (Windows, iOS, Android, etc.) and choose *Override* to customize the texture settings for *that* platform. ▶15

Arriving at the right settings in practice for your project takes some trial and error, and tweaking. In general, it's good practice to keep *Max Size* as small as you can get away with, without compromising on the quality you need. This refers to the maximum texture dimensions (in pixels) allowed. The smaller the texture, the less data your game has to process. ▶16

The *Format* value will vary depending on your target hardware. For desktops, *RGB Compressed DXT1* often works well for power-2 sized, nontransparent textures. For transparent textures, try a format of *RGBA Compressed DXT5*. For the iOS platform, I recommend starting with a texture format of *RGB Compressed PVRTC 4 Bits* for nontransparent textures, and *RGBA Compressed PVRTC 4 Bits* for transparent textures. For Android, I recommend starting with *RGB Compressed ETC 4 Bits* for nontransparent textures, and *RGBA Compressed ETC 4 Bits* for transparent textures.

Alternative Applications: Sizing Textures

When creating game art and displaying it in-game, the following rule applies: if it *looks* right, then it *is* right. Because of this, there're usually many texture settings and sizes that produce a result that looks right. This gives us flexibility for optimizing texture size. To preserve best quality in your textures, make them *exactly* the size you need. No smaller and no larger, and always strive for the smallest size you can get away with. However, when making cross-platform games that display on varied hardware and at different screen resolutions, this strategy isn't always feasible. You'll typically need *different* sizes for *different* systems. In this case, create your textures at the largest size needed so you can downscale them to lower resolutions with the least quality loss. Never create textures smaller and then upscale. Upscaling is a shortcut to degraded images and blurriness. True, some blurriness can be fixed by sharpening filters or custom shaders, but sharpening only gets you so far. For this reason, make textures at the largest size necessary whenever you're not sure about sizes or which variations you'll need.

2.5 Assets and Run-Time Loading

Every scene in Unity depends on assets (except for empty scenes), though they usually depend on only a subset of all the assets used across an entire game. For example, only *some* textures from among the *total* will be used in a single level. Unity usually does a good job of detecting which assets are needed for each specific scene. It uses this knowledge for two main purposes: first, at Build-Time to determine which assets in a project are really used at all and which should be included in the final asset file distributed with the built game executable. Second, at Run-Time to load and unload assets in memory whenever scene changes occur to keep memory usage at optimal levels. However, there might be times when you'll want to manually manage resource loading at Run-Time, loading some assets and unloading others in script. This will typically be for memory usage reasons, as well as to force Unity to include specific assets in the final assets file. To achieve this, you can use the *Resources* class in combination with *Resources* folders.

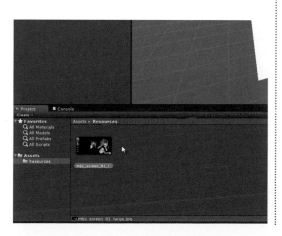

17

If you have a mesh, texture, or other asset that you want to load or unload manually *at Run-Time* from script, and if you don't want to risk Unity excluding that asset from the build, then be sure to put the asset inside a folder named *Resources* in the Project Panel. The *Resources* folder can be nested inside other folders, and your project can contain potentially many *Resources* folders. Unity is smart enough to detect them all. ▶17

18

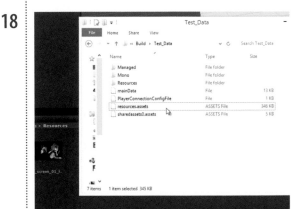

You can confirm that Unity has detected your *Resources* folder, and its contained assets, by building your project and examining the list of generated files. There will be a file named *Resources.assets* inside the *Data* folder. ▶18

To load an asset at Run-Time in script from any *Resources* folder, you call the *Resources.Load* function. To unload an asset, call *Resources.UnloadAsset*. Once an asset is loaded, it can be used as any regular asset in the scene. The code in Code Sample 2.2 loads a texture asset from a *Resources* folder, assigning the texture to a mesh renderer component, such as a plane mesh.

Code Sample 2.2: (DynamicLoad.cs)—A Class for Loading Assets at Run-Time

```
01   using UnityEngine;
02   using System.Collections;
03
04   //Class to dynamically load an asset from a resources folder
05   public class DynamicLoad : MonoBehaviour
06   {
07     //Internal reference to Renderer Component
08     private MeshRenderer ThisRenderer = null;
09
10     //Maintain an internal reference to resource object
11     private Object MyAsset = null;
12
13     //Called at object start
14     void Start ()
15     {
16       //Get Mesh Renderer component on this object
17       ThisRenderer = GetComponent<MeshRenderer>();
```

```
18
19      //Load resource
20      MyAsset = Resources.Load("MyTextureFile", typeof
        (Texture2D));
21
22      //Assign to material
23      ThisRenderer.material.mainTexture=MyAsset as Texture2D;
24   }
25
26   //Called when object is destroyed
27   void OnDestroy ()
28   {
29      //Unload asset
30      Resources.UnloadAsset(MyAsset);
31   }
32 }
```

> **NOTE**
>
> You can also unload all unused assets from memory with one call, using *Resources.UnloadUsedAssets*. An "unused" asset means any asset not being referenced by any component variables on any object in the active scene. Take care, because local variables inside functions may be referencing assets, and these are not included in this calculation.

Alternative Applications: Asset Bundles

Another motivation for loading assets at runtime is for creating plug-in, customization, add-on, or DLC (downloadable content) data for your games. The idea is to externalize a range of assets outside of the main game package so it can be edited, modified, or replaced to provide dynamic content in-game. One way to achieve this in Unity is through Asset Bundles. Using Asset Bundles, you can essentially select a range of assets in the Project Panel and compile them to an external package, known as an Asset Bundle. This bundle exists as a stand-alone and separate resource package and can be loaded dynamically by any Unity game. To create an Asset Package, add the Editor Class in Code Sample 2.3 to your project, inside an Editor folder. It won't work if it's located outside a folder named "Editor."

Code Sample 2.3: (AssetBundleBuilder.cs)—Editor Class for Generating Bundles from Selected Assets in the Project Panel

```
01   using UnityEditor;
02   //————————————
03   //Editor class to export asset bundle
04   public class AssetBundleBuilder
05   {
06     //Adds item to menu for exporting labelled asset bundles
```

```
07    [ MenuItem ("Assets/Build AssetBundles")]
08    static void BuildAllAssetBundles ()
09    {
10       //Replace "e:\bundles" with your own folder
11       BuildPipeline.BuildAssetBundles (@"e:\bundles");
12    }
13  }
14  //——————————————
```

After Code Sample 2.3 has been added to your project, you can create Asset Bundles from selected assets. In the Project Panel, select all assets to be included in the bundle, then from the Object Inspector preview window, click the Asset Bundle drop-down menu and choose New to create a new category that collects together all similarly tagged assets into one Bundle. Then use the same drop-down menu to pick and assign the tag to the

▼19

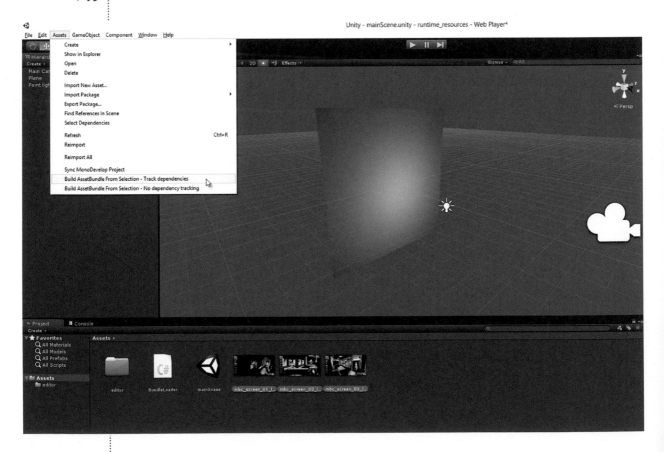

selected assets in the project panel. In this example, I've used the group *MyTextures* to collect together some textures into a single Bundle. To generate the Bundle, then choose *Assets > Build Bundle Assets* from the application menu, and a single Bundle file will be generated at the file location specified in Line 11 of Code Sample 2.3. ▶19

With the Asset Bundle file generated, you can load the file (either from a URL or local file) and any resources inside using the code in Code Sample 2.4. This code loads a texture from a bundle file and assigns it as the main texture for a *MeshRenderer* component, such as Quad Mesh displaying a texture asset.

Code Sample 2.4: (BundleLoader.cs)—Loads an Asset from an External Bundle File

```
01  using UnityEngine;
02  using System.Collections;
03  [ RequireComponent(typeof(MeshRenderer))]
04  public class AssetBundleLoader : MonoBehaviour
05  {
06    //Internal reference to Renderer Component
07    private MeshRenderer ThisRenderer = null;
08
09    //------------ ----
10    IEnumerator Start()
11    {
12      //Get Mesh Renderer Component
13      ThisRenderer= GetComponent<MeshRenderer>();
14
15      //For windows, local file loading should be prefixed with
        three / characters
16      //Replace this path with your own location for your asset
        bundle
17      string URL = "file:///e:/bundles/mytextures.unity3d";
18
19      //Log loading path
20      Debug.Log ("Loading bundle from: " + URL);
21
22      //Load bundle from URL
23      WWW www = WWW.LoadFromCacheOrDownload (URL, 1);
24
25      // Wait for download to complete
```

```
26      yield return www;
27
28      // Load and retrieve the AssetBundle
29      AssetBundle bundle = www.assetBundle;
30
31      // Load the object asynchronously
32   //Replace "MyTextureAsset" with the name of your asset, as
        assigned in the Project Panel
33   AssetBundleRequest request = bundle.LoadAssetAsync
        ("MyTextureAsset", typeof(Texture2D));
34
35      // Wait for loading to complete
36      yield return request;
37
38      // Get the reference to the loaded object
39      Texture2D TexAsset = request.asset as Texture2D;
40
41      //Assign texture to material
42      if(ThisRenderer.material != null && TexAsset != null)
43        ThisRenderer.material.mainTexture = TexAsset;
44
45      // Unload the AssetBundles compressed contents to
        conserve memory
46      bundle.Unload(false);
47
48      // Frees the memory from the web stream
49      www.Dispose();
50    }
51    //-----------------
52  }
```

NOTE

More information on Asset Bundles and their use can be found at the online Unity documentation here:
https://docs.unity3d.com/Documentation/Manual/abfaq.html

2.6 Organizing and Searching Assets

Many developers neglect to adequately organize their project assets, and they usually end up regretting it further along the line. If your project uses many different asset types (such as meshes, textures, and materials), then you'll likely benefit from a rigorous organization practice. It'll make assets faster and easier to find, and that can save you a lot of time, as well as make development smoother and more intuitive. Unity offers several features to organize assets: *filenames*, *folder names*, and *labels*.

Filenames are important and should be descriptive. Try scaling down the thumbnails in the Project Panel to see only filenames for your assets. Then ask yourself whether the names really tell you much about the files and their contents. To improve filenames, try breaking down the name into at least three main parts: *Type Prefix*, *Main Content,* and *Descriptor*. The general form of the name is given as:

20

> *TypePrefix_MainContent_Descriptor*

Examples:

> *mesh_monster_greeman*
>
> *tex_background_level01*
>
> *mat_diffuse_shinyarmour*

Start a filename with a three- or four-letter word describing the asset type: such as *mesh*, *tex* (texture), *mat* (material), etc. Then follow this with a general title or name discussing the asset association: is it for an enemy character, the player, or a GUI element? And then append the name with a descriptor to further narrow the meaning of the name: if the asset is for an enemy character, then which enemy? If it's for a weapon, then which weapon? ►20

Folders are important for grouping assets into related areas, but they can be a risk too. Take care with folder naming and arrangement. They have the potential to make your organization clearer and easier when used appropriately, but also to obscure and confuse when used without due consideration. ►21

21

Avoid too many levels of nesting, sticking to two or three levels at most. Nested folders can help arrange related assets together and emphasize structure, but overuse of nesting can make it difficult to quickly reach the assets you need—as well as making your Project Panel more cluttered.

Avoid making folder names too specific or narrow, too. Folder names should be sufficiently general and abstract to permit the grouping together of many assets, not just one or two. For my own projects, the topmost level of folders usually contains names, such as: meshes, materials, prefabs, scripts, audio, scenes, animations, and textures. These define high-level groups among assets based on asset type. But within each of these groupings, additional folders could be created based on the needs of your project.

Overall, there's no right or wrong way to name or arrange folders, but always ask yourself whether your system is making your life easier or harder. If the latter, then it's time to rethink your organization.

The *LODGroup* component displays a list of LOD groups. By default, there are three main groups. *LOD: 0* (Near), *LOD: 1* (Mid) and *LOD: 2* (Far). These groups are presented in a line, and as the scene camera is moved in the viewport, further or nearer to the object, the camera will automatically scrub through the sequence and give you a real-time preview of the detail levels. Select each LOD group in turn by clicking on it, and then drag and drop a mesh from the Project Panel into the appropriate LOD slot to assign the mesh to that level of detail. When dragging and dropping, Unity may ask about re-Parenting objects. If so, accept the Parenting operation. Be sure to drag the high-detail mesh to the *LOD: 0* slot, and the lowest detail version to the last slot. ▶27

27

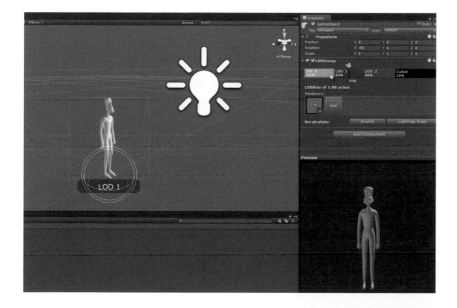

Each level of detail mesh is added as a child of the new game object. The *LODGroup* component essentially changes the visibility of each mesh depending on the distance of the active camera. ▶28

28

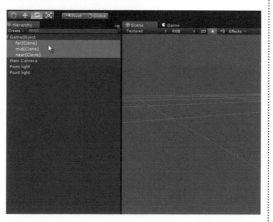

2.8 Alpha Textures

If you're creating particle effects, GUIs, sprites, fog effects, or billboard objects in your game, then you'll probably need to use transparent textures. That is, textures with transparent pixels allowing gamers to see through them to the objects behind. Among these textures, there are two main kinds: textures that contain only fully transparent and fully opaque pixels (Cut-Outs), and textures that feature a range of transparencies, including fully opaque, fully transparent, and degrees of semi-transparency. The details on how to create these textures for Photoshop are explained at the Unity documentation here: http://docs.unity3d.com/Documentation/ Manual/HOWTO-alphamaps.html. In creating alpha textures, there are, however, some helpful principles to keep in mind when configuring them as texture and material assets in Unity.

NOTE

If you're using GIMP (www.gimp.org/) instead of Photoshop to create Alpha Textures in the transparent PNG format, then be sure to export your PNG (using *File > Export*) with the setting *Save Color Values from Transparent Pixels* enabled. ▶29

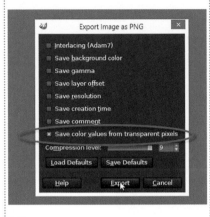

29

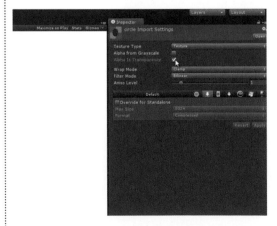

30

On importing a transparent PNG texture to be used on a standard mesh, be sure to enable the Texture option *Alpha is Transparency* from the Object Inspector. If you don't, transparency data will be ignored by default. If the texture type is set to *GUI* or *Sprite*, the transparency data will be automatically configured. ▶30

If your alpha texture is a Cut-Out (features only fully opaque or fully transparent pixels), then why not configure your materials to use either the Standard Shader with the Rendering Mode set to *Cut-Out* for desktop platforms, or the *Sprites > Default Shader*? These can boost performance. If your texture should be immune from scene lighting (self-illuminated), then you can optimize even further by using an *Unlit > Transparent Cut-Out* shader. ▶31

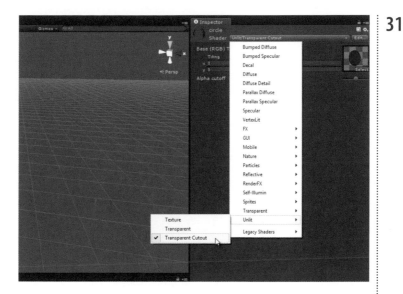

For mobile devices, the Cut-Out shaders will typically result in worse performance and should be avoided. For mobile devices and general alpha textures with a complete range of transparency, try the *Mobile > Particles > Alpha Blended* Shader. ▶32

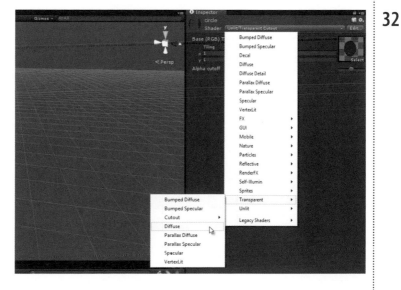

2.9 Assets and Dependencies

Assets don't usually exist in isolation. They rely on other assets. Materials and meshes, for example, rely on textures. And prefabs can potentially rely on any combination of lower-order assets, from meshes and sounds to materials and videos. This means that whenever you manually export a selected asset from a project to use elsewhere, you may not necessarily export everything you need because of unforeseen dependencies that you didn't notice at first sight.

33

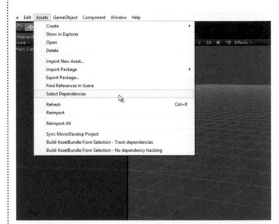

Unity provides you with a convenient method for selecting all dependencies of an asset, directly from the Project Panel. Select the asset to export, and right-click with the mouse to display a properties context menu. From there, choose *Select Dependencies*. Or else choose *Assets > Select Dependencies* from the application main menu. ▶33

34

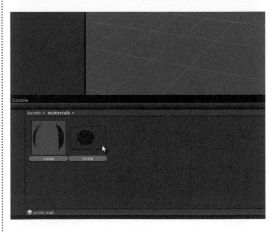

This selects all assets in the Project Panel that depend upon the previously selected asset. If there are no dependencies, then no new assets will be selected. ▶34

You can even find all references of the selected assets in the scene by choosing *Assets > Find References in Scene* from the application menu. This will select all game objects in the scene whose components are known to reference or connect with the selected assets in some way. ▶35

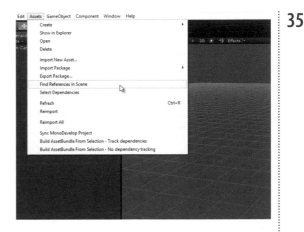

35

Alternative Applications: Deleting Assets

Deleting an asset can be troublesome and have unintended consequences, because of the dependencies between assets. It's easy, for example, to delete a texture that several materials or meshes depended upon, and this in turn "breaks" or disrupts the high-order asset. In the context of assets, I use the term "higher-order asset" to mean any asset that has dependences, such as a mesh or a material or a prefab. A lower-order asset is one that has no dependencies itself, but it may be an asset on which others depend — these include: textures, audio clips, text files, and animation data. Although Unity offers the *Select Dependencies* feature to find and select all lower-order assets from a selected higher-order asset, there's no native way to perform the reverse process. That is, you can select a material to find all dependent textures, but you can't select a texture and automatically find all materials that depend on it. This makes deleting lower-order assets risky.

One principle or general workflow to avoid this issue is always to start by deleting higher-order assets, and then moving on to lower-order assets. This method is certainly not "foolproof." But it makes things easier. Start by deleting meshes and prefabs and materials. And before deleting each, select its dependencies to see other assets connected to it, as these too may become eligible for deletion.

T--I--P

In Unity, assets are typically thought to include image files, meshes, animations, materials, audio data, videos, scripts, and scenes. Indeed, these are assets. But it doesn't have to stop here. You can import any file type into a Unity project, including word processor documents, PDF files, charts, diagrams, text files, XML files, and more. When double-clicking these files from the Project Panel, they will open in their default viewing application. It can be useful to include these nonstandard assets to share game design documents and other plan or schedule data with members of the team.

2.10 Formats, Sizes, and Compression

Textures (image files) and audio files are two assets especially prone to data loss. Extra care should be applied when saving these files for import into Unity, because not all formats and settings are made equal. In theory, Unity accepts many different formats for images and audio data, but in practice only a few give you the best results. The following general rules apply.

Rule #1. For images, use the PNG, PSD, or TGA formats. Always avoid JPG.

Rule #2. For audio files, import in WAV or AIFF format—otherwise quality loss will result. One exception to this is for desktop games (Windows, Mac, or Linux): for these platforms, you can import using OGG files without incurring any quality loss.

Rule #3. For best performance, save your texture files at power-2 dimensions in pixels: 2, 4, 8, 16, 32, 64, 128, 256, 512, 1024, 2048, and 4096. Example sizes include: 512x512, 1024x512, 256x512, etc. For sprite and GUI graphics, you can use any size at 4096 or below. But for most textures, use a power-2 size.

NOTE

More information on importing images files can be found at the Unity documentation here:

http://docs.unity3d.com/Documentation/Manual/ImportingAssets.html.

For audio files, see the dedicated audio page here:

https://docs.unity3d.com/Documentation/Manual/AudioFiles.html.

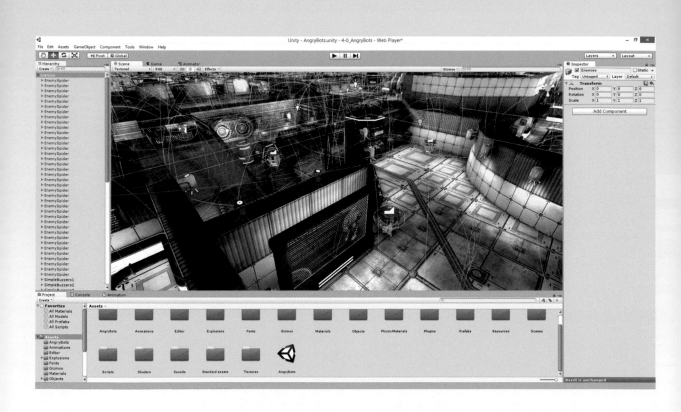

3

Scene, Component, and GameObject Cheats

The Scene is a critical asset in Unity. You'll make use of them frequently. A **Scene** is a collection of related GameObjects, and a **GameObject** is a collection of related **Components**. There's an object hierarchy at work here. The Scene encapsulates the "world" or "level", a 3D space where things exist. The concept of a *thing* is represented as a GameObject, a complete and self-contained entity with its own unique position, rotation, and scale in the Scene. And a Component represents one specific aspect or part of a GameObject. An object may exhibit many different but coordinated behaviors. A wizard character for an RPG, for example, will navigate around the environment, cast spells, take damage, *and* deal damage. Each of these behaviors might be defined by a unique Component. By using a combination of Scenes, GameObjects, and Components, tremendous complexity can be assembled. This chapter explores the many tips and tricks for working with these highly important entities.

3 Scene, Component, GameObject

3.1 The Power of Empties

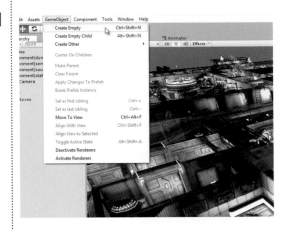

It's easy to create an empty GameObject in Unity. Simply press the keyboard shortcut *Ctrl + Shift + N*, or select *GameObject > Create Empty* from the application menu. The empty object features just one component by default: a Transform component to maintain its position, rotation, and scale in the Scene (or a RectTransform component for 2D Objects). This means an empty object cannot be seen in-game; it's not a mesh or a renderable, but herein rests the object's true power. ▶1

Think of empty objects like folders or directories for organizing your scenes: other objects can be Parented to them as children. To do this, just drag and drop your child objects onto the Parent. When you do this, a neatness is introduced into the Hierarchy panel, because you can close and expand your objects like a tree view, hiding and showing only the objects you need to see. ▶2

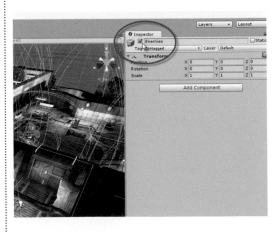

Parenting objects gives you lots more benefits than simply hierarchical tidiness. When you activate or deactivate a Parent object, all its children will automatically be activated and deactivated too, recursively. Plus, all children inherit transformations from the Parent. Specifically: Moving Parent objects will move child objects, but all children still *maintain* their *relative* position from the Parent. In code, this means the transform component for every object maintains *two* position and rotation values: *transform.position* and *transform.rotation*, describing the position and rotation of an object in *absolute* units measured in world space, and *transform.localPosition* and *transform.local Rotation*, measured in local space—that is, *relative* to the Parent. ▶3

Once you establish a Parent-child relationship between objects in the scene, you'll want direct access to that relationship in code. You'll want to access all children of a Parent, or the Parent object of a specific child. You can do this through the Transform component. Code Sample 3.1 demonstrates how to loop through all child objects belonging to a single Parent, and Code Sample 3.2 shows how to access the Parent of a child object.

Code Sample 3.1: Looping Through All Child Objects

```
01   //Loop through all child objects parented to
       this object
02   for(int i=0; i<transform.childCount; i++)
03   {
04     //Get child
05     GameObject Child = transform.GetChild(i).
       gameObject;
06   }
```

Code Sample 3.2: Getting the Parent of the Current Object

```
GameObject ParentObject = transform.parent.gameObject;
```

Alternative Applications: Root Object

It can be very helpful to apply GameObject Parenting in a thoroughgoing way in your Scenes. You can do this by creating just one, empty GameObject as the *Ultimate* Parent of a scene, an object to which all others are Parented in a complete and nested hierarchy. By doing this, you gain high-level control over all objects in the scene. You can move or rotate everything in one operation, simply by

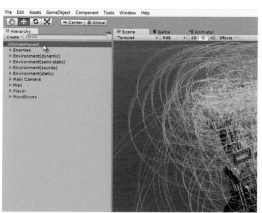

NOTE

More information on the position and rotation properties for the Transform component can be found at the Unity documentation here:

http://docs.unity3d.com/ScriptReference/ Transform.html.

T--I--P

You can activate and deactivate an object and its children in code using the *Game Object.SetActive* function. Deactivated objects are effectively non-visible and switched off in the scene. More information on the *SetActive* function can be found at the Unity documentation here:

http://docs.unity3d.com/ScriptReference/ GameObject.SetActive.html.

4

transforming the Parent. And you can use API functions like *BroadcastMessage* on the Parent to invoke other functions automatically on every child object, in just one call. To create an Ultimate Parent like this, simply drag and drop every scene object beneath an empty GameObject. ▶4

3.2 *SendMessage* and *BroadcastMessage*

5

BROADCAST MESSAGE
Call: *MyFunction*

GAME OBJECT 01
Call: *MyFunction*

GAME OBJECT 02
Call: *MyFunction*

GAME OBJECT 03
Call: *MyFunction*

GAME OBJECT 04
Call: *MyFunction*

Let's imagine you're making a fantasy RPG game. The player may engage in combat with many different enemies, including undead creatures like skeletons, zombies, mummies, and ghosts. The player has a magical spell for use in combat called "Turn Undead." When cast, it causes all undead creatures to flee in terror. But, of course, it doesn't affect other *enemy types*, like dwarves, elves, and goblins—because they're not undead. Now, when the "Turn Undead" spell is cast, it'd be great if we could simply say to Unity, "Call a function *TurnUndead* on all enemy objects involved in combat to notify them that the spell was cast. Some objects may support this function (specifically undead enemies), and some may not. I don't know which ones will for certain. But, if the object supports it, then call it. Otherwise, ignore that object and move on." Fortunately, we can do this using the *SendMessage* and *BroadcastMessage* functions. ▶5

With *SendMessage*, unity lets you specify a function name *by string*, and it'll invoke that function on *every* component attached to a *single* GameObject. By default, if the function is not present on a component, then an error will be generated. However, this default behavior can be overridden. Code Sample 3.3 demonstrates how to use *SendMessage*. If the named function is not found on a component, Unity will ignore the component and move on to the next one.

NOTE

Further details on *SendMessage* and *BroadcastMessage* can be found in the online Unity Documentation at the following URLs:

http://docs.unity3d.com/ScriptReference/ GameObject.SendMessage.html

and

http://docs.unity3d.com/Script Reference/GameObject.Broadcast Message.html.

Code Sample 3.3: Using *SendMessage* to Invoke a Named Function on All Components

```
SendMessage("TurnUndead", SendMessageOptions.DontRequire
Receiver);
```

BroadcastMessage works much like *SendMessage*. However, *SendMessage* applies to only a single object. *BroadcastMessage* cascades downward through the object hierarchy onto all child objects, invoking a named function on all their components, if the function is supported. In combination with an Ultimate Parent object therefore, as mentioned earlier, you can invoke a function on *all* components in the scene, simply by calling *BroadcastMessage* on the Ultimate Parent. This technique can be useful especially for *Load* and *Save Game* functionality, where every object must be given the opportunity to write its data to a persistent file. See Code Sample 3.4 for *BroadcastMessage* usage.

Code Sample 3.4: Sending a Message to an Object and its Children with BroadcastMessage

```
BroadcastMessage("TurnUndead", SendMessageOptions.DontRequire
Receiver);
```

Alternative Applications: Interfaces and Delegates

BroadcastMessage, *SendMessage*, and *SendMessageUpwards* form a trio of invocation functions requiring you to specify function names by string. This technique for calling functions relies internally on a process called "Reflection," which is computationally expensive. For performance reasons, then, it's not recommended to make frequent use of *BroadcastMessage*, *SendMessage*, or *SendMessageUpwards*, especially in *Update* functions and other frame-based events. Instead, consider using neater methods for achieving similar behavior with either *Interfaces* or *Delegates*.

Code Sample 3.5 demonstrates a *C# Interface* implementation of *SendMessage* behavior that doesn't involve reflection. This technique requires all components to implement an *iEventCaller* interface, and uses the *MyEvent* function to support event handling. This approach places stricter requirements on your classes than the *SendMessage* trio of methods, but the performance improvements typically make it well worth it.

T--I--P

Sometimes you may need to send a message upward through the hierarchy, from a child to a Parent. You can achieve this through the function *SendMessageUpwards*: http://docs.unity3d.com/ScriptReference/Component.SendMessageUpwards.html.

NOTE

Both the *SendMessage* and *BroadcastMessage* functions will not be received by deactivated GameObjects.

3 Scene, Component, GameObject

Code Sample 3.5: Sending Messages with Interfaces

```
01   using UnityEngine;
02   using System.Collections;
03   using System.Linq;
04   //-------------------------------
05   //Common interface to be shared by all objects supporting
     event calls
06   public interface iEventCaller
07   {
08     //-------------------------------
09     //Function to be invoked for an event
10     void MyEvent(string EventName, int Param = 0);
11     //-------------------------------
12   }
13   //-------------------------------
14   //This is a custom class supporting an EventCaller interface
15   public class InterfaceCalling : MonoBehaviour, iEventCaller
16   {
17     //-------------------------------
18     //Implement event calling function here
19     public void MyEvent(string EventName, int Param = 0)
20     {
21       //[ ...]
22       //Handle event functionality
23     }
24     //-------------------------------
25     //Custom SendMessage function. Will invoke event for all
       components on this object
26     //All components must implement the interface iEventCaller
27     void SendCustomMessage()
28     {
29       //Get list of all components attached to this object
30       Component[] MyComponents = GetComponents<Component>();
31
32       //Use Linq to get array of only components implementing
         interface
33       iEventCaller[] Callers = (from a in MyComponents where
         a.GetType().GetInterfaces().Any(k => k == typeof
```

```
        (iEventCaller)) select (iEventCaller)(object)a).
        ToArray();
34
35      //Loop through all interfaces and invoke event
36      foreach(iEventCaller C in Callers)
37      {
38        //Call event
39        C.MyEvent("TurnUndead", 0);
40      }
41    }
42    //-------------------------------
43  }
44  //-------------------------------
```

3.3 Empties and Visibility

Empties are useful but lack visibility. They don't render in the *Game* tab, unless a *MeshRenderer* component or other renderable component is attached. And they don't show up in the *Scene* tab either, except for the conventional Gizmo axis that appears when the object is selected. When the object is deselected, then it doesn't show up in any viewport at all, making it impossible to select it using the mouse from the viewport. By default, the only way to select a deselected empty is by using the Hierarchy panel. That can be frustrating, but there's a way around this problem. ▶6

6

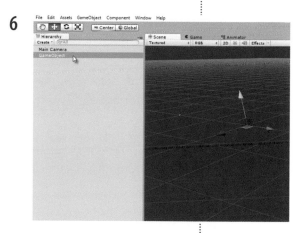

You can assign a custom icon to each empty object, allowing it to display in the Scene Viewport, even when deselected, making mouse picking and selection possible. To achieve this, select your empty object, and click the *Object Icon* button from the Object Inspector. This appears beside the *Object Name* field. From the drop-down box that appears, pick an icon and you're done! ▶7

7

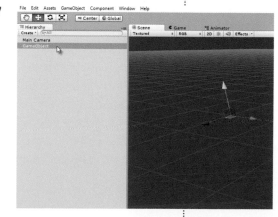

3.4 Snapping and Rounding

Level design is an important part of game development. During that process, you'll assemble prefabs and position your meshes and game objects in the scene. There are no absolute rules here, no right and wrong way to approach the task specifically. But there are some seasoned guidelines and recommendations worth considering. ▶8

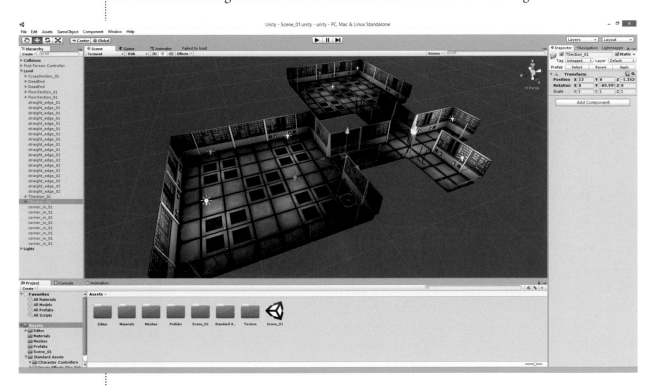

8　When building game environments, including towns, buildings, and forests, try to break down the environment into reusable pieces. Identify smaller sections and areas that could be made tile-able or modular, and create the meshes as individual pieces. Such pieces may include: corridor sections, corner sections, T-junctions, rubble piles, wreckage zones, bridges, doorways, archways, staircases, and lots more. This initial process of division is usually performed by artists during the modeling and texturing phase of mesh assets. When environment meshes are created as an interchangeable, modular set, each piece can be imported separately into Unity and fitted together like Lego bricks with other pieces in the set, forming a potentially limitless number of combinations and environments. ▶9

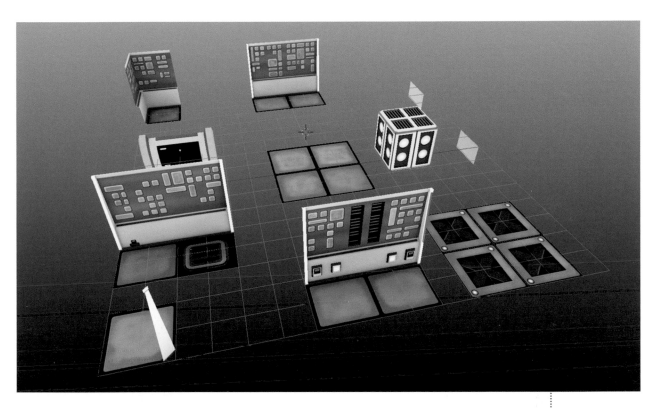

When using this "modular method" of environment creation, you'll frequently need two or more mesh pieces to "match up" or "fit exactly" alongside each other, such as two, separate corridor sections that must fit together to appear as one continuous piece. If you try to align them manually with the mouse and translate tool, you'll likely end up with meshes that overlap at the edges, or with gaps between where the meshes don't quite match. You could manually type in position and rotation values via the Object Inspector, if you know the dimensions of your models, but that'd grow tedious. To achieve precision quickly, then, Vertex Snapping can be used. This allows you to precisely

9

10

align a mesh with another by using its corner vertices as an alignment point. To access Vertex Snapping, select a mesh and switch to the Translate tool (*W*). Then hold down the *V* key on the keyboard. With *V* held down, move your cursor over a corner vertex in the selected mesh that should be the alignment point. Click and hold that point with the mouse, still with the *V* key held down. ▶10

11

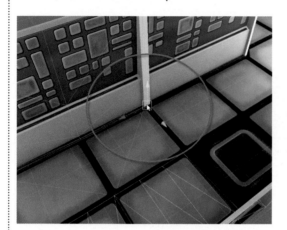

While holding down the *V* key, move your cursor over a corner vertex in the destination mesh, the point to which the selected mesh should align. Often the two vertices (the source and destination) will be the corners of the floor or walls. In the viewport, you'll see the meshes align exactly, and you can release your mouse and the *V* key. ▶11

In addition to snapping, you'll often want to move and rotate your meshes by clean, discrete increments, such as rotating 90 degrees or 180 degrees exactly, or moving a mesh by 1 unit exactly. By default, both the *Translate* and *Rotate* tools (when used with the mouse) operate continuously. That is, they allow for decimal numbers and fractions inside your Transform values. By default, you can move a mesh half a unit or a quarter of a unit, and you can rotate a mesh by a fraction of a degree. Generally, it's solid practice to keep your transforms with clean, rounded numbers wherever possible. Not only does this make an object's Transform easier and simpler to read from the Inspector, it also makes measurements and distance calculations faster and more efficient in code. To achieve quicker and easier transformations with objects using the mouse, you can use *Translate*, *Rotate*, and *Scale* Snap. To access this feature, hold down the *Ctrl* key while using the *Translate*, *Rotate*, and *Scale* tools. This locks your transformations to discrete steps only. ▶12

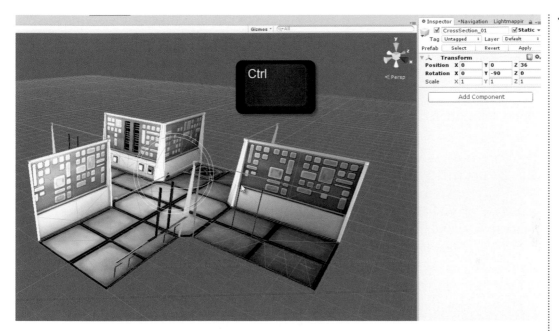

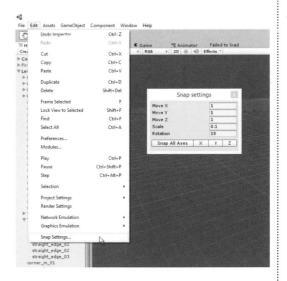

You can control the size of snapping increments for Translation, Rotation and Scale, using the Snap Settings dialog, accessible via the application menu with *Edit > Snap* Settings. ▶13

Alternative Applications: Floor at 0

The *Floor* is the lowest vertical point in your scene. It *may* correspond to the actual in-game floor for indoor environments as they appear to the gamer, but it may not. The Floor simply represents the lowest *possible* point (in the Y axis) that an object can go in any circumstances. In general, make this point always equal to 0, unless you have a very good reason not to. Having the floor set to 0 can improve Run-Time performance for mobile platforms, it reads easier from the inspector, and it helps with general physics calculations and object comparisons. Plus, it's more intuitive. If your object is at 0 on the Y axis, then you know implicitly that it can only move higher, and never lower. You'll never need to check for subzero values, or work with wraparounds at the 0 point, and you'll never need to use math functions, such as *Mathf.Abs*, to retrieve the Y value minus its sign. The principle of "keep it simple" applies strongly to game development, and here's a classic case where a simple convention can make a big difference.

3.5 Searching and Tagging

Searching for, and referencing, objects in the scene from script during gameplay is a common task, and there are many ways to do it. One way is to use the static function *GameObject.Find*. But this is not usually the most efficient way, since it searches for objects by name using string values. Instead, consider assigning all objects a descriptive tag, and search by tag instead. This can lead to significant performance gains, especially if you're searching for objects frequently. For this method to work, make sure all objects in the scene have an appropriate tag. Get into the habit of giving every object a tag, not just one or two objects. Add new, custom tags where necessary, but also make use of the built-in tags, like *Player* and *GameController*. To create a new, custom tag, select an object in the scene (it doesn't matter which), and click the *Tag* drop-down box from the Object Inspector. From the context menu, choose *Add Tag*.

14

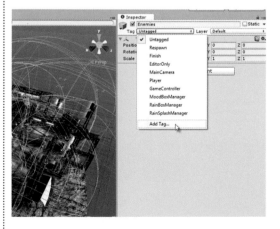

To search for objects by tag in C# script, the *GameObject* class exposes two static functions: *FindWithTag*, and *FindGameObjectsWithTag*. The former searches the scene for an object with a matching tag and returns the first matching instance, while the latter returns an array of all matching objects. Code Sample 3.6 finds all objects with a matching tag. ▶14

Code Sample 3.6: Getting Objects with a Matching Tag

```
01    //Find all objects marked with the 'Enemy' tag
02    GameObject[] Objects = GameObject.FindGameObjectsWithTag
      ("Enemy");
03
04    //Loop through all found objects
05    foreach (GameObject O in Objects)
06    {
07      //Print name of this object
08      Debug.Log (O.name);
09    }
```

> **NOTE**
>
> More information on *FindWithTag* and *FindGameObjectsWithTag* functions at the Unity Documentation here:
>
>   http://docs.unity3d.com/ScriptReference/ GameObject.FindWithTag.html
>
> and
>
>   http://docs.unity3d.com/ScriptReference/ GameObject.FindGameObjectsWithTag. html.

3.6 Object Sorting in the Hierarchy Panel

It can be useful to sort and arrange GameObjects in the Hierarchy panel according to your needs. Sometimes, it's acceptable for them to be sorted in alphabetical order. But often this is not what you want. For example, how about clustering together frequently selected objects, making them easier to pick—saving you from scrolling up and down the Hierarchy panel? Prior to Unity 4.5, objects were sorted in the hierarchy by simply changing their names; for example, inserting [] braces to the beginning and end of object names would filter them to the top. But newer behavior now allows you to simply drag and drop GameObjects into any order you like.

Clicking and dragging objects to rearrange them may be just what you need, especially if you need to rearrange only a few objects. But what about for large scenes with many objects, and cases where you need to sort them all alphabetically, or according to a custom criteria? For this, you can write an Editor plug-in, customizing the Hierarchy panel. Consider Code Sample 3.7, adding this code to an Editor folder in your project. This code sorts the Hierarchy panel by name, arranging objects alphabetically, from lowest to highest. ▶15

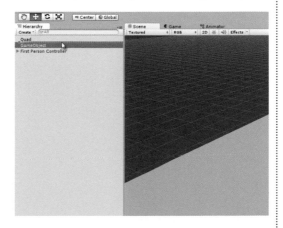

15

3 Scene, Component, GameObject

Code Sample 3.7: Sorting Objects in the Hierarchy by Name

```
01  //-------------------------------
02  using UnityEngine;
03  using UnityEditor; //Don't forget to include UnityEditor
    namespace
04  using System.Collections;
05  //-------------------------------
06  //Derive class from BaseHierarchySort
07  public class HierarchySortAlpha : BaseHierarchySort
08  {
09    public override int Compare(GameObject lhs, GameObject rhs)
10    {
11      if (lhs == rhs) return 0; //If they are the same, then
        exit
12      if (lhs == null) return -1; //If one or other object is
        null, then exit
13      if (rhs == null) return 1;
14
15      //Now compare the names of two objects and sort
16      return EditorUtility.NaturalCompare(lhs.name, rhs.name);
17    }
18  }
19  //-------------------------------
```

16

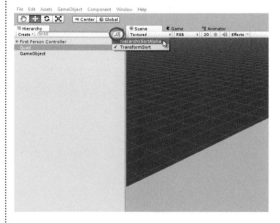

After adding this code to your project, a new button will appear in the Hierarchy panel allowing you to choose your sorting options. ▶16 Click this button and select your new sorting method!

3.7 Lines with the Line Renderer

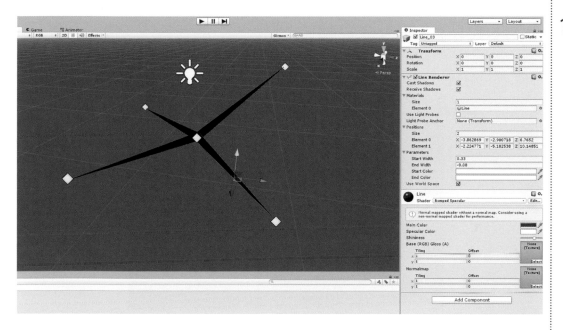

17

If you're making strategy games, RPG games, or any games where GameObjects in the scene are connected in some way, in a web of relationships, it can be useful to visualize these connections in the viewport using lines. There are many ways to draw lines in Unity—another method is considered later in the book. But if you need to display the lines to the user in-game, the *LineRenderer* component could be just what you need. It features many options for customization. The *LineRenderer* effectively takes an array

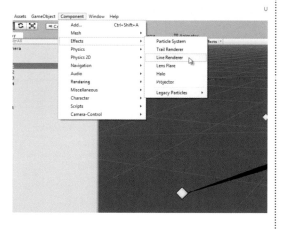

18

of Vector3 structures and draws a continuous and connected line between them in 3D space. To add a *LineRenderer* component to an object, select a GameObject and choose *Component > Effects > LineRenderer* from the application menu. ▶17, 18

Each GameObject may have only one *LineRenderer* component attached. And though a single *LineRenderer* can draw a connected line through many points, you'll need to create multiple GameObjects if you need the line to branch in multiple directions, like a verb. ▶19

19

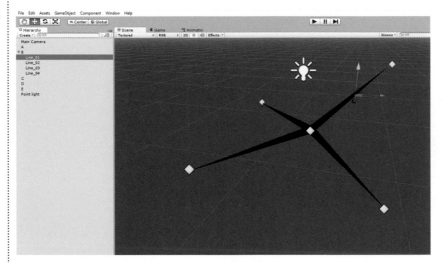

20

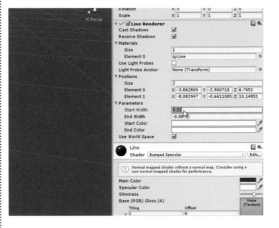

The *LineRenderer* component features several significant properties. As expected, the *Positions* property lets you specify the array of points through which the line travels (X, Y, and Z), and the *Materials* property assigns a material to the selected line. The line is essentially a billboard mesh—that is, a plane object oriented to always face the camera. In addition, the *Start* and *Width* properties allow you to taper the line, making it wider or narrower at one end: this can be useful for graphically expressing direction or strength through the lines. And finally, the *Use World Space* checkbox is enabled by default, indicating that line positions are measured from the world origin. If you need the lines to animate or move with specific game objects as they move around, then you will likely need to disable this check box, fixing the line positions relatively to a parent. ▶20

3.8 Procedural Geometry

Though Unity accepts meshes in many formats and offers many built-in primitives, like Quads and Spheres, there are times when you'll need to edit meshes manually or build them programmatically. This can be useful for creating deformations and special effects, like an expanding shockwave from an explosion, or a wibbly-wobbly jelly terrain that bends and distorts as the player moves around. Meshes created like this are called "procedural geometry" or "procedural meshes." Meshes can be generated using the *Mesh* class. Consider Code Sample 3.8 (MeshBuilder.cs). This class generates a simple quad mesh at Run-Time, demonstrating how to create vertices in code, and UVs, and how to configure them into triangles. At minimum, a mesh needs vertex and triangle data. The vertices array defines all corner points in the model, and the triangle array defines all triangles (groups of three vertices). The values for the triangle array are integer offsets into the vertices array. ▶21

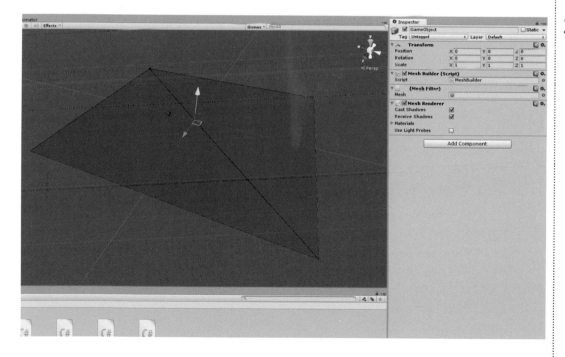

21

Code Sample 3.8: Class to Construct a Basic Mesh

```
01  //-----------------------------------
02  using UnityEngine;
03  using System.Collections;
04  //Class to make a quad mesh
05  //-----------------------------------
06  public class MeshBuilder : MonoBehaviour
07  {
08    //Vertices of mesh (four corner vertices)
09    private Vector3[] Vertices = new Vector3[ 4];
10
11    //----------------------------------
12    // Use this for initialization
13    void Start ()
14    {
15      //Add a mesh filter component - needed to store mesh
         data
16      gameObject.AddComponent<MeshFilter>();
17
18      //Add a mesh renderer component - need to display mesh
19      gameObject.AddComponent<MeshRenderer>();
20
21      //Run mesh generation function
22      BuildMesh();
23    }
24    //----------------------------------
25    //Generate Mesh (simple quad)
26    void BuildMesh()
27    {
28      //Build new mesh
29      Mesh mesh = new Mesh();
30
31      //Assign mesh to mesh filter
32      GetComponent<MeshFilter>().mesh = mesh;
33
34      //Create four corner vertices
35      Vertices[ 0] = new Vector3( 1, 0, 1);
```

```
36        Vertices[ 1] = new Vector3( 1, 0, -1);
37        Vertices[ 2] = new Vector3(-1, 0, 1);
38        Vertices[ 3] = new Vector3(-1, 0, -1);
39
40        //Set triangles (2 triangles for a quad)
41        mesh.vertices = Vertices;
42
43        //Configure mesh UVs
44        mesh.uv = new Vector2[ ]
45        {
46          new Vector2(1, 1),
47          new Vector2(1, 0),
48          new Vector2(0, 1),
49          new Vector2(0, 0),
50        };
51
52        //Define triangles for mesh
53        mesh.triangles = new int[ ]
54        {
55          0, 1, 2,
56          2, 1, 3,
57        };
58
59        //Recalculate boundaries of mesh based on vertices
60        mesh.RecalculateBounds();
61      }
62  }
63  //-----------------------------------
```

> **NOTE**
>
> Code Sample 3.8 automatically adds *MeshFilter* and *MeshRenderer* components to an empty game object. The *MeshFilter* component contains all mesh data, including vertex, uv and triangle information. The *MeshRenderer* component accepts a *MeshFilter* as input and renders it in the game, making it visible. Meshes need both a *MeshFilter* and *MeshRenderer* component to be seen in-game.

> **NOTE**
>
> For a free add-on that creates a plane mesh, allowing extra customization, consider the following C# sample code, which is an Editor plug-in:
>
> http://wiki.unity3d.com/index.php?title=CreatePlane.

3 Scene, Component, GameObject

3.9 Camera Frustum Drawing

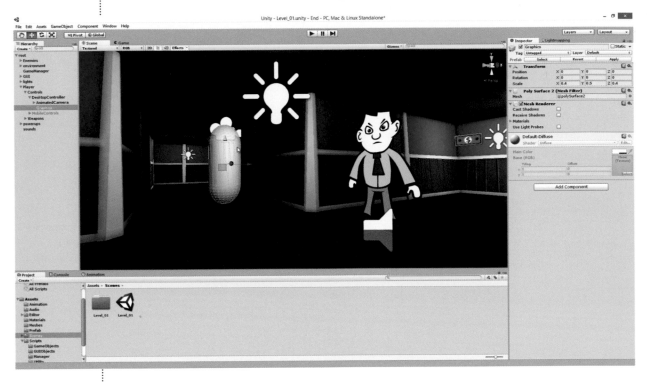

22 When you select a camera in the scene viewport, it displays a wireframe region extending from the camera lens, which represents the viewing frustum. This trapezoidal volume defines the total area within the scene that the camera can see from its current position. ▶22

23 The viewing frustum is useful for positioning the camera to get the best possible shots and angles inside the scene. However, sometimes, you want to *move and position objects within* the camera view, as opposed to moving the camera towards the objects. And yet, when you deselect the camera to select other objects, the frustum wireframe disappears, making it difficult to know visually whether an object can be seen by the camera. ▶23

We can fix this easily, however, by creating a new Script (DrawFrustum Refined.cs) as shown in Code Sample 3.9, which can be added to any Camera as a component. The component has just one adjustable property, determining whether the Camera frustum should be permanently drawn. ▶24

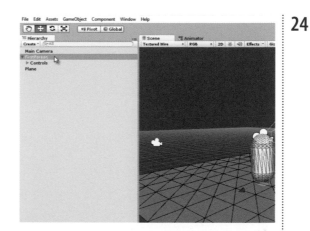

24

When the camera is deselected, the Frustum will remain visible, allowing us to easily move objects within the camera view. ▶25

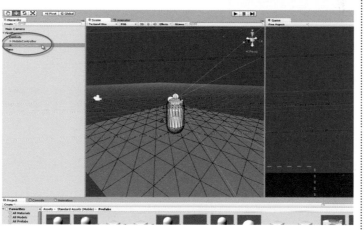

25

Code Sample 3.9: DrawFrustumRefined.cs

```
01   using UnityEngine;
02   using System.Collections;
03   //----------------------------------------
04   [ExecuteInEditMode]
05   [RequireComponent(typeof(Camera))]
06   //----------------------------------------
07   public class DrawFrustumRefined : MonoBehaviour
08   {
09      //----------------------------------------
10      private Camera Cam = null;
11      public bool ShowCamGizmo = true;
12      //----------------------------------------
```

```
13   void Awake()
14   {
15     Cam = GetComponent<Camera>();
16   }
17   //----------------------------------------
18   void OnDrawGizmos()
19   {
20     //Should we show gizmo?
21     if(!ShowCamGizmo) return;
22
23     //Get size (dimensions) of Game Tab
24
25     Vector2 v = DrawFrustumRefined.GetGameViewSize();
26 float GameAspect = v.x/v.y; //Calculate tab aspect ratio
27     float FinalAspect = GameAspect / Cam.aspect; //Divide by
       cam aspect ratio
28
29     Matrix4x4 LocalToWorld = transform.localToWorldMatrix;
30 Matrix4x4 ScaleMatrix = Matrix4x4.Scale(new Vector3
   (Cam.aspect * (Cam.rect.width / Cam.rect.height), Final
   Aspect,1)); //Build scaling matrix for drawing camera gizmo
31     Gizmos.matrix = LocalToWorld * ScaleMatrix;
32 Gizmos.DrawFrustum(transform.position, Cam.fieldOfView,
   Cam.nearClipPlane, Cam.farClipPlane, FinalAspect);
   //Draw camera frustum
33     Gizmos.matrix = Matrix4x4.identity; //Reset gizmo matrix
34   }
35   //----------------------------------------
36   //Function to get dimensions of game tab
37   public static Vector2 GetGameViewSize()
38   {
39     System.Type T = System.Type.GetType("UnityEditor.
       GameView,UnityEditor");
40 System.Reflection.MethodInfo GetSizeOfMainGameView =
   T.GetMethod("GetSizeOfMainGameView",System.Reflection.Binding
   Flags.NonPublic | System.Reflection.BindingFlags.Static);
41     return (Vector2) GetSizeOfMainGameView.Invoke(null,null);
42   }
```

```
43   //---------------------------------------
44   }
45   //---------------------------------------
```

Before testing this script, be sure to activate the desktop controller object in the scene (default), and deactivate the mobile controller. The *ControlSwitcher* script will invert the active status of these objects if a mobile platform is being used. Remember also to drag and drop both the desktop and mobile controller objects into the *DesktopFirstPerson* and *MobileFirstPerson* input fields for the *ControlSwitcher* component in the Object Inspector.

3.10 First-Person Mesh Renderer

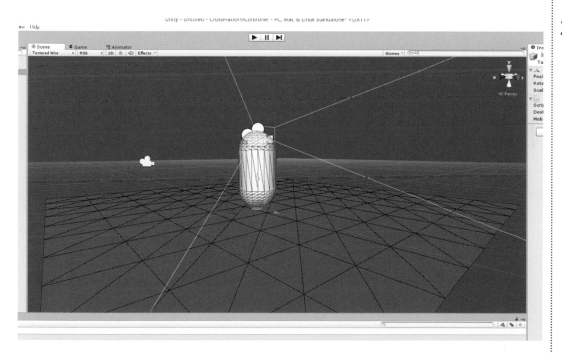

26

Whether you're using the desktop or mobile first-person controller, you'll probably want to disable its *MeshRenderer* component at game start-up, responsible for showing the capsule mesh. In most cases, you'll never see the capsule mesh during gameplay, even if it's visible. It primarily exists for the Scene Viewport, allowing you to see where the controller is and approximate its size. But there are times it can become visible and disruptive to your game during gameplay. The capsule mesh could become visible if the game camera ever leaves first-person mode, or if the player sees him or herself in a reflective surface, or during multiplayer modes, and some other occasions too. To prevent the capsule mesh becoming visible like this, simply add a script to the GameObject, hiding the controller's mesh renderer at start-up. Code Sample 3.10 (HideControllerMeshes.cs) demonstrates how to do this. This script should be attached to the root object of the first-person controller. ▶26

Code Sample 3.10: HideControllerMeshes.cs

```
01  //------------
02  using UnityEngine;
03  using System.Collections;
04  //------------
05  public class HideControllerMeshes : MonoBehaviour
06  {
07    //------------
08    // Use this for initialization
09    void Start ()
10    {
11      //Get mesh renderer components in first person controller
12      MeshRenderer[] Renderers = GetComponentsInChildren<Mesh
        Renderer>();
13
14      //Disable all renderer components
15    foreach(MeshRenderer MR in Renderers)
16        MR.enabled = false;
17    }
18    //------------
19  }
20  //------------
```

3.11 Filling the Screen with Color

You'll commonly want to fade out or fade into black, or another color, to effect scene transitions. Or you'll often need to flood fill a texture with a color, to create icons or markers for mini-maps and other features. You could achieve these results by manually creating flood-filled textures, or preconfigured materials ahead of time. But it's useful to know how to flood fill textures programmatically. ▶27 Take a look at Code Sample 3.11, representing an entire class for flood filling a texture, configuring a new material and then assigning it to an attached mesh. Just drag and drop this on your mesh, and voila!

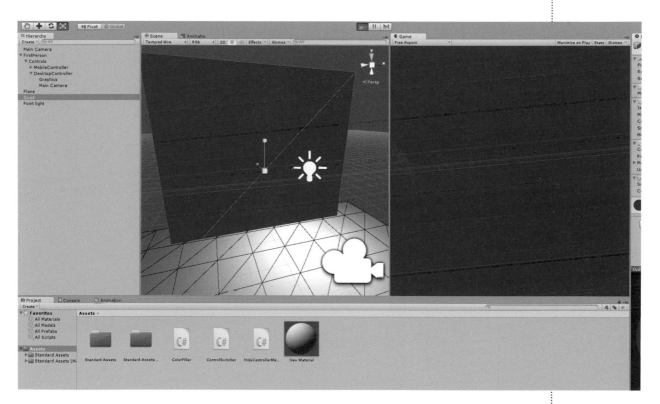

27

Code Sample 3.11: ColorFiller.cs

```
01   //----------------------------------------
02   using UnityEngine;
03   using System.Collections;
04   //----------------------------------------
05   public class ColorFiller : MonoBehaviour
06   {
07     //Color to fill
08     public Color ColorFill = Color.white;
09
10     //Private internal texture
11     private Texture2D FilledTexture = null;
12
13     //Reference to material
14     private Material FillMaterial = null;
15
16     //Get Mesh Renderer Component
17     private MeshRenderer MR = null;
18
19     //----------------------------------------
20     // Use this for initialization
21     void Start () {
22       //Get mesh renderer component
23       MR = GetComponent<MeshRenderer>();
24
25       //Assign fill material
26       FillTexture(ColorFill);
27     }
28     //----------------------------------------
29     //Set texture to color
30     void FillTexture(Color Fill)
31     {
32       //Create texture 1x1 pixels
33       FilledTexture = new Texture2D(1,1);
34       FilledTexture.SetPixel(0,0,Fill);
35       FilledTexture.Apply();
36
37       //Create new material
```

```
38      FillMaterial = new Material(Shader.Find("Unlit/
        Texture"));
39      FillMaterial.mainTexture = FilledTexture;
40
41      //Assign material
42      MR.material = FillMaterial;
43   }
44   //-----------------------------------------
45 }
```

To use this class, create a new Quad in the scene, and attach the *ColorFiller* script to it. Then use the Object Inspector to select your color and play the game. At start-up, the quad will be flood filled with the color of your choice.

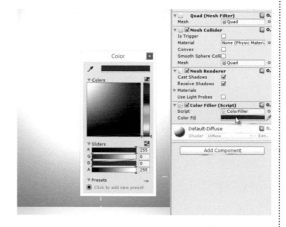

28

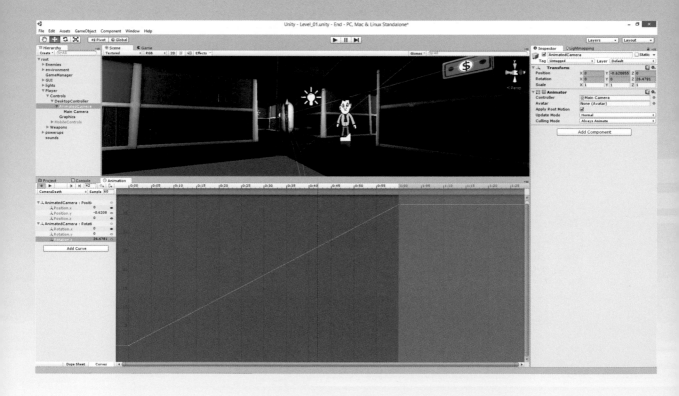

4

Animation and Time

Animation is about change over time. If your objects need to move, rotate, scale, and change in other ways, they'll need to animate. Animation in Unity comes in two main forms that may loosely be described as *Static* and *Dynamic*. Static animation refers to the *AnimationClip* and *AnimationController* assets. Together these are predefined and prerecorded animation sequences, made *in advance* of gameplay, which are either imported with mesh assets directly from modeling software, or are created via the Unity Animation Editor. Such animations include: door opening sequences, walk cycles, punch sequences, lip-syncing animations, and more. The second type of animation is dynamic, and this refers to change and movement created through scripting—such as moving enemy characters on screen, controlling the motion of vehicles, and applying physics to RigidBodies that must move over time but in ways that typically change based on user input. This latter kind of animation doesn't simply "play back"; it defines changes and updates at Run-Time based on player input or other events in-game that cannot be predicted or known in advance. This chapter considers tips and tricks for working with both animation types in Unity.

4 Animation and Time

4.1 *DeltaTime*

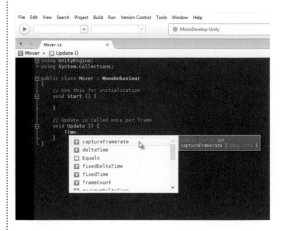

As mentioned, animation is about mapping change to time. Time is therefore a critical animation concept in games. To animate effectively, you'll need a reliable and precise method for measuring time—specifically, for measuring how much time has elapsed since a specific, earlier time. In Unity, time is encapsulated in the Time class, which can be found at the Unity documentation here: http://docs.unity3d.com/ScriptReference/Time.html. ▶1

Each and every *MonoBehaviour* component in Unity has the potential to respond to an *Update* event, which is executed automatically once per frame. This makes *Update* a great place in theory to handle behavior that must update and change over time for objects, such as objects that must move or rotate at specified speeds. However, care should be taken when animating in this function. Consider the case of translating a cube object in the scene on the X axis, starting at position 0 and moving to position 10. You could animate this object simply by using the *Update* function to add 1 to the object's X position. See Code Sample 4.1. This code sample will be "effective" in that it'll move the object by *1 unit* on the *X axis* on *each frame*.

Code Sample 4.1: Moving an Object on a Per-Frame Basis is a Bad Idea

```
01  // Update is called once per frame
02  void Update ()
03  {
04    //Translates object X position by 1 on each frame
05    transform.position = new Vector3(transform.position.x+1,
      transform.position.y, transform.position.z);
06  }
```

The problem with Code Sample 4.1 is that it'll perform inconsistently across machines. This is because the *Update* function, being called once per frame, will be called at variable frequencies on different computers, as each computer sustains a different frame rate. And the frame rate will even change over time on the same computer. So, with this code, the object will travel at different speeds on different computers, giving users an inconsistent experience. This is bad. This issue can be solved by introducing the concept of time to create a consistent speed. To help with this, Unity offers the *Time.deltaTime* variable. This variable changes on each frame and expresses the total time (in seconds) that have passed since the previous frame. Since multiple frames occur per second, this value will almost always be a small, fractional value, such as 0.01. Higher values (over 0.06, for example) indicate a lower frame rate and potential lag problems. The *deltaTime* variable is especially useful as a multiplier for speed variables, to keep an object's speed consistent over time. Code Sample 4.2 shows how Code Sample 4.1 can be changed to move an object at a consistent speed over time by using *deltaTime* as a multiplier. This code will work consistently across computers because the object's motion is linked to time as a universal measure, as opposed to system-specific frame rates.

Code Sample 4.2: (Mover.cs) Moves a GameObject at a Consistent Speed Over Time

```csharp
01  //-----------------
02  using UnityEngine;
03  using System.Collections;
04  //-----------------
05  public class Mover : MonoBehaviour
06  {
07    //Direction to move as a Vector. Eg: (0,1,0) is up,
08    //(0,-1,0) is down. (1,0,0) is right etc...
09    public Vector3 Direction = Vector3.zero;
10
11    //Movement Speed (units per second)
12    public float Speed = 5.0f;
13
14    //-----------------
15    // Update is called once per frame
16    void Update () {
17      //Translates object position using deltaTime
18      transform.position += Direction * Speed * Time.deltaTime;
19    }
20    //-----------------
21  }
22  //-----------------
```

NOTE

See the associated Unity Project in the book companion files, *Chapter04/ Mover.*

Alternative Applications: Throbber

deltaTime is not just useful for moving objects consistently. Think of it as a multiplier for any value that must change, in any way, smoothly and regularly over time. It's like the metronome for your game, always keeping track of time. However, *deltaTime* is not the only weapon in your time arsenal. There's also *Time.time*, which holds the total time in seconds to have elapsed since the game started. This value is especially useful for Ping-Pong effects: times where you need to throb values back and forth smoothly between a minimum and maximum. For example, Code Sample 4.3 Ping-Pongs the scale of an object back and forth between a minimum and maximum scale, making the object appear to pulsate or throb.

Code Sample 4.3: (Throbber.cs) Throb an Object Scale Over Time

```
01  //-----------------
02  using UnityEngine;
03  using System.Collections;
04  //-----------------
05  public class Throbber : MonoBehaviour
06  {
07    //-----------------
08    //Small scale (scale of object at smallest size)
09    public float SmallScale = 1.0f;
10
11    //Large scale (scale of object at largest size)
12    public float LargeScale = 4.0f;
13    //-----------------
14    // Update is called once per frame
15    void Update ()
16    {
17      //Throb scale
18      float ScaleFactor = SmallScale + Mathf.PingPong
        (Time.time, 1.0f) * LargeScale;
19
20      //Apply throb scale
21      transform.localScale = new Vector3(ScaleFactor,
        ScaleFactor,ScaleFactor);
22    }
23    //-----------------
24  }
25  //-----------------
```

NOTE

More information on *deltaTime* and the Time class can be found at the Unity documentation here: http://docs.unity3d.com/Script Reference/Time.html.

NOTE

See the associated Unity Project in the book companion files, *Chapter04/Throbber*.

4.2 Coroutines and Yield

Time and timing is important for animation, but so is synchronization. Not only do you need the ability to measure time, work with time, and make things happen at specific times, but you'll want to achieve more, such as: (a) making multiple events happen at the same time; (b) waiting until a specified time has elapsed before doing something else; and (c) waiting for a function to complete before continuing on with execution. One way to achieve this high level kind of synchronization in code, without resorting to flags, private variables, and multiple switch statements spanning multiple functions, is to use coroutines. Coroutines are a special kind of function in Unity. They *appear* to execute asynchronously, like threads, allowing you to achieve multi-threaded behavior—that is, allowing you to seemingly run multiple functions in parallel. Coroutines are not truly threads or parallel processes, but they act a lot like them—and that's what matters most. Creating a coroutine is much like writing a standard function, but with several additional ingredients. Coroutines must always return an *IEnumerator* type and must contain at least one *Yield* statement within their body. The basic form of a coroutine is shown in Code Sample 4.4.

Code Sample 4.4: (CoRoutineAnim.cs) Basic Coroutine Declared

```
01   //This is a CoRoutine
02   public IEnumerator MyAnimation()
03   {
04     //This line exits the coroutine
05     yield break;
06   }
```

Coroutines are not called or started like regular functions. They are initiated with the *StartCoroutine* function. There are two versions of this function, one that accepts a reference to the coroutine as an argument, and one that accepts a string (coroutine name) as an argument. The second version is generally preferable, because coroutines initiated in this way can always be terminated in mid-flow with the *StopCoroutine* function. Code Sample 4.5 demonstrates how to start and stop a coroutine.

Code Sample 4.5: Starting and Stopping a Coroutine

```
//Start a coroutine called MyAnimation
StartCoroutine("MyAnimation");

//Stop a coroutine called MyAnimation
StopCoroutine("MyAnimation");
```

Once a coroutine is started, there are many useful things you can do for animation, simply by using the *Yield* statement, which must occur at least once in the function body. The *Yield* statement acts like a *Pause* button: using it, you may suspend a coroutine for a specified time, for a single frame, or terminate it completely, and you can even wait until other coroutines complete. By using yield *WaitForSeconds*, you can suspend execution of a coroutine for a specified period, after which execution resumes on the following line. It should be emphasized that coroutines run like a separate and independent process. Pausing a coroutine doesn't pause the entire game and other functions. The following Code Sample 4.6 runs through a list of mesh objects and enables their visibility, by setting their mesh renderer to true. Each mesh is shown linearly at 2-second intervals.

Code Sample 4.6– Sample Coroutine to Show Meshes in a Timed Sequence (CoRoutineAnim.cs)

```
01  //-------------------------------
02  using UnityEngine;
03  using System.Collections;
04  //-------------------------------
05  public class CoRoutineAnim : MonoBehaviour
06  {
07    //-------------------------------
08  //Array of mesh objects
09    private MeshRenderer[] MeshRenderComps = null;
10    //-------------------------------
11    //Called at start-up
12    void Start()
13    {
14      //Get all mesh renderer components in scene
15      MeshRenderComps = Object.FindObjectsOfType
         <MeshRenderer>();
16
17      //Hide all mesh renderers
18      foreach(MeshRenderer MR in MeshRenderComps)
19        MR.enabled = false;
20
21      //Start coroutine
22      StartCoroutine("MyAnimation");
23    }
24    //-------------------------------
```

```
25    //This is a CoRoutine
26    public IEnumerator MyAnimation()
27    {
28      //Use coroutine to show all mesh render components on
        time delay
29      foreach(MeshRenderer MR in MeshRenderComps)
30      {
31        //Wait for 2 seconds, then resume next iteration of
          loop
32        yield return new WaitForSeconds(2);
33
34        //Show mesh renderer
35        MR.enabled = true;
36      }
37    }
38    //------------------------------
39  }
40  //------------------------------
```

To use coroutines effectively, it's important to understand the most common *Yield* statements available. Using *Yield*, you can easily span the execution of a coroutine across multiple frames. This is useful for creating far-reaching behavior, from artificial intelligence to cutscenes. The most common *Yields* are listed in Table 4.1.

TABLE 4.1 Common Yield Statements

yield return null

This exits the coroutine for the current frame, pausing its execution at the *Yield* line. Execution will resume automatically on the next frame from the next line.

yield return new WaitForSeconds(t)

This suspends the coroutine for the specified time *t* in seconds. Execution is suspended at the *Yield* line. Execution will resume automatically at the next line after time *t* has elapsed.

yield break

This terminates the coroutine at the current line. This is equivalent to the return statement for regular functions. The coroutine will not resume after receiving a *Yield* break statement.

yield StartCoroutine("MyOtherRoutine")

Yield, when used in combination with another coroutine, will cause the active coroutine to suspend execution until the other coroutine has fully completed. When this happens, execution resumes at the next line.

4 Animation and Time

Alternative Applications: Coroutine Update

Sometimes, when coding intelligent enemies, you need an object to switch between multiple states in an FSM (Finite State Machine), such as *patrolling*, *attacking*, *fleeing*, and other states. In these cases, you really want the *Update* function to behave differently, depending on the active state. You could use a standard, C# switch statement inside Update to manage the process, checking the current state of an object. However, a better approach is to create a unique coroutine instead, one for each state, and have it run on every frame, just like an *Update* function for as long as the state is active. This means the coroutine will be called once per frame *until* you tell it to stop. Creating this kind of coroutine relies on using an infinite loop! Let's see. Code Sample 4.7 shows you how.

Code Sample 4.7: Coroutine Acting Like an Update Function

```
01  //Coroutine behaves like update
02  public IEnumerator UpdateAttackState()
03  {
04    //Create infinite loop cycle
05    while(true)
06    {
07      //Do my actions here
08      //[ ....]
09
10      //Check if state should change
11      if(bStateShouldChange)
12      {
13        //Change to Idle State
14        StartCoroutine("Idle");
15        //Exit state here
16        yield break;
17      }
18
19      //Wait until next frame, then repeat
20      yield return null;
21    }
22  }
```

NOTE

More information on coroutines can be found at the official Unity documentation here: http://docs.unity3d.com/Manual/Coroutines.html.

NOTE

See the associated Unity Project in the book companion files, *Chapter04/coroutines*.

4.3 Animation Clips and Events

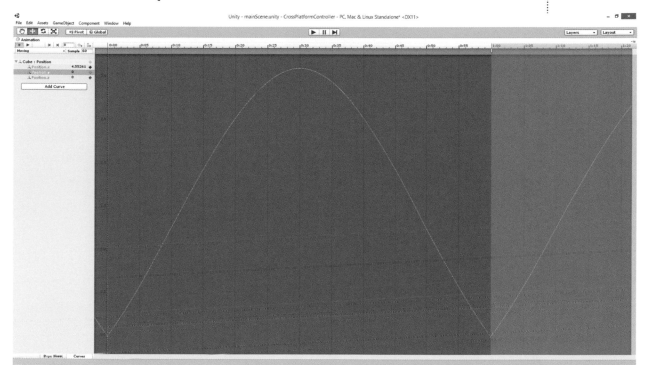

The Animation Editor in Unity is excellent. It lets you define custom animations for your objects using curves directly from the Unity Editor. With this editor, you can make moving objects, traveling cars, rotating doors, elevator platforms, crushing steel presses, flickering lights, and more. You can open the Animation Window by selecting *Window > Animation* from the application menu. ▶2

2

When animating, you'll typically need to call or execute specific code on an object during the animation, to make specific events happen at the correct time.

One way to achieve synchronized behavior is by configuring the timing of a coroutine using *yield WaitForSeconds*, to execute in time as the animation plays back. *However*, it's easier to use Animation Events instead.

4 Animation and Time

3

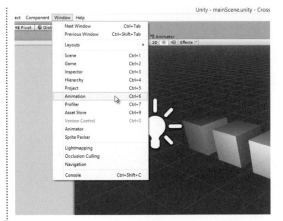

To get started, you'll first need to create a new script file with at least one function you want to call from the animation clip. To work with the Animation Editor, this function should have a void return type and accept only one argument, which can be either an integer, a float, a string, or an object—such as a GameObject. Code Sample 4.8 demonstrates a list of functions that could be called from an animation as an event. ▶3

Code Sample 4.8: Creating Functions to Call as Animation Events

```
01  //----------------------------------
02  void MyCustomEvent()
03  {
04  }
05  //----------------------------------
06  void MyCustomEventInteger(int Param)
07  {
08     Debug.Log (Param);
09  }
10  //----------------------------------
11  void MyCustomEventFloat(float Param)
12  {
13     Debug.Log (Param);
14  }
15  //----------------------------------
16  void MyCustomEventString(string Param)
17  {
18     Debug.Log (Param);
19  }
20  //----------------------------------
21  void MyCustomEventObject(Object Param)
22  {
23     Debug.Log (Param);
24  }
25  //----------------------------------
```

After creating functions to call, be sure to add all relevant script files to the object in the scene that you need to animate. Select your object, open the Animation Editor, and create your animation as usual by defining key frames and curves. To call an Animation Event from the Animation Window during the animation, position the play head at the frame where the call should be made, and right-click in the play head bar, choosing *Add Animation Event* from the context menu, or else click the *Add Event* button from the Animation toolbar. ▶4

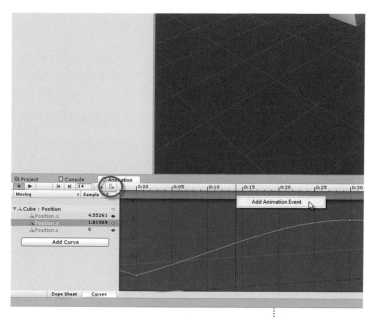

4

Once you've added an Animation Event, an Event marker appears in the play head bar. Double-click this marker to display the Animation Event window where you can customize the function to call and the argument passed when the frame is reached during playback. Remember, if your animation loops, then your Animation Event will also be executed on each loop, not just once. ▶5

NOTE

NOTE. See the associated Unity
Project in the book companion files,
Chapter04/animation_events.

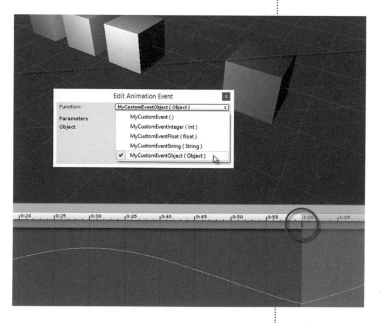

5

4.4 Animation Curves

You'll often want to move objects in the scene over time using script instead of predefined animations, objects like the player character, spaceships, enemies, and other objects that move dynamically based on player input and actions. To achieve this, you can often use lerping techniques like *Mathf.Lerp*, as well as basic vector arithmetic, to interpolate the position of an object linearly. But what if you need the object to follow a non-straight path, or to curve and bend, and to ease in and ease out. In these cases, the properties of an object should be animated according to a curve rather than a line. To achieve this programmatically, you can use the *AnimationCurve* object. Consider the short Code Sample 4.9 (CurveMover.cs) script, which uses three *AnimationCurve* variables. ▶6

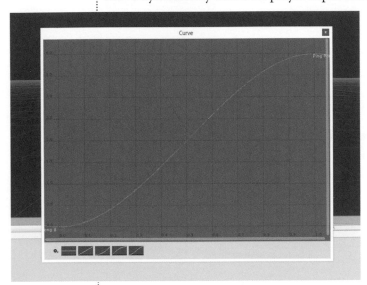

6   **Code Sample 4.9: (CurveMover.cs) Script to Translate Object Position Based on Curves**

```
01  //-----------------
02  using UnityEngine;
03  using System.Collections;
04  //-----------------
05  public class CurveMover : MonoBehaviour
06  {
07      //-----------------
08      //Curves for X Y and Z axes
09      public AnimationCurve XMovement;
10      public AnimationCurve YMovement;
11      public AnimationCurve ZMovement;
12      //-----------------
13      void Update()
14      {
```

```
15      transform.position = new Vector3
        (XMovement.Evaluate(Time.time),
        YMovement.Evaluate(Time.time), ZMovement.
        Evaluate(Time.time));
16    }
17    //-----------------
18  }
19  //-----------------
```

> **NOTE**
>
> Code Sample 4.9 uses the *Evaluate* function of *AnimationCurve* to return a value in the graph. *Evaluate* accepts a horizontal (time value) as an argument and then returns the associated vertical value. More information on the *AnimationCurve* class can be found online at: http://docs.unity3d.com/Script Reference/AnimationCurve.html.

Code Sample 4.9 features three variables of type *AnimationCurve*, each controlling movement for an object on the X, Y and Z axis over time. This script should be added to any object you need to move using animation curves. When added to the object, the Object Inspector will show three animation curve inputs for creating a curve defining motion. ▶7

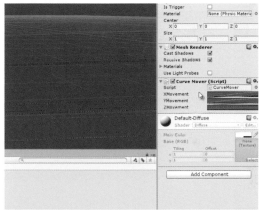

7

Click inside the Curve Thumbnail to open the Graph Editor to build a curve. By default, the graph editor maps values in the range of 0–1 on both the X and Y axis. The horizontal axis typically refers to *Time*, and the vertical refers to *Value* (whichever properties you want to animate). ▶8

8

For demonstration purposes, let's animate an object (a cube, for example) to move in the X axis 4 units on a loop, back and forth over again. That is, over 1 second a cube object will move forward 4 units and then back 4 units on a cycle, with an ease-in and ease-out motion so that the object starts slow and then accelerates, and then finally slows down before coming to a stop and beginning the loop again. This is an example of nonlinear motion, because the object changes speed over the course of traveling. To get started, follow along with me by clicking the Animation Curve in the Object Inspector. From the graph editor, create an initial linear curve, by choosing the linear curve preset from the bottom toolbar. This inserts two key frames into the graph, one at each end, defining a perfectly straight line inclining upward at a constant speed, from 0 to 1. ▶9

9

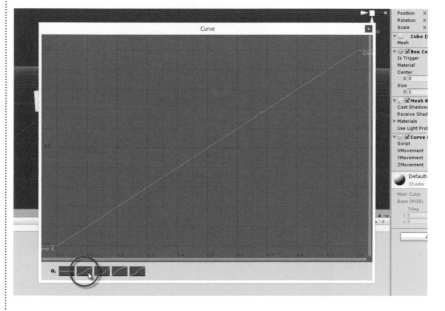

By default, the linear graph ranges from 0 to 1, both horizontally and vertically. The vertical axis represents the object's X movement, and this should range (for our sample) from 0 to 4. To fix this, click the last key frame, hold down the *Ctrl* key on the keyboard to activate snapping, and then click and drag the last key frame upward on the vertical axis, positioning it at 4. Use the middle mouse scroll wheel, if required, to zoom in and out from the graph, bringing the required regions into view. You can also press *F* on the keyboard to frame the selected key frame and curve.

The looping mode of the graph is set, by default, to clamp for both the first and last key frame. The word *Clamp* will be printed in the graph above the end key frames. This means that for time values outside 0 and 1, the vertical axis will always be clamped within the minimum and maximum range, in this case 0–4 on the X axis. Time values above 1 will always result in 4 on the X axis, and time values before 0, if possible, will always result in 0 on the X axis. For our animation, a Ping-Ping looping behavior is required. The object should move backward and forward within the range continually. To change the *Clamp* behavior, click on the *Clamp* marker in the graph and choose *Ping-Pong* from the context menu. In choosing this, the curve is now repeated and mirrored in a wave, infinitely across the graph. This means that all horizontal time values will evaluate to a vertical value that is meaningful. ▶10, 11

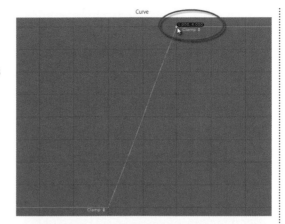

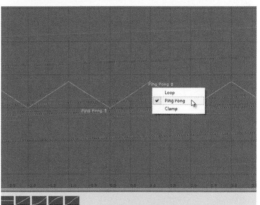

The graph is almost completed. In its current form, it will successfully animate an object back and forth over time, between 0 and 4 on the axis. But, right now, there's no ease-in or ease-out behavior. To achieve that, change the handle type for both the start and end key frames. This affects how the curves will be interpolated for the in-betweens. Start by right-clicking the first key frame, changing its value to *Free Smooth*. When you do this, a Bezier handle appears, which can be clicked and dragged to affect the curve of the line. Move the Bezier handle to an outward inclining curve, and do the same for the end key frame. This produces a sine curve in the graph. ▶12

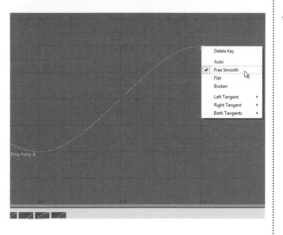

NOTE

See the associated Unity Project in the book companion files, *Chapter04/ animation_ curves*.

Now simply take your object for a test drive in Play-Mode, using the *CurveMover* script, to observe its motion. You can further refine the motion by applying animation curves to other axes, and even other properties generally, including material color, scale, rotation, and others.

4.5 Animating UVs

If you need to create moving skies or water or clouds or lava, or any other texture that should scroll across its mesh geometry while the geometry itself remains in place, then you'll need to animate an object's UVs. That is, its mapping coordinates. There are several methods to achieve this kind of behavior. The simplest is perhaps to edit the Material offset for a mesh at Run-Time. To achieve this, you can use the script file shown in Code Sample 4.10 (MatScroller.cs). This script should be attached to any mesh, like a Plane or Quad (with a *MeshFilter* and *MeshRenderer* component) to scroll its associated material over time at a specified speed. ▶13

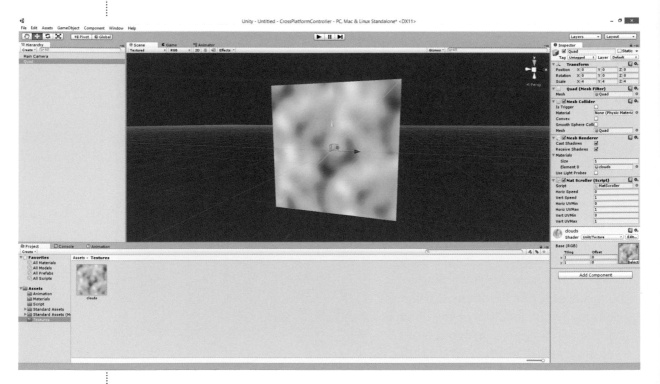

13

Code Sample 4.10: (MatScroller.cs) Script to Scroll a Texture

```
01   //CLASS TO SCROLL TEXTURE ON PLANE. CAN BE USED FOR MOVING
     SKY
02   //---------------------------
03   using UnityEngine;
04   using System.Collections;
05   //---------------------------
06   [ RequireComponent (typeof (MeshRenderer))] //Requires
     Renderer Filter Component
07   public class MatScroller : MonoBehaviour
08   {
09     //Public variables
10     //---------------------------
11     //Reference to Horizontal Scroll Speed
12     public float HorizSpeed = 1.0f;
13
14     //Reference to Vertical Scroll Speed
15     public float VertSpeed = 1.0f;
16
17     //Reference to Min and Max Horiz and Vertical UVs to scroll
       between
18     public float HorizUVMin = 1.0f;
19     public float HorizUVMax = 2.0f;
20
21     public float VertUVMin = 1.0f;
22     public float VertUVMax = 2.0f;
23
24     //Private variables
25     //---------------------------
26     //Reference to Mesh Renderer Component
27     private MeshRenderer MeshR = null;
28
29     //Methods
30     //---------------------------
31     // Use this for initialization
32     void Awake ()
33     {
34       //Get Mesh Renderer Component
```

To get the best results from this class, your texture should be tile-able and seamless, preventing the texture scrolling from being noticeable.

NOTE

See the associated Unity Project in the book companion files, *Chapter04/ animating_UVs*.

```
35        MeshR = GetComponent<MeshRenderer>();
36    }
37    //---------------------------
38    // Update is called once per frame
39    void Update ()
40    {
41        //Scrolls texture between min and max
42        Vector2 Offset = new Vector2((MeshR.material.mainTexture
          Offset.x > HorizUVMax) ? HorizUVMin : MeshR.material.
          mainTextureOffset.x + Time.deltaTime * HorizSpeed,
43        (MeshR.material.mainTextureOffset.y > VertUVMax) ?
          VertUVMin : MeshR.material.mainTextureOffset.y +
          Time.deltaTime * VertSpeed);
44
45        //Update UV coordinates
46        MeshR.material.mainTextureOffset = Offset;
47    }
48    //---------------------------
49 }
50 //---------------------------
```

4.6 Pausing a Game

If you need to pause your game, then don't rely on the *timeScale* variable of the Time class. The Time class offers *timeScale*, which is a multiplier applied to almost all time values, including *deltaTime*. When *timeScale* is 0, therefore, *deltaTime* will also be 0. This initially seems to make *timeScale* useful for creating paused behavior, because a *deltaTime* of 0 will pause all movement. But, using it for this purpose can be problematic. If your class doesn't rely on *Time*, or if you're using the *realtimeSinceStartup* variable, or if you have active coroutines in execution, Unity will continue to run your code, even when *timeScale* is 0. Plus, you may want menus and other GUI elements to move or animate even when the game is paused!

For this reason, get into the habit of creating your own, customized *Pause* behavior. Consider adding a floar *Paused* variable to your *GameController* or *GameManager* class, which everything else can read and access to determine if the game should pause. A value of 1.0f means normal speed, and 0.0f means paused. By using a float instead of a bool, you get extra control; specifically, the ability to increase and decrease the speed of your game independently of the *timeScale* variable.

4.7 *FixedUpdate* versus *Update* versus *LateUpdate*

If you search the Unity documentation for the *MonoBehaviour* class, you'll see it supports three kinds of *Update* events, all of which are critical to animation and moving objects over time. These events are: *Update*, *FixedUpdate*, and *LateUpdate*. It's important to know how these work, the order in which they're executed, and when to use them. A good understanding of this will help you get the behavior you need.

Update

Update is a frame-rate-specific event, and thus is related to hardware and not time. It's called *once* per frame, and thus its consistency varies over time and between computers. Consequently, this event is called more frequently per second on a system with a higher frame rate. In general, this function should be treated as the default method for updating the motion of objects and the changing of their properties. If you need to check for user input, or you need to move objects manually outside the physics system, then you'll probably need *Update* to do it.

FixedUpdate

FixedUpdate is frame-rate-independent and is, instead, called at a fixed, regular interval that Unity determines. This means *FixedUpdate* may be called *more* than once per frame, or *less* than once per frame, depending on the frame rate. This function is called once before an update of the physics system. For this reason, *FixedUpdate* is useful for updating objects with physics enabled, such as rigid bodies and colliders. Consequently, if you're animating objects using functions, such as *Rigidbody.AddForce* or *Rigidbody.AddTorque*, then do so inside *FixedUpdate*.

LateUpdate

LateUpdate is called once per frame, at the end of the frame. When *LateUpdate* is called, every other object and script will be guaranteed to have received and completed their *Update* events. *LateUpdate* will always be called after all *Updates*, on each frame. This makes *LateUpdate* best suited for animating "meta-objects," such as the game camera, which must track the motion of other moving objects. By updating the camera in *LateUpdate*, as opposed to *Update*, you can be always sure the camera will be focusing on objects at their final positions for the current frame.

> **NOTE**
>
> More information on the execution of events in Unity can be found at the official Unity documentation here: http://docs.unity3d.com/Manual/ExecutionOrder.html.

Animation and Time

4.8 Importing Animated Meshes

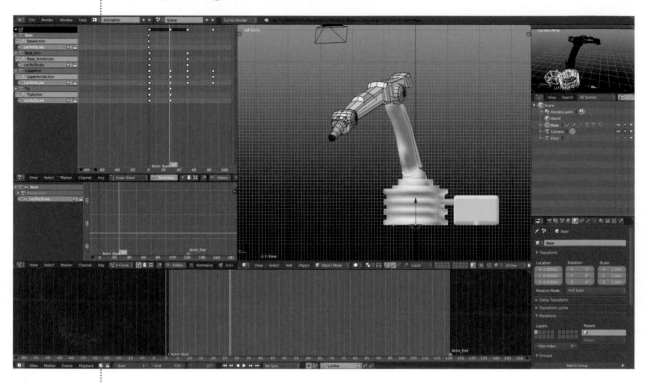

14

Unity accepts animated mesh files from many third-party applications, including 3DS Max, Maya, Strata3D, Blender, and others. Among the many possible animations you can create in 3D software, Unity recognizes two main kinds. These are *Humanoid* and *Generic*. The first refers to animated humanoid characters using Bones, with arms and legs and heads, like humans, and the latter refers to all other animation kinds, such as moving cars, opening doors, spaceships, and others. Unity is able to import the complete mesh file, including the mesh, and both the skeletal rig (if any) and its associated animation data in the form of key frames. Importing this data is often an impressively painless process (just dragging and dropping your mesh in Unity). But, there are still many things you can do, both in Unity and your 3D software, to optimize your meshes and animations, making them perform even better in Unity. Let's look at some of these. ▶14

Give Bones Appropriate Names

When rigging humanoid characters with skeletons, give all bones unique and conventional names. The hipbone (or root) should be called *hip*, or *root*. And symmetrical bones, such as the arms and legs, which appear on either side of a character, should be post-fixed with .l or .r, indicating the left or right sides of the body. The upper left arm, for example, could be named *ArmUpper.l* or *ArmUpper.left*. There's no formal standard for naming bones, but adopting a convention like this helps Unity automatically locate and configure bones in your skeletal mesh at import. Plus, it helps you identify each bone from the other when viewing their names in the Scene hierarchy panel! ▶15

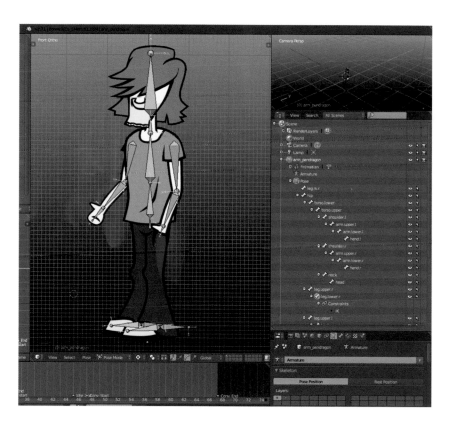

15

Delete Inverse Kinematic Nodes or Bones

Different 3D modeling programs work differently with Inverse Kinematics (IK) for rigging arms and legs. Most programs (including Blender) expect you to create additional nodes or bones, marking end points of an IK chain, like the end of an arm where it meets the hand or the end of a leg where it meets the feet. This allows the 3D software to calculate IK effectively. The final IK motions and animations, however, will be baked into the key frames themselves for the bones, effectively converting the animation data from Inverse Kinematics to Forward Kinematics. This means any additional IK-helper bones for a chain don't need to be exported into Unity, because they don't really correspond to the character mesh itself. You can therefore optimize your character meshes by removing the IK bones before export. ▶16

16

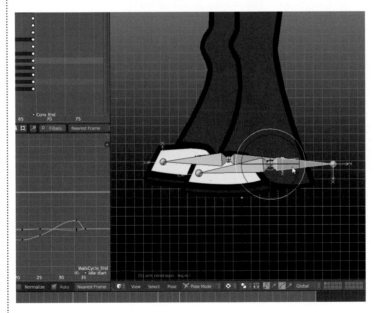

Group Skinned Meshes

Unity automatically attaches a *SkinnedMeshRenderer* component to every active and rigged character meshes in the scene. Each visible *SkinnedMeshRenderer* demands at least one draw call from the Unity renderer at Run-Time, meaning that an increase in skinned meshes will lead to a resultant increase in draw calls. Draw calls are associated with a performance hit—less of them is better. For this reason, in scenes where there are multiple skinned meshes interacting in predefined animations, consider grouping the meshes together in your modeling software, making them part of one larger rigged mesh. In other words, make sure the arms and legs and torso and head of a character are part of a single mesh, instead of separate meshes. Doing this is not always possible or convenient but, where possible and useful, give it a try! ▶17

17

Reduce Key Frames

Every key frame in an animation represents data that Unity must process and blend between. Get into the habit of reducing key frames, seeing animation as partly a logistical exercise in achieving your goals with the fewest key frames possible. Actively look for ways to reduce key frames in your modeling software while keeping the results you need. Make creative use of tools, such as the Graph Editor and Dope Sheet. For example, if you're moving an object in the X axis only, then you don't need key frames for the Y and Z axis, and you don't need key frames for rotation or scale. ▶18

18

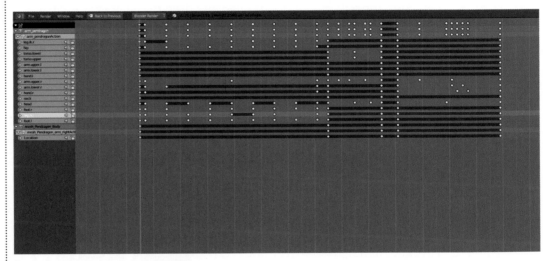

▼19

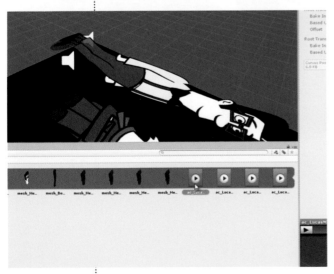

Import Multiple Animations from One File

One of the great things about Unity is that it allows separation between a mesh, its rig, and its animation data. This means that different animations, from different files, can be applied to the same rig and used to animate the same or a different mesh. It's possible to recombine meshes with rigs and animations to create variation from the same data. Even so, it helps to be organized in your workflow. For this reason, try to export all related animations together on the same timeline from the same file. This provides a convenient and useful mechanism for grouping together your animations. ▶19

4.9 Shape Keys

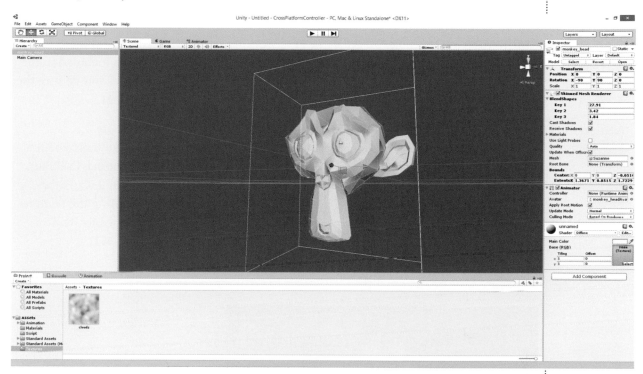

20

Many people don't seem to know that Unity supports shape keys (or blend shapes). A shape key effectively stores a copy of all vertices in the mesh at a specified time in the animation. By creating multiple shape keys at different times, with vertices in different arrangements, Unity can then blend or morph between the multiple states. This is especially useful for facial animation, such as lip-synching and facial expressions. Each state or Shape Key has its own unique

21

NOTE

See the associated Unity Project in the book companion files, *Chapter04/ blendshapes*.

weighting between 0 and 1, indicating how strongly the key factors into the final topology of the mesh shown in the game. This weighting means you can blend not just between two different keys, but multiple keys at the same time, each with different weights contributing to the whole. To get shape keys working in Unity, be sure to export your meshes from your 3D modeling software with the shape key information included in the FBX file. Once imported into Unity, select your mesh in the Project Panel and be sure the *Import BlendShapes* checkbox is enabled from the Object Inspector. ▶20, 21

Then just drag and drop your mesh into the scene, select it, and examine its *SkinnedMeshRenderer* component in the object inspector. Provided the keys are enabled and configured, it'll feature an array variable for all *BlendShapes* in the model. Each key has its own numerical field that can be edited, specified, and even animated using the native Unity animation tools. Each key can range from 0 to 100%, indicating the relative strength the key has in influencing the final topology of the mesh in the scene. By increasing the values of keys, you strengthen the influence of the morph. ▶22

22

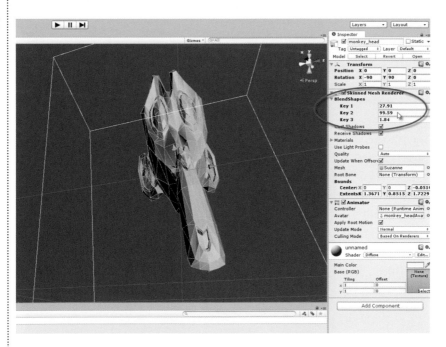

File Edit Search View Encoding Language Settings Macro Run TextFX Plugins Window ?

SaveGame.xml

```xml
<?xml version="1.0" encoding="Windows-1252"?>
<GameData xmlns:xsi="http://www.w3.org/2001/XMLSchema-instance" xmlns:xsd="http://www.w3.org/2001/XMLSchema">
    <Enemies>
        <DataEnemy>
            <PosRotScale>
                <X>6.53815556</X>
                <Y>0.019997187</Y>
                <Z>4.971764</Z>
                <RotX>0</RotX>
                <RotY>14.361268</RotY>
                <RotZ>0</RotZ>
                <ScaleX>1</ScaleX>
                <ScaleY>1</ScaleY>
                <ScaleZ>1</ScaleZ>
            </PosRotScale>
            <EnemyID>3</EnemyID>
            <Health>100</Health>
        </DataEnemy>
        <DataEnemy>
            <PosRotScale>
                <X>1.64043438</X>
                <Y>0.019997187</Y>
                <Z>-8.93423748</Z>
                <RotX>0</RotX>
                <RotY>339.341339</RotY>
                <RotZ>0</RotZ>
                <ScaleX>1</ScaleX>
                <ScaleY>1</ScaleY>
                <ScaleZ>1</ScaleZ>
            </PosRotScale>
            <EnemyID>1</EnemyID>
            <Health>100</Health>
        </DataEnemy>
        <DataEnemy>
            <PosRotScale>
                <X>2.82607913</X>
                <Y>0.019997187</Y>
                <Z>-3.47039962</Z>
                <RotX>0</RotX>
                <RotY>2.94075561</RotY>
                <RotZ>0</RotZ>
                <ScaleX>1</ScaleX>
                <ScaleY>1</ScaleY>
                <ScaleZ>1</ScaleZ>
            </PosRotScale>
            <EnemyID>2</EnemyID>
            <Health>100</Health>
        </DataEnemy>
        <DataEnemy>
            <PosRotScale>
```

5

Persistence and Accessibility

This chapter considers the distinct but related issues of persistence and accessibility in Unity. Persistence is about how data, like variables and objects, remain over time, not just between scenes, but also across play sessions. That is, across days and weeks, and months, even after the user has quit your game and returned to it much later. It's about how you can keep objects like save-games in external files. Second, the chapter also considers accessibility. By "accessibility," I mean the ways you can *scope* objects in code, making it easier and simpler for separate game objects to communicate and share data efficiently between scenes. The tips and techniques covered here are important if you're making games that span multiple scenes and let the user save and restore data from external files, and also if you need objects—like *Manager* classes—to be globally and instantly accessible to all other objects in the scene, without having to rely on dedicated, local variable references.

5 Persistence and Accessibility

5.1 Player Preferences

The quickest and simplest means of saving persistent data in Unity between play sessions is through the *PlayerPrefs* class. This class is especially useful for permanently saving isolated settings and parameters, such as the game resolution or the master volume level. It's typically used for creating option or preference screens for games, allowing you to save player settings to the system where they can be reliably accessed and restored across play sessions. Documentation for this class can be found online at: http://docs.unity3d.com/ScriptReference/PlayerPrefs.html. Code Sample 5.1 demonstrates a sample C# class for saving and loading settings via *PlayerPrefs*.

Code Sample 5.1: Loading and Saving Data via *PlayerPrefs*

```
01  using UnityEngine;
02  using System.Collections;
03
04  //Sample class for an option screen
05  public class Database : MonoBehaviour
06  {
07    //Width of game in pixels
08    int ScreenResX = 1920;
09
10    //Height of game in pixels
11    int ScreenResY = 1080;
12
13    //Should game run in full screen mode
14    bool FullScreen = true;
15
16    //Normalized volume 0-1
17    float MasterVolume = 1.0f;
18
19    //Player name
20    string PlayerName = "John";
21
22    //Function to save values to system
23    void SaveDatabase()
24    {
25      //Save screen dimensions
26      PlayerPrefs.SetInt("ScreenWidth", ScreenResX);
```

```
27      PlayerPrefs.SetInt("ScreenHeight", ScreenResY);
28
29      //Covert bool to int
30      PlayerPrefs.SetInt("FullScreen", FullScreen ? 1 : 0);
31
32      PlayerPrefs.SetFloat("MasterVolume", MasterVolume);
33      PlayerPrefs.SetString("PlayerName", PlayerName);
34
35      //Call save function. This is optional. Will be called
        automatically on application quit
36      PlayerPrefs.Save();
37    }
38
39  //Function load values from system to variables, if the key
    exists
40  void LoadDatabase()
41  {
42    //Always specify a default value to return if key doesn't
      exist
43    ScreenResX = PlayerPrefs.GetInt("ScreenWidth",
      ScreenResX);
44    ScreenResY = PlayerPrefs.GetInt("ScreenHeight",
      ScreenResY);
45    FullScreen = (PlayerPrefs.GetInt("FullScreen", FullScreen
      ? 1 : 0) == 1) ? true : false;
46    MasterVolume = PlayerPrefs.GetFloat
      ("MasterVolume", MasterVolume);
47    PlayerName = PlayerPrefs.GetString
      ("PlayerName", PlayerName);
48  }
49 }
```

T--I--P

The physical location of *PlayerPrefs* data on the local computer differs, depending on the operating system—as explored in the Unity documentation. It should be noted for Web player games that all data for a *unique URL* will be saved to the same local file. This file should not exceed 1 MB in size. If it does, all subsequent save operations will fail and raise an exception.

Alternative Applications: Data Transfer

PlayerPrefs isn't limited to saving only options or preference data, despite its name. It can also be used to save data between scene changes during a single play session. That is: you can use it to transfer information from one scene to another. For example, if you need to save player health or a time value or a game statistic as the scene transitions from one to the next, you can use *PlayerPrefs*. You can save the data before exiting the first scene, during an *OnDestroy* event using any of the *PlayerPrefs Set* methods, and then retrieve the data back on starting the second scene, during a *Start* event using any of the *Get* methods. This approach isn't ideal for transferring large quantities of data and, as we'll see, there are plenty of slicker alternatives. But, when you need to transfer just a few integer or string values, *PlayerPrefs* can be your friend. When using this method, however, be sure to call either the *DeleteAll* or *DeleteKey* methods as appropriate to delete the relevant keys when they're no longer needed as the play session ends. If you don't, the keys will remain stored on the local computer even when the player exits the game, and even if they uninstall the game!

5.2 XML and Binary Files: Serialization

Using the *Scene* tab to move an object at Run-Time, and then saving its position data to a file. Both Binary and XML serialization techniques can be used to save any kind of data.

For creating save-state behavior, and for permanently storing more substantial data than just numbers and strings, you'll frequently need to save data to a file, and then load it back again. Unity has no native feature set for save-game states. For this reason, you have to create save-game files manually. The files you create can be either human-readable XML files, or proprietary binary files—both have advantages and disadvantages, depending on your requirements, as we'll see. There are many ways to achieve save-states using Unity and the Mono Framework, which is included. Perhaps the simplest and most convenient way for general-purpose saving-and-restoring behavior is to use object *serialization*. This is the process of converting an instance of a class into a linear stream of bytes that may be either transmitted over a network or written directly to a file. In addition, the bytes can be loaded back from the network, or from a file, at any time to accurately reconstruct the object again as it was when it was serialized; this process is known formally as de-serialization. By default, serialization to a file or to XML in Unity requires your classes to use only simpler, value-type objects: objects like *ints*, *floats*, *strings*, and *bools*, as well as arrays of these. More complex reference type objects, like *Transform*, *GameObject*, *Component*, and others, cannot be serialized as they are: they

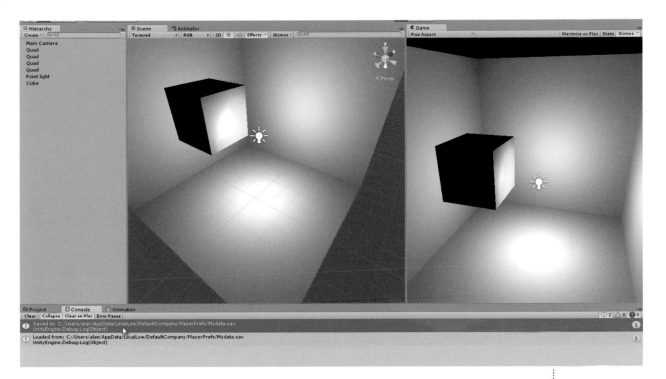

should be converted to simpler types. Code Sample 5.2 demonstrates loading and saving using both XML and binary files. It's a complete class that can be attached to any game object in the scene to save and load a transformation component to a file, allowing an object's position, rotation, and scale to be saved and restored across play sessions. Comments follow the source code. ▶1

Code Sample 5.2: Loading and Saving Data with XML and Binary Files

```
001    //-------------------------------------
002    using UnityEngine;
003    using System.Collections;
004    using System.Collections.Generic;
005    using System.Xml;
006    using System.Xml.Serialization;
007    using System.Runtime.Serialization.Formatters.Binary;
008    using System.IO;
009    //-------------------------------------
010    public class ObjSerializer : MonoBehaviour
011    {
```

NOTE

A complete Unity project demonstrating this class (as shown in Figure 5.1) is included in the book companion files inside the *Chapter05/ XML_and_ Binary* folder.

```
012    //Data to save to file XML or Binary
013    [System.Serializable]
014    [ XmlRoot ("GameData")]
015    public class MySaveData
016    {
017      //Transform data to save/load to and from file
018      //This represents a conversion of a transform object
019      //into simpler values, like floats
020      [System.Serializable]
021      public struct DataTransform
022      {
023        public float X;
024        public float Y;
025        public float Z;
026        public float RotX;
027        public float RotY;
028        public float RotZ;
029        public float ScaleX;
030        public float ScaleY;
031        public float ScaleZ;
032      }
033
034      //Transform object to save
035      public DataTransform MyTransform = new DataTransform();
036    }
037
038    //My Save Data Object declared here
039    public MySaveData MyData = new MySaveData();
040    //-------------------------------------
041    //Populate structure MyData with transform data
042    //This is the data to be saved to a file
043    private void GetTransform()
044    {
045      //Get transform component on this object
046      Transform ThisTransform = transform;
047
048      //We got the transform component, now fill data structure
049      MyData.MyTransform.X = ThisTransform.position.x;
```

```
050       MyData.MyTransform.Y = ThisTransform.position.y;
051       MyData.MyTransform.Z = ThisTransform.position.z;
052       MyData.MyTransform.RotX = ThisTransform.localRotation.
          eulerAngles.x;
053       MyData.MyTransform.RotY = ThisTransform.localRotation.
          eulerAngles.y;
054       MyData.MyTransform.RotZ =
          ThisTransform.localRotation.eulerAngles.z;
055       MyData.MyTransform.ScaleX = ThisTransform.localScale.x;
056       MyData.MyTransform.ScaleY = ThisTransform.localScale.y;
057       MyData.MyTransform.ScaleZ = ThisTransform.localScale.z;
058     }
059     //---------------------------------------
060     //Restore the transform component with loaded data
061     //Call this function after loading data back from a file
        for restore
062     private void SetTransform()
063     {
064       //Get transform component on this object
065       Transform ThisTransform = transform;
066
067       //We got the transform component, now restore data
068       ThisTransform.position = new Vector3(MyData.
          MyTransform.X, MyData.MyTransform.Y, MyData.
          MyTransform.Z);
069       ThisTransform.rotation = Quaternion.Euler
          (MyData.MyTransform.RotX, MyData.MyTransform.RotY,
          MyData.MyTransform.RotZ);
070       ThisTransform.localScale = new Vector3(MyData.
          MyTransform.ScaleX, MyData.MyTransform.ScaleY,
          MyData.MyTransform.ScaleZ);
071 }
072     //---------------------------------------
073     //Saves game data to XML file
074     //Call this function to save data to an XML file
075     //Call as SaveXML(Application.persistentDataPath +
        "/Mydata.xml");
076     public void SaveXML(string FileName = "GameData.xml")
```

```
077  {
078    //Get transform data
079    GetTransform();
080
081    //Now save game data
082    XmlSerializer Serializer = new XmlSerializer
       (typeof(MySaveData));
083    FileStream Stream = new FileStream(FileName, FileMode.
       Create);
084    Serializer.Serialize(Stream, MyData);
085    Stream.Close();
086  }
087  //-------------------------------------
088  //Load game data from XML file
089  //Call this function to load data from an XML file
090  //Call as LoadXML(Application.persistentDataPath +
       "/Mydata.xml");
091  public void LoadXML(string FileName = "GameData.xml")
092  {
093    //If file doesn't exist, then exit
094    if(!File.Exists(FileName)) return;
095
096    XmlSerializer Serializer = new XmlSerializer
       (typeof(MySaveData));
097    FileStream Stream = new FileStream(FileName,
       FileMode.Open);
098    MyData = Serializer.Deserialize(Stream) as MySaveData;
099    Stream.Close();
100
101    //Set transform - load back from a file
102    SetTransform();
103  }
104  //-------------------------------------
105  public void SaveBinary(string FileName = "GameData.sav")
106  {
107    //Get transform data
108    GetTransform();
109
```

```
110      BinaryFormatter bf = new BinaryFormatter();
111      FileStream Stream = File.Create(FileName);
112      bf.Serialize(Stream, MyData);
113      Stream.Close();
114 }
115   //------------------------------------
116   public void LoadBinary(string FileName = "GameData.sav")
117   {
118     //If file doesn't exist, then exit
119     if(!File.Exists(FileName)) return;
120
121     BinaryFormatter bf = new BinaryFormatter();
122     FileStream Stream = File.Open(FileName, FileMode.Open);
123     MyData = bf.Deserialize(Stream) as MySaveData;
124     Stream.Close();
125
126     //Set transform - load back from a file
127     SetTransform();
128   }
129   //-------------------------------- ---
130   void Update()
131   {
132     //If 1 key is pressed,then data saved to XML file
133     if(Input.GetKeyDown(KeyCode.Alpha1))
134     {
135       SaveXML(Application.persistentDataPath +
              "/Mydata.xml");
136       Debug.Log ("Saved to: " + Application.persistent
              DataPath + "/Mydata.xml");
137     }
138
139     //If 2 key is pressed,then data loaded from XML file
140     if(Input.GetKeyDown(KeyCode.Alpha2))
141     {
142       LoadXML(Application.persistentDataPath +
              "/Mydata.xml");
143       Debug.Log ("Loaded from: " + Application.persistent
              DataPath + "/Mydata.xml");
```

```
144      }
145
146      //If 3 key is pressed,then data saved to binary file
147      if(Input.GetKeyDown(KeyCode.Alpha3))
148      {
149        SaveBinary(Application.persistentDataPath +
           "/Mydata.sav");
150        Debug.Log ("Saved to: " +
           Application.persistentDataPath + "/Mydata.sav");
151      }
152
153      //If 4 key is pressed,then data loaded from binary file
154      if(Input.GetKeyDown(KeyCode.Alpha4))
155      {
156        LoadBinary(Application.persistentDataPath +
           "/Mydata.sav");
157        Debug.Log ("Loaded from: " + Application.persistent
           DataPath + "/Mydata.sav");
158      }
159    }
160    //-----------------------------------
161    }
162    //-----------------------------------
```

Comments

- **Lines 002–008**. Using serialization for saving objects either to XML or binary files, or both, relies on several namespaces within the Mono Framework. Be sure to include them all at the top of your source files to get access to serialization.

- **Lines 013 and 014**. If you plan on serializing a class, make sure it's marked with the *[System.Serializable]* attribute at the top, and for XML Serialization also include an *XmlRoot* attribute for naming the root node in the file. The latter is optional.

- **Lines 043–058**. The serializable class *DataTransform* will eventually be streamed to a file, saving the position, rotation, and scale variables for the *Transform* component. *DataTransform* is populated with the *Transform* member variables, in the functions *GetTransform* and *SetTransform*. Remember, this is necessary because reference objects (like *Transform* and *Component*) cannot be serialized by default.

- **Lines 076–086**. The *SaveXML* function serializes the object's transform data to a specified XML file on the local computer. This file is "open" and human-readable: this means a player or developer can open the file and edit its contents. This makes XML files good for debugging save-data, and for creating user-customizable features, including level editors.

- **Lines 091–103**. The *LoadXML* function de-serializes an XML file back to the object's *Transform* component, restoring its position, rotation, and scale in the scene. It also uses the *File.Exists* function to first check whether the specified file is present on the computer.

- **Lines 105–114**. The *SaveBinary* function serializes the object's transform data to a specified binary file on the local computer. This file is closed, meaning that it cannot be understood or meaningfully edited by the user. This makes binary files a great choice for preventing "user tampering or cheating."

- **Lines 116--128**. The *LoadBinary* function de-serializes a binary file back to the object's *Transform* component, restoring its position, rotation and scale in the scene. It also uses the *File.Exists* function to first check whether the specified file is present on the computer.

- **Lines 130–159**. Here, a temporary *Update* function has been added to the class, simply to demonstrate the general usage of the other functions and on how they can be used to save and restore persistent data. When the user presses a range of keys, between 1 and 4, it will initiate different save-restore methods. Notice that the *Application.persistentDataPath* variable is used to construct a string representing a valid file path on the computer. This variable always expresses a valid, persistent storage location on the computer.

Alternative Applications: XML Debugging

Saving object data to human-readable files like XML is valuable not only for creating save games or player-customizable data, it can be useful for you during development too, especially when testing. When your beta testers (who could be on the other side of the world!) encounter an error or problem with your game and you need to track down the source of the problem quickly, you can use XML files. By outputting the states of objects at critical times to an XML file, testers can then send you the generated file for examination, letting you judge how objects are responding and behaving to player input on their system at the time of the error. This can help you better diagnose the source or causes of problems, and also to reconstruct test cases on your own system to reproduce their error. More information on debugging and text files is considered later in this chapter.

5 Persistence and Accessibility

5.3 JSON Parsing

NOTE

A sample JSON file can be found online here: http://json.org/example.

▼2

An increasingly popular file format for saving persistent data in games generally is the *JSON* file (*JavaScript Object Notation*). The main reason for its popularity is that it offers an open, human-readable standard, like XML, but with a more abbreviated syntax and structure, making the file smaller in size, faster to parse, and faster to send over network connections. This makes JSON significantly more attractive than XML. However, neither Unity nor Mono have native classes supporting JSON parsing or serialization. Thus, developers must either code a JSON system themselves from the ground upward, or turn to community-made or asset store plug-ins. In this book, I'll refer you to a popular and free JSON parser, known as *SimpleJSON*, which is accessible online here: http://wiki.unity3d.com/index.php/SimpleJSON. More information on the JSON standard can be found here: http://json.org/. ▶2

Page   Discussion

SimpleJSON

Navigation

Main Page
Extensions
Particle Library
Programming
Scripts
Shaders
Wizards

Extras

Tips, Tricks, Tools
Tutorials
Unity Projects
Contests
IRC Chatroom

Quick Links

Community portal
Recent changes
New Pages
Help

Toolbox

What links here
Related changes
Special pages
Printable version
Permanent link

Contents [hide]
1 Description
2 Usage
  2.1 CSharp
  2.2 UnityScript (Unity's Javascript)
3 Examples (C# / UnityScript)
4 Download
5 SimpleJSON.cs

Description

SimpleJSON is an easy to use JSON parser and builder. It uses strong typed classes for the different JSONTypes. The parser / builder does **not** distinguish between different value types. Number, boolean and null w JSON string that requires the actual types.

In short: The parser conforms to rfc4627 ⮧, the generator does **not**.

Usage

To use SimpleJSON in Unity you just have to copy the SimpleJSON.cs file into your projects "plugins" folder inside your assets folder.

If you want to use the compression feature when it comes to saving and loading you have to download the SharpZipLib ⮧ assembly and place it next to the SimpleJSON.cs file. In addition you have to uncomment th

For language specific usage see below.

CSharp

Like most assemblies SimpleJSON is contained in it's own namespace to avoid name collisions.

To use SimpleJSON in C# you have to add this line at the top of your script:

```
using SimpleJSON;
```

UnityScript (Unity's Javascript)

To use SimpleJSON in UnityScript you have to add this line at the top of your script:

```
import SimpleJSON;
```

For UnityScript it's vital to place the SimpleJSON.cs (and SharpZipLib if needed) into a higher compilation group ⮧ than the UnityScript file that should use it. The usual place is the Plugins folder which should work

Examples (C# / UnityScript)

This is the JSON string which will be used in this example:

```
{
    "version": "1.0",
    "data": {
        "sampleArray": [
            "string value",
            5,
            {
                "name": "sub object"
```

5.4 Transferring Data between Scenes—with GameObjects

Sometimes you only need to transfer data between scenes *within the same play session*, and you don't need to save data persistently to local storage. Typical cases include keeping track of player health, or inventory items, or the game score whenever the player leaves one scene and enters another. The only time you'd actually need to save this data would be if the player saved their game. But in all other cases, you only need to transfer the data between scenes. Now, by default, Unity destroys all GameObjects inside a scene whenever that scene ends, and there can technically be only one scene active at any one time. This means that, *by default*, there's no way to transfer GameObjects or their data from one scene to another. There are, however, methods available to us in script. One method, as we've seen, is to use the *PlayerPrefs* class as a temporary, global buffer for data storage, allowing us to save and restore data between scenes. The problem with this method is: first, it only retains object specific *data*, and doesn't allow *objects themselves* to survive scene changes. And second, it's ultimately slow and clumsy when working with lots of data, including sound files, meshes, textures and more. The ideal alternative, then, is to create GameObjects whose lifetime is independent of the scene and who can "jump" with the player between scenes, retaining their data and components and settings as they go. This is achieved in Unity using the *Object.DontDestroyOnLoad* method. By calling this method on an object, you make it survive all subsequent scene transitions. See Code Sample 5.3.

Code Sample 5.3: Creating Objects that Survive Scene Changes

```
01 u  sing UnityEngine;
02  using System.Collections;
03
04  public class Survivor : MonoBehaviour
05  {
06    // Use this for initialization
07    void Start () {
08      //Make me survive scene transitions
09      DontDestroyOnLoad(gameObject);
10    }
11  }
```

An object marked with *DontDestroyOnLoad* will survive a scene change. This has important performance and workflow implications that are worthwhile keeping in mind.

1. The Object, its components, *and all its child objects and components* will survive a scene transition, including any textures, meshes, and assets used by those components. Take care to manage your assets and memory carefully.

2. The Object will *keep* its name and tagging information, unless you explicitly change it from code. This can have implications if other scenes search for objects by name or tag and don't expect to find your persistent object.

3. The Object will maintain any *coroutines* or pending *Invoke* operations, even after changing scenes. The *Invoke* function can be called to run a function after an interval elapses. This means an *Invoke* call made in one scene will still be honored after the scene change unless a cancellation call is made with *CancelInvoke*. See: http://docs.unity3d.com/ScriptReference/MonoBehaviour.CancelInvoke.html.

4. Indirect references to assets or objects in script will be invalidated on changing scenes. If your script has variable references to other game objects that are not its children, then those references will be nullified when the scene change happens, unless the references themselves are also marked with *DontDestroyOnLoad*.

DontDestroyOnLoad configures an object to survive a scene change, but to actually change scenes you'll need to call *Application.LoadLevel*. Before calling this function, however, make sure each of your scenes is assigned a unique identifier. To do this, access the *Build Settings* dialog by choosing *File > Build Settings* from the application menu, or press the keyboard shortcut *Ctrl + Shift + B*. ▶3

3

Next, drag and drop all scenes from the Project Panel into the *Scenes in Build* list, inside the *Build Settings* window. On doing this, each scene will automatically be assigned a unique identifier. The order of scenes in the list is important: specifically, the topmost scene will have an ID of 0 and will represent the first scene Unity will load when the compiled application starts. ▶4

4

After you assign every scene a Unique ID, close the *Build Settings* dialog, and then use the scripting method *Application.LoadLevel* to change the active scene to the specified one, as shown in Code Sample 5.4. For more information on *LoadLevel*, see the official Unity documentation at: http://docs.unity3d.com/ScriptReference/Application.LoadLevel.html.

Code Sample 5.4: Changing the Active Level with *Application.LoadLevel*

```
01  using UnityEngine;
02  using System.Collections;
03
04  public class SceneChanger : MonoBehaviour
05  {
06    public int LevelID = 0;
07
08    // Use this for initialization
09    void Start ()
10    {
11      //Changes to scene 1
12      Application.LoadLevel(LevelID);
13    }
14  }
```

5.5 Transferring Data between Scenes—with Scenes

In the previous section, we transferred data between scenes by creating GameObjects that persisted. This approach is useful for single, specific objects like the player character, which need to "carry data with them" as they move from scene to scene. The limitation of this method is that it works only from the current scene onwards. That is, the scene containing the persistent object must first be started and entered to allow that object to continue into later scenes. But sometimes you'll want to import objects from a non-active scene into the current one. This is useful for creating level streaming behavior in large open-world RPG games where the environment seems to expand endlessly across forests and deserts and towns with no perceptible break or disconnection in the experience. And it's also useful for creating "scene *within* scene" style scenarios, such as when the player character *in the scene* plays a game on a handheld console, seeing the level (which is a separate scene) through the device screen—*a game within a game*. To create this behavior, importing one scene into another, you can use the method *Application.Load LevelAdditive*. This method works much like *LoadLevel*, except it retains the contents of the active level and simply adds the contents of the imported level one. More information on this function can be found online at the Unity documentation here: http://docs. unity3d.com/ScriptReference/Application.LoadLevelAdditive.html. Code Sample 5.5 demonstrates its usage.

Code Sample 5.5: Adding a Level to the Existing One

```
01   using UnityEngine;
02   using System.Collections;
03
04   public class SceneAdder : MonoBehaviour
05   {
06     // Update is called once per frame
07     void Update ()
08     {
09       //When you press the space bar, load a new level into the
          existing one
10       if(Input.GetKeyDown(KeyCode.Space))
11       {
12         Application.LoadLevelAdditive(1);
13       }
14     }
15   }
```

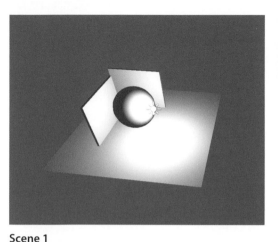

Scene 1

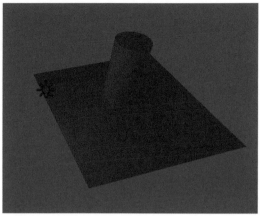

Scene 2

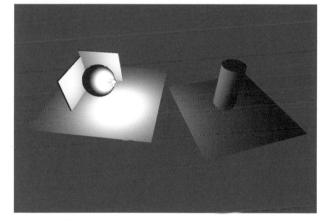

Scene 1 + Scene 2

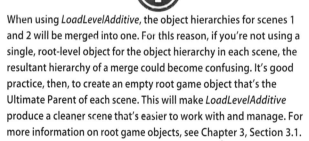

T--I--P

When using *LoadLevelAdditive*, the object hierarchies for scenes 1 and 2 will be merged into one. For this reason, if you're not using a single, root-level object for the object hierarchy in each scene, the resultant hierarchy of a merge could become confusing. It's good practice, then, to create an empty root game object that's the Ultimate Parent of each scene. This will make *LoadLevelAdditive* produce a cleaner scene that's easier to work with and manage. For more information on root game objects, see Chapter 3, Section 3.1.

5.6 Global Functionality with Singletons

Even when working in a single scene, you'll still need objects to communicate effectively with each other, sending and receiving messages backward and forward. The *SendMessage* and *BroadcastMessage* functions can be helpful for this, but with important limitations (see Chapter 3, Section 3.2). However, you'll often need more than these in the long term—specifically, you'll need a more streamlined communication system. Typically, you'll want *all* objects to have *direct* access to a *common*, baseline functionality. That is, there are some features every object may need access to, at potentially any time: the ability to set the game score and access player health, and call methods for exiting the game, showing the main menu, pausing the game, loading and saving the game, and for invoking and detecting game-wide events that trigger behaviors elsewhere in the scene. This baseline functionality will typically be centralized into a single game object: a *Game Manager*. This object should be accessible *globally* to every other object. This is efficient design because it saves us from having to maintain a vast network of private variable references and interconnections across many different objects, simply to get access to the range of features we need. With a centralized design, every object just needs access to one, central manager to get its main work done. Objects like the Game Manager, of which there's only one, are known as singleton objects: with these, you cannot have more than one instance in the scene, and they're typically accessible to everything else. To create these, you must use a very specific style of class design. Consider Code Sample 5.6 for a singleton *GameManager* class, with variables for game score and player health, as well as functions to restart the level. The following Code Sample 5.7 demonstrates how a completely separate object can have direct access to the manager at any time, with no additional code required. Comments follow each sample.

Code Sample 5.6: Singleton GameManager

```
01  //---------------------------
02  using UnityEngine;
03  using System.Collections;
04  //---------------------------
05  public class GameManager : MonoBehaviour
06  {
07      //---------------------------
08      //Read-Only Public access to singleton instance
09      //Make static. Is globally accessible as GameManager.
        instance
10      public static GameManager instance
11      {
12      get{return gm;}
13      }
14      //---------------------------
15      //Internal reference to static singleton instance
16      private static GameManager gm = null;
17  //---------------------------
18      //Game Manager member variables for global access
19      public int PlayerHealth = 100; //Can be accessed with
        GameManager.instance.PlayerHealth
```

```
20    public int GameScore = 0; //Can be accessed with
      GameManager.instance.GameScore
21
22    //---------------------------
23    // Use this for initialization
24    void Start ()
25    {
26      //Now make sure this is a singleton object: only one
        instance
27
28      //If we are not null, then instance already exists. So
        destroy this instance and exit
29      if(gm != null)
30      {
31        DestroyImmediate(gameObject);
32        return;
33      }
34
35      //If null, then we are first and only instance
36      DontDestroyOnLoad(gameObject);
37
38      //Assign gm reference as singleton instance
39      gm = this;
40    }
41    //---------------------------
42    //Function to restart game
43    //This object is singleton. This function is accessed
      globally as: GameManager.instance.RestartGame()
44    public void RestartGame()
45    {
46      //Re-load active level
47      Application.LoadLevel(Application.loadedLevel);
48    }
49    //---------------------------
50  }
51  //---------------------------
```

Comments

- **Lines 10–13**. A C# instance property is declared as static, offering global but read-only access to the internal singleton instance of the GameManager. This ensures that only one protected instance of the class is available in memory at any one time.

- **Lines 16**. Here, we keep an internal reference to the singleton instance. Read-only access to this variable is controlled by the instance property.

- **Lines 29–33**. In the start function, we either keep the created object as the one and only instance of GameManager, or else we destroy the object immediately, if an instance already exists in the scene.

By using the GameManger class, any other object and script can get direct and shared access to its members, as shown in Code Sample 5.7.

Code Sample 5.7: Sample Class Interacting with the GameManager

```
01   using UnityEngine;
02   using System.Collections;
03
04   public class TestObject : MonoBehaviour
05   {
06     // Update is called once per frame
07     void Update ()
08     {
09       //If press space, access game manager and set some
         properties
10       if(Input.GetKeyDown(KeyCode.Space))
11       {
12         //Access game manager
13         GameManager.instance.PlayerHealth = 50;
14         GameManager.instance.GameScore += 1;
15       }
16
17       //If press R key, then restart level via game manager
18       //This gives the gamemanager the opportunity to handle
         additional code for this event, if required
19       if(Input.GetKeyDown(KeyCode.R))
20       {
```

```
21          GameManager.instance.RestartGame();
22      }
23    }
24  }
```

Alternative Applications: Finding Objects of a Type

The singleton design shown here, along with static members, is not the only way to create a globally accessible Singleton object for your games. The concept of a singleton class means only that there can be one instantiation at once, and no more than that. To achieve that effect, there are, in fact, too many different ways to list in a single chapter. But there is one alternative that I do want to list here, because of its general usefulness, though it is slow in terms of performance—so use it sparingly. You can use the static function *Object.FindObjectOfType* to retrieve a reference to the first instance of a specified type in the scene. This means that, for singleton objects (with just one instance), *FindObjectOfType* will always return the global object you need. See Code Sample 5.8.

Code Sample 5.8: Get Singleton Instance

```
01  //----------------------------------
02  using UnityEngine;
03  using System.Collections;
04  //----------------------------------
05  public class GetSingleton : MonoBehaviour
06  {
07    //Reference to singleton in scene
08    private GameManager MySingleton = null;
09
10    // Use this for initialization
11    void Start () {
12      //Searches scene and gets GameManager
13      MySingleton = Object.FindObjectOfType
          <GameManager>();
14    }
15  }
16  //----------------------------------
```

T--I--P

As an aside, when dealing with multiple instances of objects (like all enemies, all power-ups, or all weapons), you can also call the *Object.FindObjectsOfType* function to retrieve an array of all objects in the scene of a specified type. Again, take care when using this function: it's performance-intensive and should be avoided inside events, like *Update* or *OnGUI*. For more information, see the online Unity documentation here: http://docs.unity3d.com/ScriptReference/Object.FindObjectsOfType.html.

5.7 Handling Errors with Log Files

There's another way you can work with files in Unity, and that's to log Run-Time exceptions. A Run-Time exception is an error that Unity intentionally generates or "throws" whenever an unhandled or unexpected event happens in-game for which the application has no known response. A classic exception would be a "divide by zero" error. When this happens, Unity prints an exception to the console, indicating what occurred, its probable cause, and the associated line of code where the error happened, if known. When the final build of your game is running, exceptions can have unpredictable results: sometimes they'll be inconsequential and go unnoticed, but sometimes they'll cause your game to crash or glitch. For this reason, it's important to be very aware and alert to exceptions. One way to do this is to create an exception logging system from the outset so that, when shipping your game to testers and end users, you already have a means of "remotely" debugging and testing your game. That is, when users experience exceptions, they can send you a copy of a text-based log file, so you can inspect the exception that occurred. The hope is that the exception logged will be informative and instructive enough to help you find the problem quickly. Consider Code Sample 5.9. This class, when attached to a game object in the scene, will exist persistently and log *every* exception that occurs to a text-based log file. ▶8

8

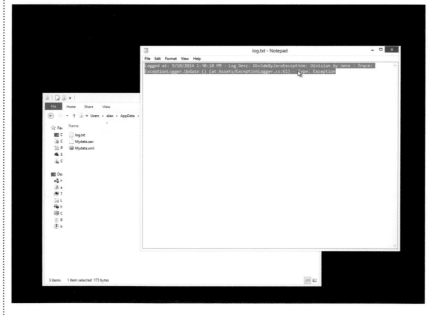

Code Sample 5.9: Writing Exceptions to a Log File

```
01   //---------------------------
02   using UnityEngine;
03   using System.Collections;
04   using System.IO;
05   //---------------------------
06   public class ExceptionLogger : MonoBehaviour
07   {
08     //Internal reference to stream writer object
09     private System.IO.StreamWriter SW;
10
11     //Filename to assign log
12     public string LogFileName = "log.txt";
13
14     //---------------------------
15     // Use this for initialization
16     void Start ()
17     {
18       //Make persistent
19       DontDestroyOnLoad(gameObject);
20
21       //Create string writer object
22       SW = new System.IO.StreamWriter(Application.persistent
         DataPath + "/" + LogFileName);
23
24       Debug.Log(Application.persistentDataPath + "/" +
         LogFileName);
25     }
26     //---------------------------
27     //Register for exception listning, and log exceptions
28     void OnEnable()
29     {
30       Application.RegisterLogCallback(HandleLog);
31     }
32     //---------------------------
33     //Unregister for exception listening
34     void OnDisable()
35     {
```

```
36        Application.RegisterLogCallback(null);
37    }
38    //---------------------------
39    //Log exception to a text file
40    void HandleLog(string logString, string stackTrace, LogType
      type)
41    {
42      //If an exception or error, then log to file
43      if(type == LogType.Exception || type == LogType.Error)
44      {
45        SW.WriteLine("Logged at: " + System.DateTime.Now.
          ToString() + " - Log Desc: " + logString + " - Trace: "
          + stackTrace + " - Type: " + type.ToString());
46      }
47    }
48    //---------------------------
49    //Called when object is destroyed
50    void OnDestroy()
51    {
52      //Close file
53      SW.Close();
54    }
55    //---------------------------
56  }
57  //---------------------------
```

5.8 Validating Data

Maybe you're making a multiplayer game where the player must enter a password, or maybe you need to save a high score or RPG statistic like Magic Points and Strength Points. If so, you'll probably want to verify that the actual values you saved maintain their integrity over time: that is, you want to be sure the player hasn't tampered with the values between sessions, trying to edit their score or stats manually. You can achieve this using an MD5 hash. The MD5 hash algorithm effectively generates a unique code (sequence of letters and numbers) from a string, and no two strings produce the same sequence. You cannot recreate the string from the hash, but the hash uniquely identifies the string. This means you can verify whether a string has been changed or edited, by comparing the hash of the original with the hash of a different string. If the two don't match, then the strings are not identical. If that happens, you should reset your data to a default value as opposed to using the saved value, because the saved value has been edited. Consider Code Sample 5.10, which converts a string to an MD5 hash, and then compares to any other string for a match.

Code Sample 5.10: Comparing Strings Based on an MD5 Hash

```
01   //-------------------------------
02   using UnityEngine;
03   using System.Collections;
04   //-------------------------------
05   public class StringEncoder : MonoBehaviour
06   {
07       //-------------------------------
08       public string StringToEncode = "";
09       //-------------------------------
10       //Function to produce MD5 hash from string
11       public string MD5Encode(string Str)
12       {
13         //Generate has as byte array
14         System.Text.UTF8Encoding Enc = new System.Text.
           UTF8Encoding();
15
16         //Convert string to bytes
17         byte[] bytes = Enc.GetBytes(Str);
18
19         //Create new md5 object
20         System.Security.Cryptography.MD5CryptoServiceProvider MD5
           = new System.Security.Cryptography.MD5CryptoService
           Provider();
21
22         //Create mdh hash
23         byte[] hashBytes = MD5.ComputeHash(bytes);
24
25         //Convert hash to string
26         string FinalStr = "";
27         foreach (byte b in hashBytes)
```

```
28        FinalStr += System.Convert.ToString(b, 16);
29
30    //return string
31    return FinalStr;
32  }
33  //------------------------------
34  void Update()
35  {
36    //Press e to encode string to registry
37    if(Input.GetKeyDown(KeyCode.E))
38      PlayerPrefs.SetString("EncodedString", MD5Encode
      (StringToEncode));
39
40    //Press c to compare StringToEncode with PlayerPrefs
      string EncodedString
41    if(Input.GetKeyDown(KeyCode.C))
42    {
43      string EncStr = MD5Encode(StringToEncode);
44      string OriHash = PlayerPrefs.GetString("EncodedString",
      "");
45
46      if(EncStr.Equals(OriHash))
47        Debug.Log ("Strings match");
48    }
49  }
50  //------------------------------
51 }
52 //------------------------------
```

6

Cameras, Rendering, and Lighting

You can't avoid using cameras in Unity scenes, unless you're only making an interface in screen-space overlay mode. Otherwise, you'll need at least one camera to make anything visible to the player. If you don't, you'll simply get a blank screen. Furthermore, the use of cameras implies an internal rendering process that converts objects in the scene into pixels on-screen, and this entails lighting calculations too—so cameras, rendering, and lighting are important and interconnected processes for your game. This chapter takes an in-depth look at some helpful and efficient ways of working with these three processes. We'll see how to control multiple cameras and rendering composites, how to configure 2D orthographic cameras for pixel-perfection, how to create split-screen games, and optimal ways to light your scenes, plus lots more.

Cameras, Rendering, Lighting

6.1 Camera Depth

Every Unity scene by default features one active camera, and this is the viewpoint from which everything is rendered when the game runs and enters that scene. For a GameObject to be a camera, it crucially needs a Camera component, which features all critical properties for a camera, including its *Field of View* and *Background Color*. In some cases, one camera may be all you need. But for most games, multiple cameras become both important and essential, for many different reasons. For example: if you need to render a user interface *on top of* an existing scene, or if you need an object to always appear *in front of* other objects, regardless of their real position in the scene, or if you need the ability to show other parts of the scene *alongside* the main game view, then you'll probably need multiple cameras. And to work effectively with them, it's important to understand camera depth. ▶1

▼1

Every camera has a *Depth* value. When multiple cameras are in the scene, the Depth value determines the render order of cameras. By default, cameras are rendered on top of each other like layers, with the lower depth cameras rendered before higher depth cameras. This means that a camera with a depth value of –1 will appear underneath a camera with a depth value of 0. Thus, if you add two cameras to a scene with the depth values of –1 and 0, and all their remaining properties are left at defaults, you'll never see the rendered data from the –1 camera, even though it exists in the scene and renders, because a higher-order camera is rendered on top on each frame. ▶2

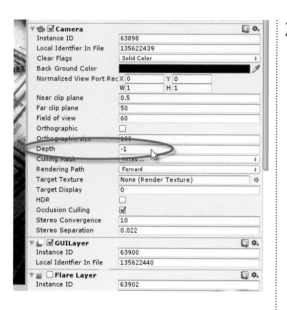

You can control how one camera is layered or blended over the camera below by using the *Clear Flags* field on the Camera component. This lets you layer camera renders on top of each other, making some parts of the render transparent, allowing the renders beneath to show through, like the layers option in Photoshop. Specifically, the *Depth Only* setting will hide the camera background, revealing any layers beneath. If you choose *Depth Only* for higher-ordered cameras, then pixels that don't render geometry (like the scene background) will be rendered as transparent. Thus, the *Depth* field combined with the *Clear Flags* field means you can overlay entire areas of your scene on top of other cameras with alpha transparency, which is especially useful for rendering user interfaces and mouse cursors, making sure they render on top of everything else. ▶3

To test this, create a new scene with two separate cameras, one with a *Depth* value of –1, and another with a *Depth* value of 0 and a *Clear Flags* setting of *Depth Only*. Be sure to remove the Audio Listener component from the second camera, as Unity allows only one Audio Listener component to be active in the scene at any one time. Position the cameras

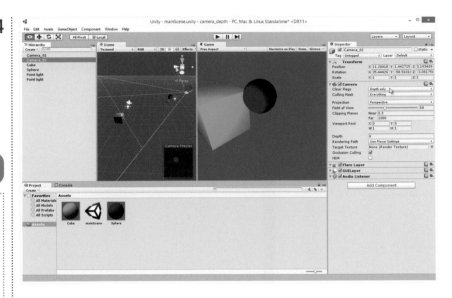

4

NOTE

More information on Layers can be found at the online Unity documentation here: http://docs.unity3d.com/Manual/Layers.html.

apart in the scene, and focus them on different objects, whether cubes or spheres or other meshes. Notice how renders of both cameras are composited together as one final output render in the *Game* tab, with the higher order camera rendered on top of the lower. ▶4

By default, every camera is configured to render *all* visible objects in the scene within its frustum, excluding nothing. Therefore, one issue that arises with layered, multiple cameras in the same scene is "double rendering." This happens when two or more cameras can see the same objects, and so those objects are effectively rendered multiple

▼5

times, once from each camera. You can, of course, use this to create various special effects, but typically you'll want to avoid it. One practical and "simple" way to do this is simply by positioning each camera, and the objects it should render, at the extremes of your scene away from each other. However, another way is to use *Culling Masks* to exclude the rendering of all objects attached to a specific layer from a specific camera. To achieve this, first mark all objects that should be hidden from a specific camera by attaching them to the same layer: select the object and assign it to a layer, picking a layer name from the Layer drop-down box in the Object Inspector. If no appropriate layer is available, you can create more by choosing *Add Layer*. ▶5

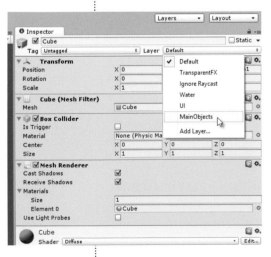

Finally, to exclude a layer from camera rendering, effectively hiding all objects on the layer from the selected camera, choose the layer name from the *Culling Mask* field in the Camera component. Alternatively, if you *only* want to render objects on *that* layer, then first choose *Nothing* to disable rendering from all layers, and then select the appropriate layer to enable it. ▶6

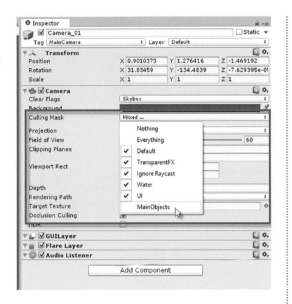

6

6.2 Split-Screen Games

Split-screen games are typically local multiplayer games where the screen is divided into two halves, allowing each player to simultaneously control an independent character in the same world. That being said, split-screen has other purposes too: for single player games, for example, the player may activate a lever or button, and a small pop-up window

7▼

6 Cameras, Rendering, Lighting

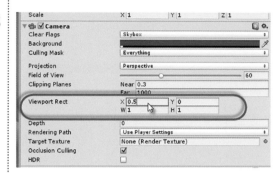

8

may display to show the effect that the lever press had on objects elsewhere in the world, such as a door-opening animation. Split-screen games clearly rely on multiple cameras in the scene, but their final presentation on-screen differs from the single, composited render in layers as discussed in the previous tip. Effectively, split-screen games should carve up the final render into *distinct spaces* inside where each camera renders its own output separately. To achieve this, you can use the *Camera Viewport* field. ▶7, 8

The *Viewport* field consists of a rectangle data structure with four members, defined in normalized space (between 0 and 1) representing the dimensions of the screen in each axis. This expresses the rectangular region inside which the camera is rendered on screen. 0 defines the left or bottom edge, and 1 defines the top or right edge. A value of (0.5 0.5), for example, represents the screen center. By default, every camera has X and Y set to 0 (bottom-left corner) and W and H to 1 (top-right corner), rendering the camera across the total surface of the screen. These values can be changed to render two cameras side by side in a split-screen format. To create a vertically divided split-screen setup, the left camera should be defined with the viewport of *(X:0 Y:0, W:0.5 H:1)* and the right camera should be *(X:0.5, Y:0, W:0.5, H:1)*. ▶9

9

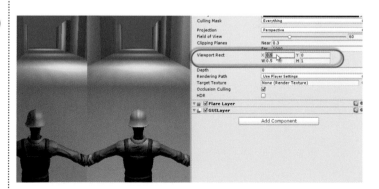

Alternative Applications: Mini Map with No Coding

By using multiple cameras, combined with a creative use of the *Depth*, *Clear Flags*, and *Culling Mask* settings, as well as the *Viewport Rect*, you can achieve so many complex behaviors. One is real-time mini-map functionality, without having to write even one line of code! First, a mini-map is a game feature that often appears in real-time strategy games and RPG games. It offers an overhead view of the surrounding level and terrain, and features diagnostics colours and icons for items of interest, such as the player character, enemies, and collectable items. The mini-map is essentially an augmented reality HUD feature, one that helps the player navigate an environment and more easily make sense of what they're doing and what is happening in-game. Here's how you can quickly make a mini-map by combining all the tips we've just seen in this chapter. Start with an empty scene, and add a third-person controller from the Character Controllers package, as well as a terrain object, giving you a basic, traversable scene. ▶10

> **NOTE**
>
> The mini-map scene discussed here can be found in the book companion files at *Chapter06/ minimap*.

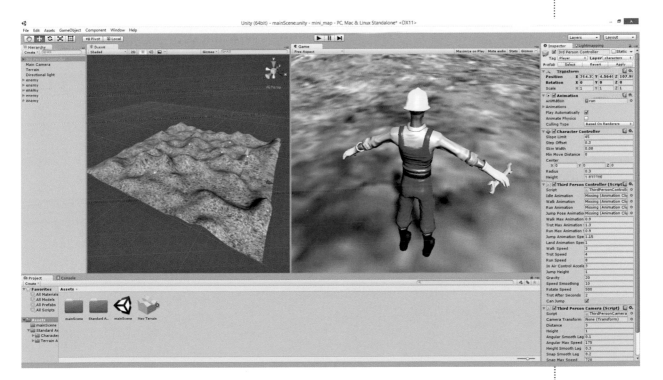

Next, add some sample enemy characters to the scene. For the test, they can simply be static boxes or any meshes. The important thing is that they're independent game objects. Then add a new, secondary camera to the scene, ensuring its depth setting is higher than the main camera's depth. This camera will act as the mini-map camera.

10

Therefore, position it overhead in the scene, looking down at the player and the terrain. Be sure to center the camera on the player object, and then Parent it to the player object in the scene hierarchy, so it follows the player as they move. ▶11

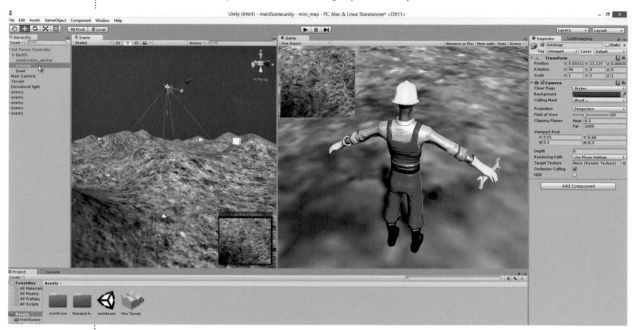

11

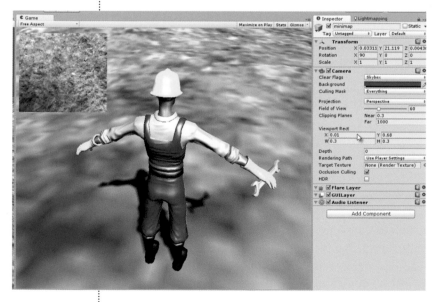

12

Right now, the mini-map camera spans the dimensions of the screen and obscures the main camera rendering. Instead, the mini-map camera should appear as a small box in the top-left corner of the screen. To achieve this, use the Viewport Rect field in the Camera component to size the mini-map. For this case, I've used the settings (*X:0.01 Y:0.68 W:0.3 H:0.3*). ▶12

The final problem with the mini-map is that bold, clear colors should stand in for the enemy and player objects, as opposed to the player and enemy meshes themselves. This makes it clearer to see the player and enemies on the mini-map. In short, the player and enemy meshes should be visible to the main camera, while approximate bold colors should represent those objects to the mini-map camera. To achieve this, add new plane objects to the scene and position them directly above the player and enemy characters, respectively. One plane per character, Parenting each plane object in the hierarchy to the character object that appears directly underneath it in the scene. This makes sure each plane follows the character to which it should be attached. Then, assign the player plane object a green material, and the enemy plane objects a red material. ▶13

13▼

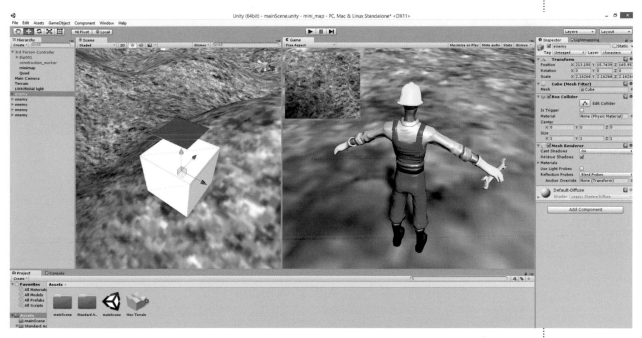

Now all that remains is to *hide* the colored plane objects to the main camera, because the main camera should display only the regular player and enemy meshes. And, show the planes to the mini-map while also hiding the player and enemy meshes, because only the colored planes should represent characters. To do this, we can use layers. Assign the regular player and enemy meshes to a characters layer, and assign the plane objects to a mini-map layer. ▶14

14

Lastly, use the *Culling Mask* field for the main camera to exclude the *MiniMap* layer. Then use the *Culling Mask* field for the mini-map camera to exclude the *Characters* layer. And now, you have a completed and functional mini-map for your level. ▶15

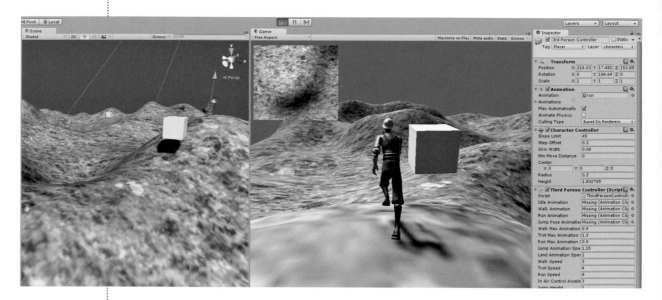

15 6.3 Render Textures

Sometimes, the "standard" camera rendering functionality is simply not enough. Sometimes, you'll want to take a render from a secondary camera elsewhere in the scene, and then project it onto a 3D surface as a texture. A common example of this is for creating an in-game security camera system: you position a camera in the scene, inside a

16

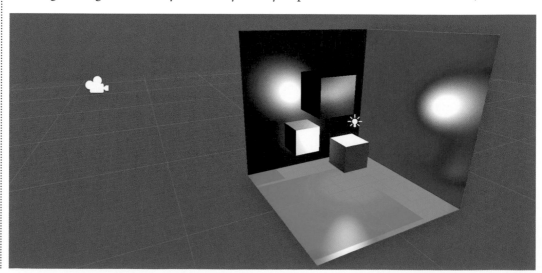

room or perhaps a secret lab, to act as the surveillance camera, and then you'll want to show the results of that camera inside a monitor mesh in-game, allowing the player to look at the monitor and to see inside the room, through the security camera. This behavior is distinct from the split-screen and mini-map camera work we've seen in the previous tips. This behavior doesn't simply render a camera view to a specified rectangle *on-screen*. Instead, a camera is rendered onto a surface *inside the scene*, which will be viewed by the player in perspective, like any other 3D object. To achieve this, we must use Render Textures. Another great benefit of Render

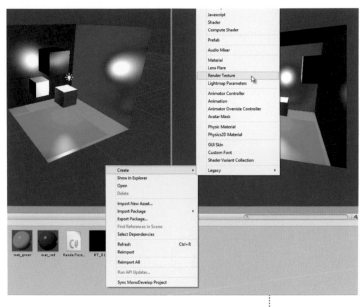

Textures is that, when a camera is rendered to a texture, the texture can be further edited and manipulated by shaders. To get started, open up the Render Texture project in Unity, which can be found in the book companion files in the folder *Chapter06/RenderTexture*. This project features a Cornell box scene, being viewed by a main camera. From there, create a render texture: right-click inside the Unity Project Panel, and choose *Create > Render Texture*. ▶16, 17

After creating the Render Texture, select it in the Object Inspector and assign it a size in pixels, as well as other texture properties. Often, the settings can be left at the defaults. ▶18

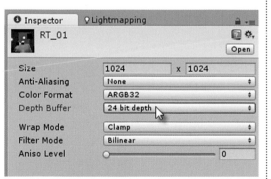

Next, select the main camera in the scene and assign its *Target Texture* member to the newly created Render Texture. When you do this, the viewport inside the *Game* tab may turn dark, if your scene has just one camera. This is because the main camera no longer renders to the screen, but to the target render texture, leaving you without any main camera for the scene. ▶19

Cameras, Rendering, Lighting

Now create a new, second camera in the scene and align it in view of a simple plane object, away from the rest of the scene objects. Then drag and drop the Render Texture asset from the Project Panel onto the Plane Object in the scene, and it will automatically display the Render Texture contents as a texture. That is, it will render into the plane object that resultant view from the original, main camera. ▶20

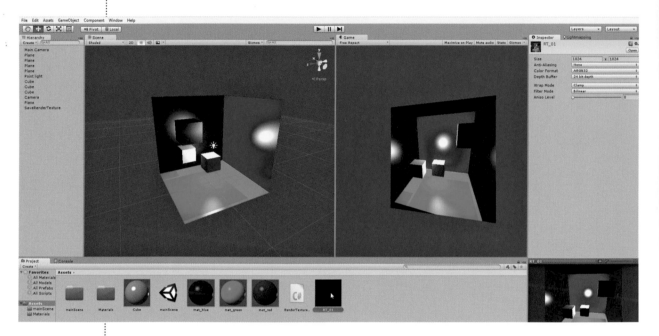

20

Alternative Applications: Screenshots

It's common practice to take a screenshot of the game view when the player saves a session, to help them more easily identify which session to restore back later. One quick and easy method is to save a screenshot to a file by calling the *Application.Capture Screenshot* function. More information on this function can be found at the Unity online documentation here: http://docs.unity3d.com/ScriptReference/Application.Capture Screenshot.html.

However, you can achieve similar behavior by using Render Textures too, by saving the Render Texture contents to a standard image file, like a PNG. Code Sample 6.1 saves a render texture to a file when the user presses the space bar.

Code Sample 6.1: Saving a Render Texture to a File

```
01  //Class to save a render texture to a file
02  using UnityEngine;
03  using System.Collections;
04  using System.IO;
05  //-----------------------------------
06  public class RenderTextureToPNG : MonoBehaviour
07  {
08     //-----------------------------------
09     public RenderTexture RT = null;
10     public string localFileName = "";
11     //-----------------------------------
12     // Update is called once per frame
13     void Update ()
14     {
15       //If press space, then save RT to file
16       if(Input.GetKeyDown(KeyCode.Space))
17         SaveRTToFile();
18     }
19     //-----------------------------------
20     void SaveRTToFile()
21     {
22       Texture2D Tex2D = new Texture2D(RT.width, RT.height);
23       RenderTexture.active = RT;
24       Tex2D.ReadPixels(new Rect(0,0, RT.width, RT.height),
          0, 0);
25       Tex2D.Apply();
26       RenderTexture.active = null;
27       byte[] bytes = Tex2D.EncodeToPNG();
28       Destroy(Tex2D);
29       File.WriteAllBytes(Application.persistentDataPath + "/" +
          localFileName, bytes);
30       Debug.Log ("Saving to: " + Application.persistentDataPath
          + "/" + localFileName);
31     }
32     //-----------------------------------
33  }
34  //-----------------------------------
```

NOTE

Please consult the book companion files at *Chapter06/ RenderTexture.*

6.4 Orthographic Cameras

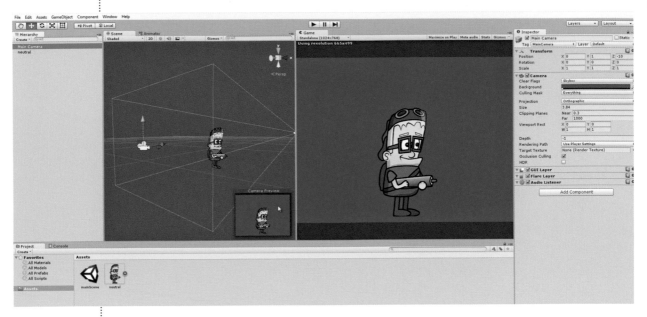

21 If you're making truly 2D games, like side-scrolling platformers or hidden object games, it's likely you'll need at least one orthographic camera. An orthographic camera is one in which perspective distortion (such as foreshortening and viewing angle) have been removed to show an entirely flattened view of the 3D scene. A view where parallel lines remain parallel and objects don't scale based on their distance from the camera. This makes orthographic cameras especially useful for 2D games, because it lets sprites render in a crisp and correct way, undistorted by 3D perspective. Creating an orthographic camera in Unity is easy, at least initially. You simply select a camera in the scene and change its *Projection Type* from *Perspective* to *Orthographic*. ▶21, 22

22 The problem with orthographic mode, by default, is that it's not immediately clear how and if the camera should be configured further for 2D games. If you add a 2D sprite to the scene and align it in view of the orthographic camera, you'll notice it probably appears either larger or smaller than the intended size. You can of course scale the sprite either up or down to fit the view, using trial and error. But, most developers want the sprite to appear on screen at exactly the same size it appears in the image file, pixel for pixel. That is, most developers require pixel perfection: for 2D images to appear on-screen based on their sizes in the texture file. To achieve this, further configuration of the orthographic camera is required. In short, you'll need to adjust the *Size* field, which only appears in the Object Inspector when the camera *Projection* type is set to *Orthographic*. The value of this field relates to the window size or game resolution. Specifically: if you set the *Size*

23

field to half the screen height, you'll map one world unit to one screen pixel. Thus, a cube sized *1x1x1 (Unity Units)* will appear 1 *pixel* wide and 1 *pixel* high on screen, if the *Size* field is *Screen.Height/2*. It's important to remember, however, that if the gamer resizes the window, then *Size* must update to reflect the new window dimensions, maintaining the world-to-pixel ratio. ▶23

The standard formula of *Screen.Height/2* will work for translating world units to pixels directly, but this doesn't always solve sizing problems for sprites. This is because sprite assets are pre-scaled by Unity. To see this, select a sprite object in the Project Panel and examine the field *Pixels to Units* in the Object Inspector. This defines how the selected sprite is scaled by Unity when added to the scene. Often, this field will be 100 pixels by default, meaning

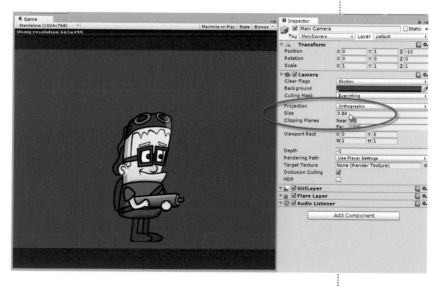

24

NOTE

Please consult the book companion files at *Chapter06/ Orthographic Camera.*

that 100 pixels in the texture is scaled down to fit inside 1 world unit. This being so, you can adjust the orthographic size formula to accommodate sprites, provided all of them share the same pixels to units scale, using the formula: *Screen.Height / 2 /Pixels to Units.* ▶24

6.5 Camera Shaking

When making action games, from first-person shooters to beat 'em ups, a camera shake effect is a common need. When objects explode, or punches land, or grenades detonate, a camera shake in response can add atmosphere and tension. *One* way to create this effect is through pre-scripted animation, using either the Unity Animation Editor or by importing animation from third-party software like Blender or Maya. Another way is through scripting. With scripting, you gain some extra Run-Time, parametric control over animation speed, extremity, and timing and movement pattern. To create camera shaking, you can use a camera shake script, as shown in Code Sample 6.2. This effect relies on the Unity function *Random.insideUnitSphere* to repeatedly pick a random point around the camera starting location, and to smoothly move toward that location until a new point is selected. This achieves both *random positioning* and a *smoothing* of camera motion. ▶25

25

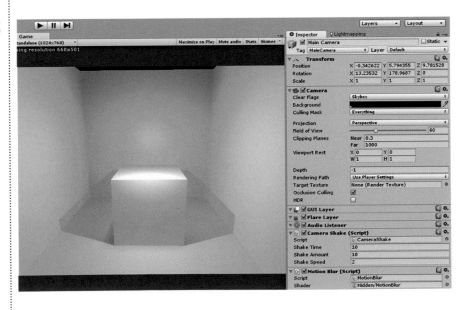

Code Sample 6.2: Camera Shake Effect

```
01  using UnityEngine;
02  using System.Collections;
03  //-----------
04  public class CameraShake : MonoBehaviour
05  {
06    private Transform ThisTransform = null;
07
08    //Total time for shaking in seconds
09    public float ShakeTime = 2.0f;
10
11    //Shake amount - distance to offset in any direction
12    public float ShakeAmount = 3.0f;
13
14    //Speed of camera moving to shake points
15    public float ShakeSpeed = 2.0f;
16
17    //-----------
18    // Use this for initialization
19    void Start ()
20    {
21      //Get transform component
22      ThisTransform = GetComponent<Transform>();
23
24      //Start shaking
25      StartCoroutine(Shake());
26    }
27    //-----------
28    //Shake camera
29    public IEnumerator Shake()
30    {
31      //Store original camera position
32      Vector3 OrigPosition = ThisTransform.localPosition;
33
34      //Count elapsed time (in seconds)
35      float ElapsedTime = 0.0f;
36
37      //Repeat for total shake time
```

```
38        while(ElapsedTime < ShakeTime)
39        {
40           //Pick random point on unit sphere
41           Vector3 RandomPoint = OrigPosition + Random.inside
             UnitSphere * ShakeAmount;
42
43           //Update Position
44           ThisTransform.localPosition = Vector3.Lerp
             (ThisTransform.localPosition, RandomPoint,
             Time.deltaTime * ShakeSpeed);
45
46           //Break for next frame
47           yield return null;
48
49        //Update time
50           ElapsedTime += Time.deltaTime;
51        }
52
53        //Restore camera position
54        ThisTransform.localPosition = OrigPosition;
55     }
56   //-----------
57 }
58 //-----------
```

Alternative Applications: Shaking and Anticipation

The shake script in Code Sample 6.2, which is included in the book companion files in *Chapter06/Camera_Shake*, is useful not only for cameras. Shaking cameras add atmosphere, but shaking objects can too. For this reason, the camera shake script can be reapplied and adapted to objects beside the camera. Specifically, shaking is useful for establishing anticipation. If a rocket is about to launch, or an object is about to explode, or an angry character is about to scream, an initial shake is an appropriate precursor to the main act. It signals what is about to come, and resonates an emotion that can significantly increase the drama and character of your games.

NOTE

Please consult the book companion files at *Chapter06/ CameraShake*.

6.6 Reflections and Reflection Probes

To get the best looking and most realistic reflections for GameObjects, be sure to use *Reflection Probes*. These let you record or sample the static environment from a specific position in the scene, and then to use that information for a reflection map on GameObjects. To create a Reflection probe, select *GameObject > Light > Reflection Probe* from the main menu. ▶26, 27

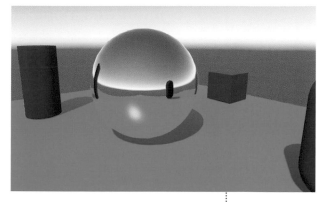

After creating the probe, assign a reflective material to an object in the scene, such as a Standard Shader with both its *Metallic* and *Smoothness* settings at 1. Then select the Reflection Probe object in the scene and control its quality settings from the Object Inspector using the Type field and Resolution field. The type can be either *Baked* or *Realtime*: *Baked* calculates reflections only for non-moving objects marked as Static, and Realtime calculates reflections for all objects in real time (at the cost of performance). You can use the Resolution setting to control the quality of reflections.

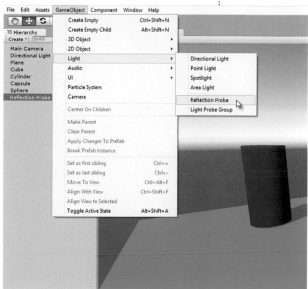

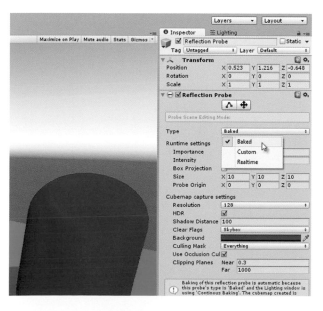

Higher values for this setting, combined with the Realtime option for Type, can dramatically damage runtime performance. In short, use High Resolution values only for Static Reflections. ▶28

26▲▲
27▲
28◀

NOTE

Please consult the book companion files at *Chapter06/Reflections*.

6 Cameras, Rendering, Lighting

6.7 Lighting and Maps

29

30

There are two quick and really easy ways to control lighting in your scene using only maps and materials, as opposed to light objects themselves. These are *Environment Lighting*, and *Emissive Lighting*. Environment Lighting lets you surround the scene with a skybox, and use the pixel information in the skybox map to illuminate the environment for both real-time and static objects. This is a great method for creating base lighting and general low-level illumination in the scene. In addition, you can create a skybox right within the Unity editor. To do this, create a new material, and then change the material type to *Skybox > Procedural*. You can use the Sun Size, Sky Tint and Ground properties to change the colour and feel of the sky. After a Sky material is created, it can be easily assigned as a sky for the active scene through the Lighting tab, which is accessible via *Window > Lighting*. ▶29, 30

You can also control lighting through Emissive Mapping via a Material using the Standard Shader. Emissive Mapping lets you use a pixel based texture map to determine how bright a surface should be, where white values represent full illumination and black values represent no illumination. This gives much more flexibility over controlling the shape and intensity of a light as it varies across a surface. ▶31

31

To create an Emissive Material, drag and drop a map into the Emissive Slot in the Standard Shader. The color picker can be used to control and set the color for the light, if the light areas inside the texture are set to white. You can also use the intensity slider to increase the light brightness, and the Global Illumination setting controls whether the emissive lighting should affect only static objects (Baked) or all objects (Realtime). ▶32

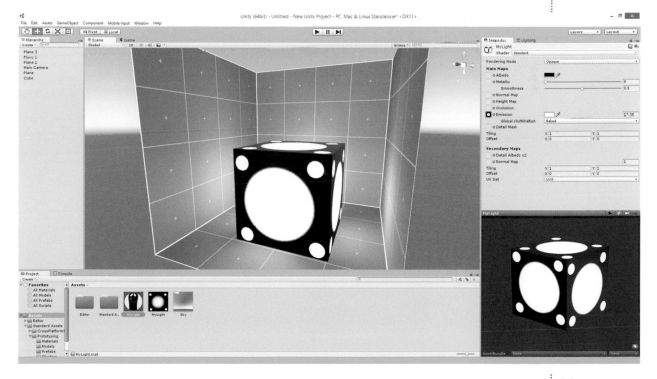

32

T--I--P

Remember, for pre-made or complete level environments whose lighting conditions remain constant, you can always light map in external tools, such as Blender, 3DS Max, or Maya. Most 3D modeling applications let you render to textures, including ambient occlusion maps, as well as other map types. Using this approach, your mesh will need only one UV map set, and possibly fewer textures too.

If you need finer control over light mapping beyond the settings offered in the regular light mapping window, you can always download the freely available add-on *Lightmapping Extended* by Michael Stevenson, from the Unity Asset Store. This add-on exposes many additional settings of the Beast Lightmapper, the render system used by Unity for generating light maps. Using *Lightmapping Extended*, you gain extensive and finer control over light map generation. The add-on can be downloaded from here: http://u3d.as/content/michael-stevenson/lightmapping-extended/3SF.

6.8 Light Probes

If your game has objects that move, and thus are not static, then don't feel restricted to simply expensive "real-time" lighting. You can instead use a "semi-real-time" system, known as *light probes*. In terms of performance, light probes are a middle ground between

33

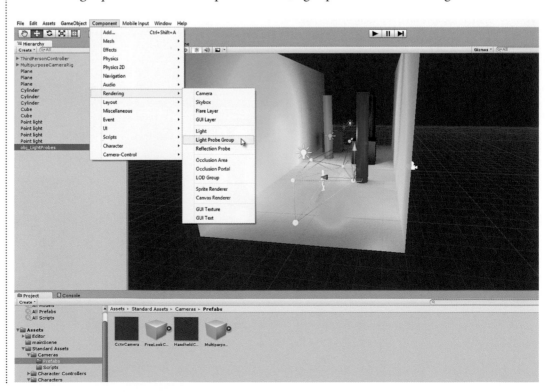

static lighting and fully dynamic lighting. Light probes can sample lighting levels at key points in the scene and then, based on the samples, interpolate lighting across moving objects to closely approximate baked lighting for pre-computed Global Illumination. Here's how to use them.

Assuming you have a scene with lights already created, add a new and empty object to the scene, and name this *obj_LightProbes*. The name is not essential, but simply descriptive. Once created, add a new *Light Probe Group* component to the object by selecting *Component > Rendering > Light Probe Group* from the application menu. ▶33

Next, add some light probes to the scene. A light probe is, essentially, a sphere object (which is invisible to the game camera) that samples an average of all scene lights at its current position, both their color and intensity. To add a light probe, click the *Add Probe* button from the *Light Probe Group* component in the Object Inspector. This adds a new light probe to the scene, which can be selected and transformed like any regular GameObject in the *Scene* view. Add at least four probes at different positions in the scene and the connections between them will become apparent. The central idea is to position a probe at a location of prominent light change in the level: at areas where light color or brightness dramatically changes. ▶34

34

6 Cameras, Rendering, Lighting

35

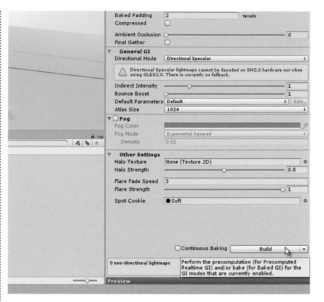

> **NOTE**
>
> Please consult the book companion files at *Chapter06/ LightProbes*.

After adding all probes, switch to the Lighting Window *Scene* tab and press the *Build* button, if Continuous Baking is not enabled. This samples the lighting across light probes in the scene. ▶35

Finally, select all moveable meshes (dynamic meshes) in the scene, and enable the *Use Light Probes* checkbox from the Object Inspector. This mesh will now use all baked light probes throughout the level for its lighting. ▶36

36

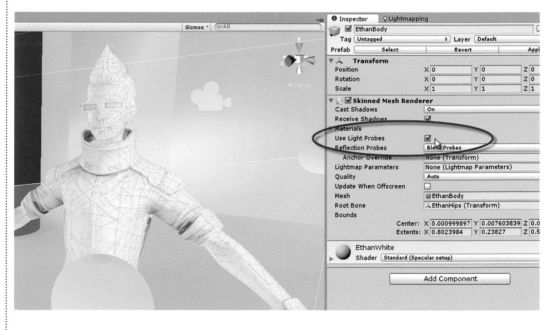

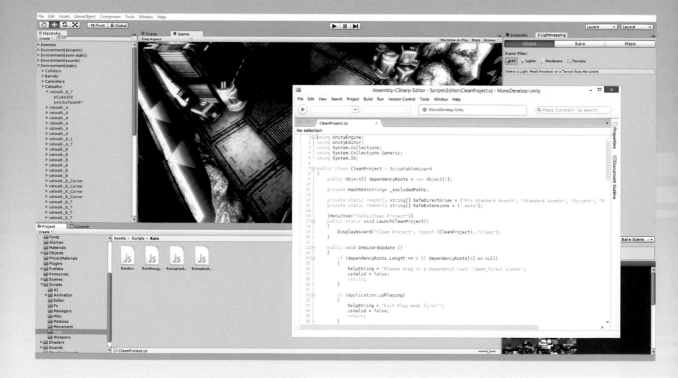

7

Coding and
MonoDevelop Tricks

Much nowadays is said within Unity circles about the "democratization of game development." This movement consists of making things "simpler" and "more accessible" to more people than ever before. But, however much this concept may be true, there's really no getting around the importance and necessity for coding in some form, and especially for optimized coding. For this reason, if you're serious about Unity development and making professional-grade games, then you'll need to start coding. And once you start, you'll need to rely on powerful and effective techniques that let you achieve both tangible results and solid performance, quickly and easily. This chapter therefore assumes you're familiar with scripting, and on that basis, it makes recommendations on extra techniques you can use along the way. Let's see these.

7 Coding and MonoDevelop Tricks

7.1 Caching

Caching refers to a process where you create and initialize objects ahead of time, holding them hidden in reserve until you actually need to use them. The main justification for doing this is performance. The act of creating an object or accessing a property entails, under the hood, the execution of functions and the dynamic allocation of memory. These processes in themselves may not appreciably impact performance when invoked occasionally, here and there, but when dealing with lots of objects and large scenes, it can quickly become the source of lag and stutters. Consider Code Sample 7.1, for example, which simply resets an object's position to the origin on each frame.

Code Sample 7.1: Setting an Object's Position
```
01  // Update is called once per frame
02    void Update () {
03        transform.position = new Vector3(0,0,0);
04    }
```

This code, if taken at face value, seems just a simple one-line statement at Line 03. But that's not correct. The reason is because *transform.position* is a *C# Property* and not a member *variable*. The result is that all statements involving *transform* will internally invoke a function call. The solution is to cache the Transform using the *Awake* function. See Code Sample 7.2.

Code Sample 7.2: Setting an Object's Position Through Cached Members
```
01  using UnityEngine;
02  using System.Collections;
03
04  public class Mover : MonoBehaviour
05  {
06    //Cached reference to the transform component
07    private Transform ThisTransform = null;
08
09    // Use this for initialization
10    void Awake ()
11  {
12        ThisTransform = GetComponent<Transform>();
13    }
```

```
14
15      // Update is called once per frame
16      void Update () {
17          ThisTransform.position = new Vector3(0,0,0);
18      }
19  }
```

T--I--P

Transform is not the only property of *MonoBehaviour*. Others include: *rigidbody, audio, collider, particle System, light,* and others.

NOTE

What's the difference, if any, between the Awake and Start events, apart from their name? They're both invoked at level start-up, right? The answer is not necessarily. The Awake event is called at level start-up for all objects, either active or non-active, before any other event. It is equivalent to a class constructor. The Start event, by contrast, is called on the first frame *after an object becomes activated*, and is always called after *every* object has received an Awake event. Therefore, with Start events: they are *guaranteed* to be called after all Awake events, but they're not always called at level start-up, because some objects may not be active when the scene begins.

Alternative Applications: Instantiation

Another common usage of caching is object instantiation, for creating objects that must appear to spawn dynamically, such as power-ups, enemies, weapons, bullets, explosion effects, and more. In almost every case, these objects seem to "come from nowhere," popping into existence during gameplay. Now, it's possible to dynamically generate these

1▼

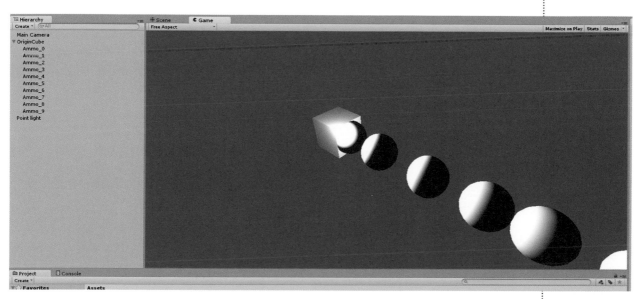

objects into the scene through code, as and when they're needed. But it's usually better to generate them either straight from the editor, or else at level start-up, holding them hidden until needed, when they can finally be "made visible," as though they've been generated immediately. Code Sample 7.3 defines a class for firing a pre-generated array of ammo prefabs. The complete source code for this project is included in the book companion files, in the folder *Chapter07\Caching*. ▶1

Code Sample 7.3: Firing Cached Ammo Prefabs

```
01  //---------------------------
02  using UnityEngine;
03  using System.Collections;
04  //---------------------------
05  public class Weapons : MonoBehaviour
06  {
07    //Number of ammo objects to pregenerate
08    public int AmmoMax = 10;
09
10    //List of ammo prefabs to pre-generate
11    private GameObject[] Ammo = null;
12
13    //Reference to ammo prefab to generate
14    public GameObject AmmoPrefab = null;
15
16    //Reference to this transform
17    private Transform ThisTransform = null;
18
19    //Reference to last generated prefab in array
20    private int LastSpawned = 0;
21    //---------------------------
22    // Use this for initialization
23    void Awake ()
24    {
25      //Get reference to transform
26      ThisTransform = transform;
27
28      //Loop through ammo list and generate now, at level
          start-up
```

```
29        Ammo = new GameObject[ AmmoMax] ;
30
31        for (int i=0; i<AmmoMax; i++)
32        {
33          //Generate new prefab
34          Ammo[ i]  = Instantiate(AmmoPrefab, ThisTransform.
            position, Quaternion.identity) as GameObject;
35
36          //Make child of this object
37          Ammo[ i] .transform.parent = ThisTransform;
38
39          //Set name
40          Ammo[ i] .name = "Ammo_" + i.ToString();
41
42          //Hide prefab
43          Ammo[ i] .SetActive(false);
44        }
45   }
46    //----------------------------
47    // Update is called once per frame
48    void Update ()
49    {
50      //If we press space, then spawn new ammo in scene from
        among pre-generated ammo
51      if(Input.GetKeyDown(KeyCode.Space))
52      {
53        //Rest ammo position back to gun barrel
54        Ammo[ LastSpawned] .transform.position = ThisTransform.
          position;
55
56        //Activate new ammo object
57        Ammo[ LastSpawned] .SetActive(true);
58
59        //Increment last spawned
60        ++LastSpawned;
61
62        //Check bounds - reset back to 0 if spawn supply
          exhausted
```

```
63          if(LastSpawned >= AmmoMax) LastSpawned = 0;
64      }
65   }
66   //-------------------------
67 }
68 //-------------------------
```

7.2 Code Commenting and Organization

Nobody wants to work with obfuscated code, even if it's code of your own creation. By obfuscated, I mean code that's difficult to read and maintain in the long term, not just for other team members, but also for the person who writes it. Some have said, humorously and cynically, that writing "unmaintainable" code (code that only you understand) is important for keeping your job, making yourself indispensable. But, assuming clearness and good craftsmanship is foremost with you, then it's critical to write clear code, with *appropriate* and concise commenting, and also with clearness of presentation. Don't underestimate the benefits to be had: clarity of code is intimately related to the speed by which you and others can understand what's written, and that can save you lots of developmental time. Thankfully, MonoDevelop can help us more easily achieve readable code.

2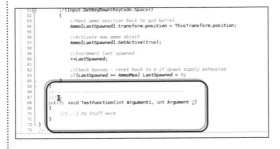

MonoDevelop supports XML comments for documenting functions, and these integrate well with tooltip menus for showing pop-up helper messages when calling those functions. To start writing XML comments, position your cursor at the line above a function definition, and enter /// (three sequential forward-slash characters). ▶2

3

When you do this, MonoDevelop automatically generates an XML comment that is specifically structured and formatted for the function below, allowing you to "fill in" the blank areas with relevant commenting. ▶3

Here, in Code Sample 7.4, is how I've written a comment for a sample function.

Code Sample 7.4: XML Code Comments

```
01  /// <summary>
02  /// Test Function - Call this to run a test function
03  /// </summary>
04  /// <param name="Argument1">This is the first argument
    </param>
05  /// <param name="Argument2">This is the second argument
    </param>
06  public void TestFunction(int Argument1, int Argument 2)
07  {
08    //[ ...] Do Stuff Here
09  }
```

This style of code commenting, apart from being conventional, has a further practical use. It integrates with MonoDevelop tooltip help, which means that as you call functions and specify arguments, MonoDevelop will display the relevant comments. This makes it easier to contextualize and understand the arguments a function expects as you write the calls, without having to revisit the function source code to check what it does. ►4

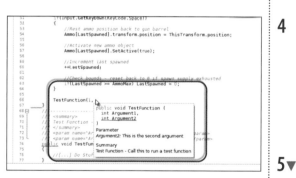

4

In addition to comments, MonoDevelop supports the #region pre-processor directive. By inserting this instruction into your source files, you can mark out the beginning and end of sections of related code, starting from a top line and moving to a bottom line. Once a region is marked, you will be able to expand and contract the region inside the code editor, using code folding. This makes it simpler to hide and

5▼

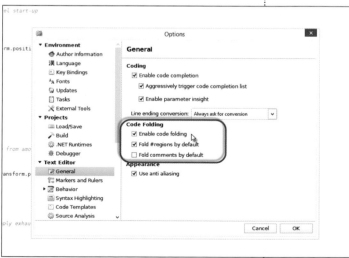

show relevant regions of the file for editing. To get started at using this feature, be sure code folding is enabled for comments in MonoDevelop. Access the options menu, by choosing *Tools > Options* from the application menu. Then from the *General* tab, enable the options *Enable Code Folding* and *Fold # Regions by Default.* ▶5

6

You can mark out a region of your source file using the *#region* and *#endregion* syntax. #region marks the top line of a region, and #endregion marks the bottom, with all lines between classified as belonging to the region. Note, this doesn't affect the validity of the code in terms of compilation; it simply makes your code easier to read. Consider Code Sample 7.5, where a *Variables* region is marked. ▶6

Code Sample 7.5: Using Regions

```
01  #region variables
02  //Number of ammo objects to pregenerate
03  public int AmmoMax = 10;
04
05  //List of ammo prefabs to pre-generate
06  private GameObject[] Ammo = null;
07
08  //Reference to ammo prefab to generate
09  public GameObject AmmoPrefab = null;
10
11  //Reference to this transform
12  private Transform ThisTransform = null;
13
14  //Reference to last generated prefab in array
15  private int LastSpawned = 0;
16  #endregion
```

7.3 Attributes

Maybe you want a script file to add entries to the Unity Editor menus, allowing you to attach the script to the selected object straight away without having to drag and drop from the Project Panel. Or, maybe you're creating a class that requires its attached object to have another component present, and which should be added automatically if it is not. Or, maybe you want to hide a global variable from the inspector, or maybe you even want to show a private variable in the inspector. You can achieve all of these things, and more, by using Attributes. In C#, Attributes are effectively metadata tags that can be attached to script files and classes within script files to change the way the script behaves with the Unity engine and other elements. They take the form of *[AttributeName]*. Let's consider the most common uses.

To add a script file as a menu entry in the editor, consider Code Sample 7.6. The *AddComponentMenu* attribute can be used.

Code Sample 7.6: The *AddComponentMenu* Tag
```
01   using UnityEngine;
02   using System.Collections;
03   //----------------------------------
04   [AddComponentMenu("CustomClasses/MyClass")]
05   public class MyTestClass : MonoBehaviour
06   {
07   }
08   //-------------------- --------------
```

The *AddComponentMenu* attribute accepts a string allowing you to specify the entry in the component menu where the script will be added as an option. ▶7

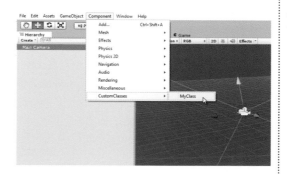

8

If you want to add a slider control to a variable in the Object Inspector, limiting its value to within a minimum and maximum range, then you can use the *Range* attribute. See Code Sample 7.7. ▶8

Code Sample 7.7: The Range Attribute

```
[ Range(0, 100)]
public int MyNumber = 0;
```

To explicitly mark one component X as depending on another Y; as requiring component Y to be attached to the object and, if Y is not attached, then to add Y automatically on adding X, then you can use the *RequireComponent* attribute. This will also prevent Component Y from being manually removed, so long as X is attached. See Code Sample 7.8.

Code Sample 7.8: The *RequireComponent* Attribute

```
//-----------------------------------
//This script will require a RigidBody Component
[RequireComponent (typeof (Rigidbody))]
public class MyTestClass : MonoBehaviour
{

}
//-----------------------------------
```

To make the script execute in the editor, as though Unity were in Run-Time mode, then use the *ExecuteInEditMode* attribute. See Code Sample 7.9. This attribute will include all calls to *Update* events too. Take care here, because infinite loops and Run-Time errors could cause the Editor to become unresponsive and crash. For this reason, only use *ExecuteInEditMode* where absolutely essential. Perhaps the most common use of this Attribute is for previewing render effects or user interfaces in the *Game* tab, when coded using the older *OnGUI* event.

Code Sample 7.9: *ExecuteInEditMode* Attribute

```
//-----------------------------------
[ ExecuteInEditMode]
public class MyTestClass : MonoBehaviour
{
}
//-----------------------------------
```

To hide a public variable of a class from the Object Inspector, as though it were a private variable, you can use the *HideInInspector* attribute. See Code Sample 7.10. This can be especially useful during debugging, when you're tracing the source of a problem, and would prefer to hide working variables to avoid distraction. This lets you focus on the problem specifically.

Code Sample 7.10: *HideInInspector* Attribute

```
//-----------------------------------
public class MyTestClass : MonoBehaviour
{
    [ HideInInspector]
    public String Name;
}
//-----------------------------------
```

Showing a private variable in the Inspector can be helpful for debugging, to see the values of variables as they change at Run-Time. There are two ways to go to achieve this. To show *all* private variables of a class for *all* components on the selected object, you can use Debug Mode from the Object Inspector. To access this, click the Object Inspector context menu icon, and choose *Debug Mode*. On choosing this, all private variables will be shown. ▶9

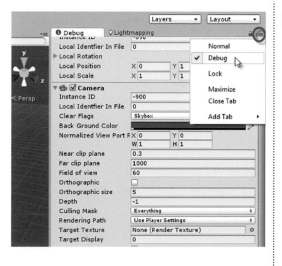

9

To show only a *specific* private variable in the Object Inspector, for either Debug or Release Mode, you can use the *SerializeField* attribute. See Code Sample 7.11.

Code Sample 7.11: *SerializeField* Attribute

```
//----------------------------------
public class MyTestClass : MonoBehaviour
{
    [ SerializeField]
    private string MyPrivateVariable = "hello world";
}
//----------------------------------
```

7.4 Platform-Dependent Compilation and Global Defines

Sometimes, when building cross-platform games for many different systems (like Android, Windows, Mac, etc.), you may need or prefer to use slightly different sections of code in some areas of your game, such as in input handling, shader selection, and lighting calculations, among others. That is, you may want to run a block of code for one platform, but not for another. You could achieve this in several different ways. One way is to use a "Run-Time platform check," such as *Application.platform*. See Code Sample 7.12.

Code Sample 7.12: Checking the Target Platform at Run-Time

```
01  //-------------------
02  using UnityEngine;
03  using System.Collections;
04    //-------------------
05  public class PlatformChecker : MonoBehaviour
06  {
07    //-------------------
08    // Use this for initialization
09    void Start ()
10    {
11      //Check if we are running on Windows
12      if(Application.platform == RuntimePlatform.WindowsPlayer
         || Application.platform == RuntimePlatform.WindowsEditor)
```

```
13      {
14          Debug.Log("Running on Windows");
15      }
16    }
17  }
18  //------------------
```

This code can be useful in some cases, where application execution must branch dynamically based on Run-Time platform. But in many cases, you can optimize your platform specific code further by using platform dependent compilation instead of performing Run-Time checks. This allows you to use pre-processor directives to mark regions of code in MonoDevelop that work or "compile" only for specific platforms. Once marked, Unity selectively compiles the relevant code depending on the active platform selected for building. This differs significantly from Run-Time checks: with Run-Time checks, code branches at Run-Time based on the active platform. But with platform dependent compilation, Unity selectively compiles code based on the active platform. Consider, for example, Code Sample 7.13, which defines input code used for desktop platforms only.

Code Sample 7.13: Check Desktop Input Using Platform-Dependent Compilation

```
01  //---------------------------------
02  using UnityEngine;
03  using System.Collections;
04  //----------------------   --------
05  public class InputHandler : MonoBehaviour
06  {
07    //---------------------------------
08    //Check for keyboard input desktop systems only
09    void Update()
10    {
11      #if UNITY_EDITOR || UNITY_STANDALONE || UNITY_WEBPLAYER
12
13        //Get horizontal and vertical axes
14        float Horz = Input.GetAxis("Horizontal");
15        float Vert = Input.GetAxis("Vertical");
16
17      #endif
```

```
18      }
19      //------------------------------------
20  }
21  //------------------------------------
```

10

The code from lines 13 to 16 will compile only for the Unity Editor, Web Player, and Desktop Builds. Remember, to change the active platform in Unity for a build, select *File > Build Settings* from the application menu. And then choose your destination platform, and finally click the *Switch Platform* button. ▶10

Alternative Applications: Custom Defines

11

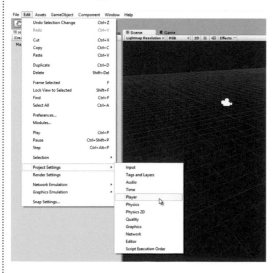

There are times when even the native platform-dependent pre-processor directives, as we've seen, may not be enough to meet your needs. This is because, even within a single platform— such as Windows—there are legitimate reasons why you may need several code branches. You may, for example, be creating two versions of your game: a free and paid version, or a demo and final version, or a debug and release build, for example. In such cases, it can be helpful to create your own pre-processor directives for conditionally compiling code, where the switches are based on global flags or settings specified from the editor. For the purposes of illustration, let's assume we're creating a specialized debug build. First, to create the global flag indicating whether this is or is not a debug build, access the *Player Settings* dialog, by choosing *Edit > Project Settings > Player* from the application menu. ▶11

From here, expand the *Other Settings* group from the Object Inspector. Under the *Configuration* field, enter *DEBUG_BUILD* into the *Scripting Define Symbols* edit box. The name *DEBUG_BUILD* can be substituted for any descriptive name you like: it effectively names the state to activate. You can remove the state by simply deleting its name from the edit box, or else renaming it with the / prefix, such as /DEBUG_BUILD. ▶12

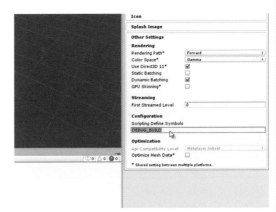

12

You can then branch your code, in any supported Unity language, by using pre-processor directives in combination with your flag name. See Code Sample 7.14.

Code Sample 7.14: Printing a Debug Message in a Code Block

```
01  //----------------
02  using UnityEngine;
03  using System.Collections;
04  //----------------
05  public class CustomFlagBranch : MonoBehaviour
06  {
07    //----------------
08    // Use this for initialization
09    void Start ()
10    {
11      #if DEBUG_BUILD
12      Debug.Log("My flag is set");
13      #endif
14    }
15    //----------------
16  }
17  //----------------
```

7.5 Working with Events

There's more to the *MonoBehaviour* class than first meets the eye or is first recognized. By that I mean: it offers a lot more functionality in terms of event notifications than is often acknowledged. Let's see some of the more surprising and useful events.

- **OnValidate**
  This event is called automatically by Unity during edit mode whenever you change a component value in the Object Inspector. It doesn't tell you *which* value was changed, but only that *some* value was changed, giving you the opportunity to check any specific values and validate them, if required. This can be useful if you need specific variables to stay inside a specific range, such as a minimum or maximum. Although, an effective alternative to clamp integers and numerical data between a range can be achieved through the *Range* attribute, as discussed in Section 7.3. For more information, see: http://docs.unity3d.com/ScriptReference/MonoBehaviour. OnValidate.html.

- **OnBecameInvisible** and **OnBecameVisible**
  These two events describe an object's visibility. The event *OnBecameVisible* is called once automatically whenever the object becomes visible to at least one camera in the scene, and *OnBecameInvisible* is called when the object leaves the visibility of any camera. There are some caveats to note with these events. Specifically: *OnBecameVisible* is not called repeatedly on each frame, but is called once unless the object becomes invisible to all cameras, in which case it's called each time it becomes visible to the first camera. Second, the term "visibility" here means only a frustum test; that is, an object is classified as visible when it enters a camera frustum, and issues such as occlusion (whether distant objects are obscured by nearer objects) are not considered. And lastly, camera visibility also includes visibility from the scene camera in the *Scene* tab, inside the Unity Editor. That means, if you're running a game with the *Scene* and *Game* tabs side by side in the Unity Editor, your object will be classified as visible if it can be seen by the Scene camera, even if no game camera can see it.

- **OnWillRenderObject**
  This event is called automatically *once per frame* on an object *for each camera* to which it's currently visible in the scene—including the scene preview camera. When inside this function, you can reference the static variable *Camera.current* to retrieve a reference to the active camera; that is, the camera currently seeing this object for this call. Again "seeing" and "visibility" here refer to being inside the viewing frustum.

- **OnLevelWasLoaded**

  This event is called automatically for persistent objects (objects that survive a scene when it ends) at level start-up, but before each object in the new scene receives its *Start* event. *OnLevelWasLoaded* is useful if your persistent object needs to perform object searching and referencing behaviors on scene changes. For more information on creating persistent objects, see Chapter 5, Section 4.

T--I--P

If your object never needs to handle an event, including *Start* and *Update* events, then get into the habit of removing them from your classes completely. Don't simply leave them blank. Blank events are classified as "handled" by Unity and incur a performance overhead, albeit marginal, in being called.

7.6 MonoDevelop: Refactoring Variables and Functions

Refactoring is the name given to a general process of safe and equivalent code amendment. In short: it's where you edit your code *after the fact*, to improve its readability and efficiency, without fundamentally changing what it ultimately does in terms of final results. Refactoring is something we do manually very often, but there are tools to automate the process in some ways. This might initially seem trivial, but it can be important: we often reflect on our code and see ways of making it better simply by changing how it's ordered or its naming conventions, and we can do that quickly and easily with Refactoring tools. Let's see these at work in MonoDevelop. ►13

13

So perhaps you've spent days creating a feature-filled and reliable class that does everything it's supposed to. The source file is long and the class contains many functions and variables. Then, finally, you realize that an important function or variable is either misspelled or could be named more descriptively. Therefore, you resolve to rename it. But, the problem is that renaming the function or variable at the declaration line will have implications elsewhere in code for wherever those names are used, either in function calls or in variable referencing. You could, by careful reading of your code, rename at each occurrence of the word in the source file, ensuring everything is adjusted properly, and

14

this might work well, but it could take a long time. For this reason, Refactoring can be helpful. To rename a function in MonoDevelop, right-click the function name wherever it occurs in the source file, and choose *Refactor > Rename* from the context menu, or else press the keyboard shortcut F2. ▶**14**

15

After selecting *Refactor*, a *Rename Method* dialog will appear asking you to enter a new name. Enter the name of the function in the *New Name* field (for my example, I will name it *RenamedFunction*). ▶**15**

You can click the *Preview* button to get a view of the source file, listing all the identified changes to make to the code, including the *Before* and *After* states. ▶**16**

16

After clicking OK, the contents of the source file will change to reflect the renaming at all appropriate locations. In addition to renaming functions, however, you can also rename variables in the same way. Simply right-click a variable name, and choose *Refactor > Rename* from the context menu. This time, a dialog will *not* show. Instead, you just need to rename your variable directly in the Editor window, and MonoDevelop automatically renames all other identified instances. Once renamed, press *Enter* or *Return* to confirm the rename operation. ▶17

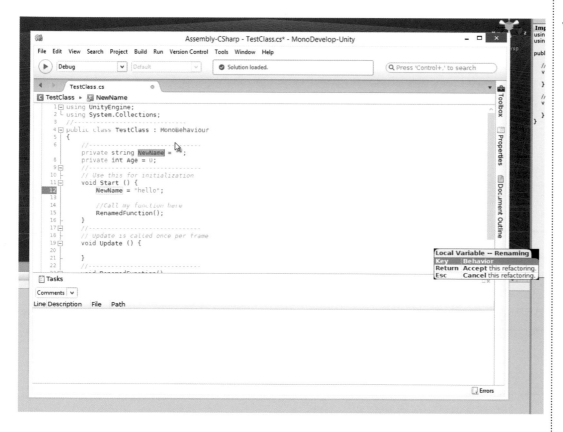

17

Alternative Applications: Properties and Refactoring

One reason for using C# properties as a front line for private variables is to validate and control the values being assigned to the variables, before they are actually assigned. This gives you control over variable "setting" and "getting," allowing you to make data validation decisions. For this reason, private and protected member variables will commonly need C# properties associated to them. You can, of course, write the property definitions manually using the appropriate syntax. But, MonoDevelop can generate them automatically for you using the Refactoring tools. To achieve this, right-click a private variable, and choose *Refactor > Create Property* from the context menu. ▶18

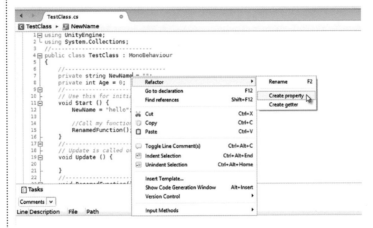

MonoDevelop will then show a line highlighter, which can be controlled using the keyboard arrow keys. Use the up and down keys to move the highlighter to the line where the property should be inserted. ▶19

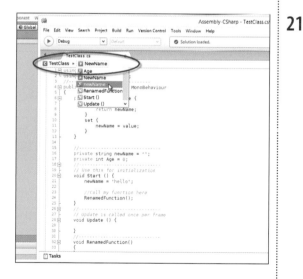

Press enter to confirm the operation and a new property for the private variable will be generated in the class. ▶20

7.7 MonoDevelop: Quick Navigation and Tasks

Two common navigational needs arise when working with long source files in MonoDevelop, as well as multiple source files. Let's see these one at a time. First, it'd be useful to jump around the source file to specific variable and function declarations without having to continually scroll up and down the file using the scrollbar or mouse wheel, searching manually for what we need. Thankfully, MonoDevelop does offer us a "bookmarking" or "navigation" feature. To access this, click your mouse cursor anywhere inside your class within the code editor, and then move your mouse up to the navigation bar and click on the first variable or function name listed to access a list of functions and variables belonging to the class. ▶21

Coding and MonoDevelop Tricks

Click on the function or variable name from the list; MonoDevelop will automatically jump to the declaration line in the editor. It's that simple!

Next, it's also useful, when debugging code and fixing errors across multiple files, to mark lines inside the file that you plan to come back to, either to implement a fix or to reference for some code. In short: it'd be useful to bookmark specific lines so you can quickly and easily return to them to implement a fix. MonoDevelop supports this in the form of tasks. To get started, you'll need to access the task panel. To do this, choose *View > Pads > Tasks* from the application menu, or else press *Alt + Shift + T* on the keyboard. ▶22

22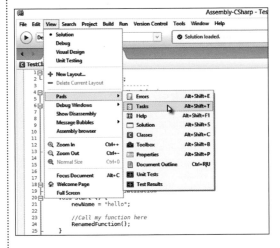

To add an entry to the tasks list, insert a new comment on any line that begins as //FIXME. See Code Sample 7.15. Remember to write "FIXME" in capitals.

Code Sample 7.15: Using FIXME Notes

```
01   using UnityEngine;
02   using System.Collections;
03   //————————————
04   public class TestClass : MonoBehaviour
05   {
06      //————————————
07      private string newName = "";
08      private int Age = 0;
```

```
09    //————————————
10    // Use this for initialization
11    void Start () {
12      newName = "hello";
13
14      //FIXME MyNewFix - This needs fixing
15
16      //Call my function here
17      RenamedFunction();
18    }
19    //————————————
20    // Update is called once per frame
21    void Update () {
22
23    }
24    //————————————
25    void RenamedFunction()
26    {
27    }
28  }
```

When you add a FIXME line, MonoDevelop will add an entry to the list. If you double-click the entry, MonoDevelop will automatically jump to that event. The great thing about this list is that it spans across multiple files, allowing you to jump between FIXME lines across files. ▶23

23

7 Coding and MonoDevelop Tricks

7.8 MonoDevelop: Code Readability

24

Many people are comfortable writing code inside MonoDevelop using the default interface colour scheme. For these people, nothing about the interface needs to change, and so no more need be said. But, some people (myself included) prefer darker colour schemes when writing code—a scheme in which the background is dark and the text is brighter. I've only disabled that colour scheme for taking screenshots in this book to make them appear clearer on the printed page. To change the MonoDevelop colour scheme, access the options window with *Tools > Options*. ▶24

25

The options dialog then appears. From here, choose the *Syntax Highlighting* tab. Be sure to enable the check box *Enable Highlighting*, if it's disabled. Then, select a colour scheme from the Color Scheme list. I personally prefer Oblivion, which offers brighter text and darker backgrounds. Once selected, click OK. ▶25

8

Performance and Optimization

When developing a game, you'll typically have target hardware in mind. That is a real or imaginary minimum system specification on which your game should run without performance problems. And ideally your game should work on all later and higher specifications too. Optimization happens when, after observing how your run game actually runs on the hardware, you decide to implement changes or amendments to make it run better. Your motivation for this might simply be a desire to technically "do better," even though you've observed no real performance problems. Or, it may be that your game displays severe or mild performance issues that need correcting to make your game playable and merchantable. Implicit in the optimization process are two main concepts: the "game" and the "target hardware," and each of these matter significantly in how you approach optimization. This necessarily means that what counts as "optimization" for one type of game and hardware may not be so for a different game and different hardware. For this reason, it's important not to consider the guidelines presented here as hard and fast rules that apply in all cases, and to be mindful to the specific conditions that apply for you.

8.1 Rendering Statistics: The Stats Panel

The best measure of performance for your game is far from "technical," as traditionally understood. Just play your game on your target hardware and see how it runs. This is the "best" method of performance assessment, and not some number on a graph, simply because it's the same experience that your gamers will have when they actually play the game for real. However, once you finally spot a performance issue, a problem to be solved because it degrades the experience, then it's time to use diagnostic tools to help identify the source, assuming the source isn't obvious. The Stats panel can help you do this. The panel can be accessed from the *Game* tab: just click the *Stats* button from the *Game* tab toolbar, and then play your game. ▶1

1

To read the Stats panel effectively, some information and background is required on each of the stats or "dimensions of performance." These are discussed below.

- **FPS**. Frames per second defines the total number of "frames" or "renders" that Unity can sustain per second. A frame refers to a final, composited render in pixels that's transferred from the graphics hardware to the screen. To produce the output, both the CPU (central processing unit) and the GPU (graphics processing unit) must perform many calculations. Together, these reflect the complexity of a render and the length of time required to produce it. Longer render times result in a lower FPS, since fewer frames are calculated per second. In general, then, the higher this number, the better. However, there's ultimately no absolute FPS that's "correct." But typically, FPS values lower than 15 will result in lag and jitter-like motions. Thus, FPS can help you make relative judgments about the performance of your game: if the FPS is consistently very low (less than 15 frames per second), then take that as a strong indication that serious optimizations need to be made.

- **SetPass Calls (Draw Calls)**. To produce a complete render, Unity must make "draw calls." Under the hood, a draw call refers to the number of requests made to the graphics hardware to "draw" data to intermediary buffers that will eventually compose a final render. It's sometimes said that there's "one draw call per object," but this definition can mislead us, as we'll see soon. Note: the "draw call" field, alongside almost all other fields in the Stats panel, will continuously change while the game is running. The Stats panel reflects the *current* state of the game, based on everything that needs to be rendered and processed for the current frame, given the position of the camera in the current scene. Overall, with draw calls, as with FPS (and optimization in general) the *less the better*. Fewer draw calls are to be preferred over more. Of course, this guidance, as elsewhere, is meant within reasonable limits. It's no doubt possible, for example, to reduce draw calls entirely by emptying your scene of everything, leaving a blank scene. The idea however is, more modestly, to reduce draw calls so far as is consistent with your target hardware and yet also respect your design and vision.

- **Tris** and **Verts**. This defines the total number of triangles and vertices being rendered "right now," and is not a total count of the triangles and vertices in the current scene. If your cameras and objects move, then the count will change as geometry is culled from entering and leaving camera frustums. Vertex count is often regarded as "less of an issue" for contemporary hardware than it once was, but still "less is generally better," as we'll see.

- **Fill Rate**. One statistic that's not explicitly mentioned or defined on the Stats panel is the fill rate. This defines the total amount of *pixel data* that a graphics card can process in *one second*. "Pixel data" here doesn't only refer to pixel data included in final output renders, but also to all the intermediary buffers created to compose the final render. It thus incorporates all pixel data output from shaders, which interact with materials and lights to produce output data. Every modern graphics card will have a maximum or a capacity regarding fill rate that if exceeded will cause lag and freezes as the hardware is pushed beyond its limits. The primary way to diagnose whether you're experiencing a fill rate performance issue is to run your game at lower resolutions, without making any other changes, so that the hardware processes fewer pixels. If performance improves to acceptable levels, then you're probably experiencing a fill rate issue. The way to solve this aligns with almost all other performance optimizations covered in this chapter, which have as their aim a relieving of the CPU and GPU from avoidable workload.

8.2 Draw Calls and Batching

Draw calls, as mentioned, play a significant role in render times: fewer draw calls are better. For this reason, some optimizations can be made by configuring your assets and objects for batching. Batching essentially allows Unity to group multiple objects together, treating them as though they were the same mesh or resource, so they can all be drawn together in a single draw call, as opposed to multiple. There are two forms of Batching: *Dynamic* and *Static*.

Static Batching
In short, for meshes that don't move at Run-Time (like walls, chairs, hills, mountains, lamp posts, and others), always mark them as static. This signals that the meshes may be batched together, which Unity will do automatically. To mark an object as static, either click the check mark *Static* from the Object Inspector when the object is selected (marking it as static for all categories), or at least open the *Static* drop-down and mark the object as *Batching Static* from the context menu. ▶2

2

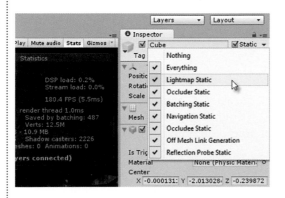

T--I--P

You can select multiple GameObjects, marking them as static simultaneously. For environment meshes, I typically group them together under one, Parent GameObject— even an empty GameObject. If you do this, you can mark the Parent as static and the setting will cascade downward to all children.

The extent to which multiple objects are reduced to smaller batches depends on additional factors. Specifically, all objects *sharing the same material* will be batched together. Thus, multiple objects are typically divided into as many batches as there are materials among them. This will result in an equivalent number of draw calls at Run-Time (5 batches = 5 draw calls), unless there are additional real-time lights and shaders that artificially increase that count.

Dynamic Batching

Dynamic batching is a collection process that Unity performs automatically to all non-static objects wherever possible to further reduce draw calls at Run-Time. In short: all non-static *MeshRenderer* and *ParticleSystem* objects sharing the same material and scale will be batched together, with some notable exceptions. Specifically, objects receiving real-time shadows will not be batched. In addition, *SkinnedMesh* renderers and *Cloth* renderers will always render separately, incurring at least one additional draw call.

> **NOTE**
>
> Limitations of Static. So long as an object is marked as static, it cannot move independently at Run-Time. This is because Unity is using a "copy" of the original, separate meshes that have been batched together as a single, complete mesh. The resultant batched meshes are copies: this means that Unity maintains a duplicate of all statically batched meshes. This could have performance implications both for your game and for development in the Editor, if you have very large and dense meshes. Consequently, you'll need to reach an acceptable balance that works best for you.

> **NOTE**
>
> For more detailed information on batching, see the Unity documentation at: http://docs.unity3d.com/Manual/DrawCallBatching.html.

8.3 Avoid Reflection: Event Systems

Reflection is the ability for a program to be "self-conscious" in a limited sense—to see and know itself, including the classes, functions, and variables it contains. Reflection in practice allows programmers to invoke functions and reference variables by way of their user-defined names in code, specified as strings. Common functions native to Unity that depend on reflection are the *BroadcastMessage*, *SendMessage* and *Invoke* functions. Using these functions, other methods can be invoked just as though we had a direct reference to them by simply passing a string, specifying the name of the function to call. This makes *SendMessage* and *BroadcastMessage* simple and appealing, because we can invoke methods on components without even knowing their class type—we thus achieve a certain degree of type agnosticism or "Run-Time polymorphism." However, reflection comes at a performance cost that can be prohibitive if used frequently, such as inside Update events. For this reason, consider using C# class inheritance to implement an application-wide event handling system to substitute *SendMessage* functionality.

Let's take a specific case—which can be found in the book companion files at *Chapter08\Events*. This sample application considers just one GameObject with multiple components that want to communicate with each other, *without using SendMessage* and *without having to know the data type of each other*. First, take a look at Code Sample 8.1, which defines a base class from which all components should inherit.

Code Sample 8.1: Events.cs—Base Class for an Event System

```
01   using UnityEngine;
02   using System.Collections;
03   //-------------------------------
04   //Base class for all components that must handle events
05   public class EventHandler : MonoBehaviour
06   {
07     //-------------------------------
08     //List of events to support for all objects application-
       wide - add your events here
09     public enum EVENT {ON_START, ON_END, ON_DAMAGE};
10
11     //List of event handlers attached to this object
12     private EventHandler[] AttachedHandlers = null;
13
14     //-------------------------------
15     //Base start function to cache all event handlers attached
       to this object
16     public virtual void Start()
17     {
18       //Get attached handlers
19       AttachedHandlers = GetComponents<EventHandler>();
20     }
21     //-------------------------------
22     //Post an event to all attached handlers - like sendmessage
23     public void SendEvent(EVENT Event_Type, object Data = null)
24     {
25       //Loop through all attached handlers
26       foreach(EventHandler EH in AttachedHandlers)
27         EH.OnEvent(Event_Type, Data);
28     }
29     //-------------------------------
```

```
30    //Event to override in derived classes
31    public virtual void OnEvent(EVENT Event_Type, object Data =
      null){}
32  }
33 //--------------------------------
```

To test this class in your application for replacing *SendMessage*, create a new
GameObject in the scene and attach two new components to it: each component should
be derived from the base class *EventHandler*, and not *MonoBehaviour*. Consider Code
Samples 8.2 and 8.3.

Code Sample 8.2: CustomHandler.cs—Class to Handle an OnStart Event

```
01  using UnityEngine;
02  using System.Collections;
03  //--------------------------------
04  public class CustomHandler : EventHandler
05  {
06    public override void Start ()
07    {
08      //Call base start event
09      base.Start();
10    }
11
12    //----------------------------- ----
13    public override void OnEvent(EVENT Event_Type, object Data
      = null)
14    {
15      switch(Event_Type)
16      {
17        case EVENT.ON_START:
18        Debug.Log ("This was called on start");
19        break;
20      }
21    }
22    //--------------------------------
23  }
24  //--------------------------------
```

Code Sample 8.3: CustomCaller.cs—Class to Call an Event on Another Component

```
01  using UnityEngine;
02  using System.Collections;
03  //-------------------------------
04  public class CustomCaller : EventHandler
05  {
06    //-------------------------------
07    // Use this for initialization
08    public override void Start ()
09    {
10      //Call base start event
11      base.Start();
12
13      //Invoke event on other component
14      SendEvent(EVENT.ON_START, null);
15    }
16    //-------------------------------
17  }
18  //-------------------------------
```

The class *EventHandler* defines a base that supports a *SendEvent* function, which can be used to dispatch an event call to components attached to the GameObject derived from *EventHandler*. Thus, the class *CustomCaller* will invoke an event specified in class *CustomHandler* at scene start-up. This configuration in many respects mimics the *SendMessage* behavior without relying on its reflection approach.

8.4 Use Atlas Textures

It's tempting to think of textures always as separate images: as though each and every graphic in your game (from sprites to GUI elements) must be chopped apart into separate files. The problem with doing this is that, when separate textures are used, separate materials must be created and assigned to objects. And yet separate materials incur performance penalties because they increase the draw call count, since only objects sharing the same material can be batched. For this reason, try where possible to consolidate your sprites and graphics together by copying and pasting them orderly into a single, larger texture—known as an *atlas texture*. In the case of 2D sprites specifically,

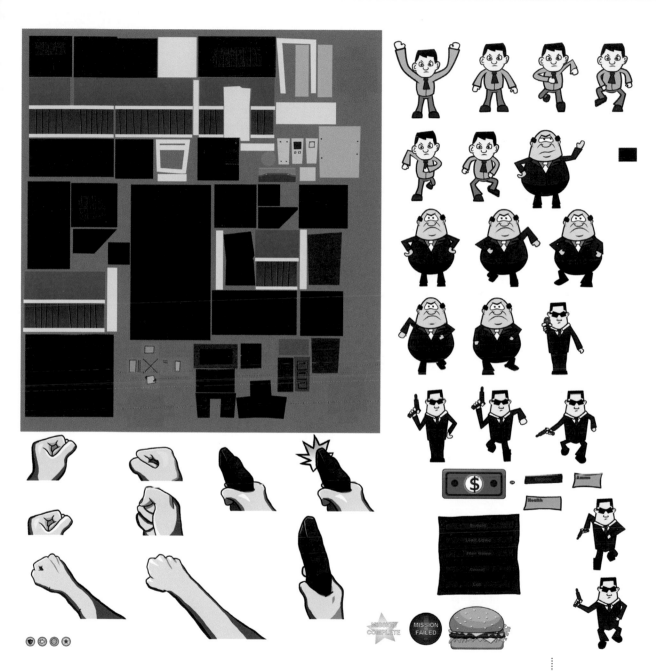

3

using the Unity sprite system, you can also have Unity pack textures into an atlas automatically. Let's see how: Import several textures into your project (some are included in the book companion files, *Chapter08\Atlas_Textures* folder). ▶4

4

Next, convert all the imported textures to sprites by selecting the textures and choosing *Sprite* from the *Texture Type* drop-down list in the Object Inspector. ▶5

Then, to make sure all sprites are compiled together into the same atlas texture, assign them all an identical *Packing Tag*. In the Packing Tag field, assign them a name—for this example: *MySprites*. Then click *Apply*. ▶6

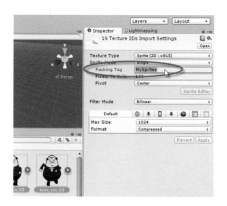

To activate the Sprite Packing feature, you'll need to enable it for your project specifically. To do this, choose *Edit > Project Settings > Editor* from the application menu. ▶7

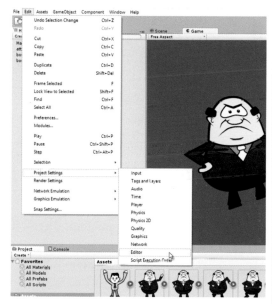

From the Object Inspector, change the Sprite Packer mode to *Always Enabled*. ▶8

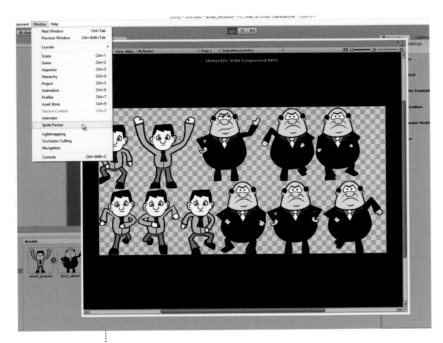

Now, on running your game, Unity will automatically compile all sprites with a matching tag into a single atlas texture that will be used for sprite instances in the scene, allowing them to be batched. To see the generated sprite atlas textures, while the game is running, select *Window > Sprite Packer* from the application menu. ▶9

9

8.5 Optimizing Meshes

Marking non-moving meshes as static from the Object Inspector is an important step toward optimizing your game, but there's still more you can do. Specifically, you can make in-game optimizations even at the modeling and mapping stages of your meshes. Here are some important considerations:

- **Minimize Vertex Count and Topology**
  Vertices are the raw ingredients of a mesh because they define its structure, or topology. When modeling a mesh, then, keep vertices to a minimum. True, both Unity and modern GPUs are very capable at processing large numbers of vertices, and this perhaps makes them less of a concern than in former times. But even so, you can still have "too many," which can reduce performance and cause lag. These means that no vertices are practically "free" in terms of computational expense, and so seeking to minimize their number makes sense. However, always be sensitive to good topology during the minimizing process: use only tris or quads (three- or four-sided polygons) and, for animated meshes, make sure their edges flow predictably and neatly along the contours of the model. ▶10

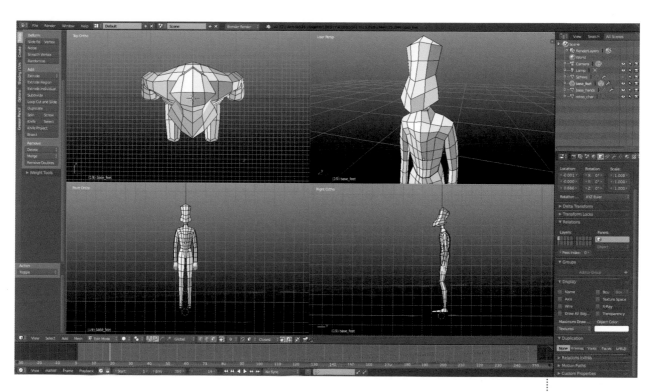

10▲ 11▼

- **Minimize UV Seams**

  Textures are flat 2D images mapped into the 3D surface of a mesh. The mapping information is known as UV mapping, and it is defined by seams. Seams mark edges in a model where imaginary cuts or splices can be made, allowing the mesh to unravel or unfold itself onto a 2D surface. This means a direct correspondence is made between a model and its texture. In general, seek to minimize the number of seams in a model. The reason is because Unity will actually cut the model at the seams, "doubling up" all vertices along every seam. This is why the vertex counts of a model between Unity and 3D modeling software, like Blender and Maya, can differ for the same model: since each software counts the vertices by a different standard. ▶11

- **Minimize Bones and Keyframes**

  Again, in keeping with the minimize strategy, reduce bones and animation keyframes as far as possible, while remaining true to your creative vision. This is, of course, a matter of reductionism and not brutality. That means: don't cut out bones or keyframes simply for its own sake or because you can, regardless of the results. Rather: remove those bones and keyframes wherever the effects will be negligible. And actively seek ways to achieve the same results more efficiently: looking to create the same skeletal structure or animation using less. ▶12

12

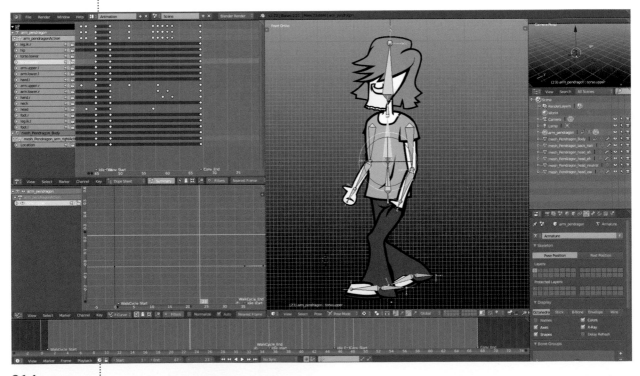

- **Orient Local Axis**
  Each GameObject in Unity has its own local axis (X, Y, and Z axes) whose origin marks the object's pivot point—its center and anchor point. The pivot point of an object defines its position in world space, and the object's local space is a measured offset from its pivot. If you're making character meshes, or vehicles, or spaceships, or objects that move and have a clearly defined direction, then take extra care about the position and orientation of an object's pivot. For character meshes, position the pivot at the character's feet (between each foot), marking the point where the feet touch the ground. In addition, the local axes should be oriented so that the local Z axis points in the direction of the character nose: the Z axis effectively expresses "which way" an object is looking—its "look at" vector. ▶13

13

- **Combine Meshes From Proximity**
  For an example, consider two house meshes that stand side by side in-game to form two houses in a street. If these houses always appear side by side in-game and never move independently of each other, then it's a good idea to merge the two meshes together as one integrated mesh, as opposed to leaving them as separate meshes. The general rule here is to combine, where possible, any meshes that always appear "close together" and never move independently. The idea of "close together" here is relative to your game and refers mainly to whether the player will *see* the objects together in-game. If the objects are small enough and near enough to the camera to be seen together (and thus must be drawn by the Unity engine), then these represent candidates for merging. Doing this can reduce draw calls, if multiple materials and lights would otherwise be involved, and can even improve the speed of existing draw calls.

8.6 MipMaps

MipMapping is a form of "detail modulation" based on camera distance, and it can significantly improve performance for large, open-world games with lots of objects and large textures. The term "Mip" in "MipMap" means *multum in parvo* (MIP) (which is often translated as "much in little"). And so MipMap can be thought to mean "much in a little map." The idea is that, by importing the largest sized texture needed, Unity automatically generates progressively smaller and lower-detail versions, which it holds internally. These lower-detail versions will then be substituted for the high-res texture in-game, whenever it's seen on objects *in the distance*. Thus, smaller and lower-detail textures will replace high-res textures when seen in the distance, reducing texture overhead on the CPU and GPU. When used effectively, MipMap transitions are often imperceptible to the gamer, because distant objects do indeed appear less detailed than nearer ones. To configure MipMaps for imported textures, select a texture in the Project Panel, and change its texture type in the Object Inspector to *Advanced*. ▶14

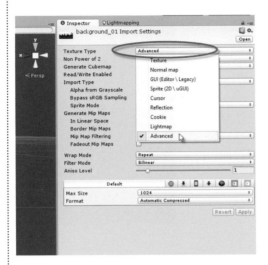

Then enable the *Generate MipMaps* check box, and click the *Apply* button. Remember, MipMaps should only be generated for texture maps that will be shown in perspective and can potentially appear in the distance. Textures used for 2D games and for GUIs should not typically be enabled for MipMaps. If they are, texture quality may appear significantly reduced. ▶15

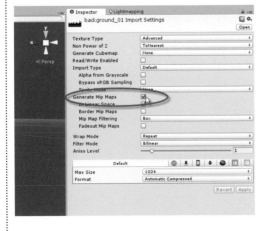

8.7 Miscellaneous Rendering Optimizations

If your game is running slow, or if it doesn't look as good as intended, and if you've tried all the above tips, there are still additional issues to consider. These are included as below.

16▼

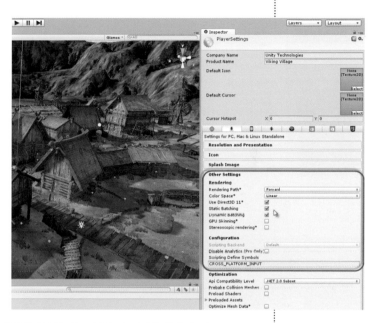

First, open the *Player Settings* dialog by choosing *Edit > Project Settings > Player* from the application menu. Then expand the *Other Settings* tab inside the Object Inspector. If you need real-time shadows from point lights and spotlights, be sure to enable the *Forward Rendering* Path from *Rendering Path* drop down menu. When activated, you may then enable real-time shadow casting from point and spotlights in the scene. ▶16, 17

17◀

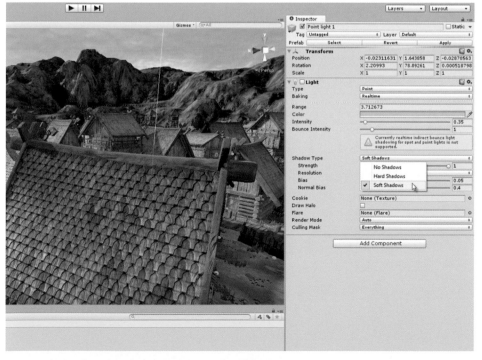

8 Performance and Optimization

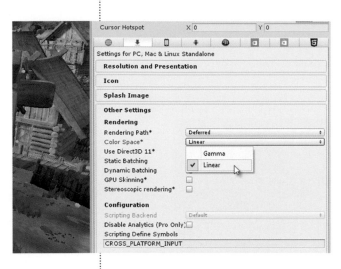

18

To achieve greater realism with lighting, use *Linear Space* instead of *Gamma Space* for the *Color Space* setting. Linear Space ensures shaders and color-based arithmetical operations are applied to textures and other pixel-based inputs with Gamma Correction removed, allowing higher graphical fidelity. More information on Linear Space lighting can be found at the online Unity documentation here: http://docs.unity3d.com/Manual/LinearLighting.html. ▶18

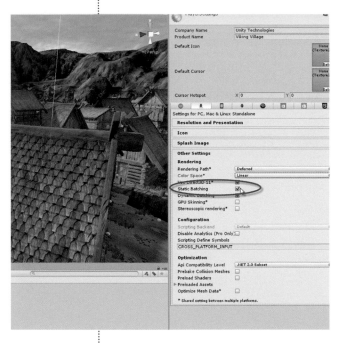

19

In Unity, Static Batching is a form of optimization where Unity combines together all separate meshes in the scene, which are marked as Static and share the same material, as one single, larger and unified mesh. Static Batching offers faster Run-Time performance because Unity can send the combined "mesh unit" to the renderer in one batch, as opposed to using multiple draw calls. But the combined mesh typically requires a larger memory footprint, both in RAM and on the graphics hardware. Consequently, you'll need to decide carefully about whether Static Batching should be enabled or disabled for your project. If you're seeking a performance boost and can safely use extra memory to achieve it, then it's probably worthwhile enabling Static Batching. More information on Batching can be found at the online Unity documentation here: http://docs.unity3d.com/Manual/DrawCallBatching.html. ▶19

Don't forget to disable the *Cast Shadows* and *Receive Shadows* settings on all objects where Shadows are not required, using the *Mesh Renderer* component. ▶20

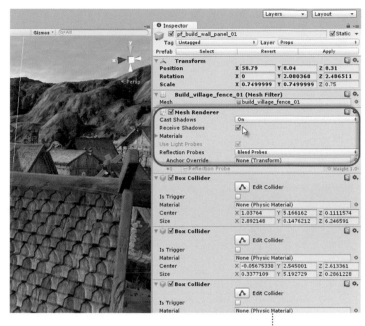

If a light never changes or moves at Run-Time, then consider changing its mode to either *Mixed* or *Baked*, to prevent Run-Time calculations. ▶21

20▲

21

Reducing shadow quality can have a big impact on Run-Time performance where real-time lighting is used. To access the Master Shadow Quality Settings for the entire game, select *Edit > Project Settings > Quality* from the application menu. Then reduce *Shadow Quality* using the *Shadow Resolution* drop-down list in the Object Inspector. ▶22

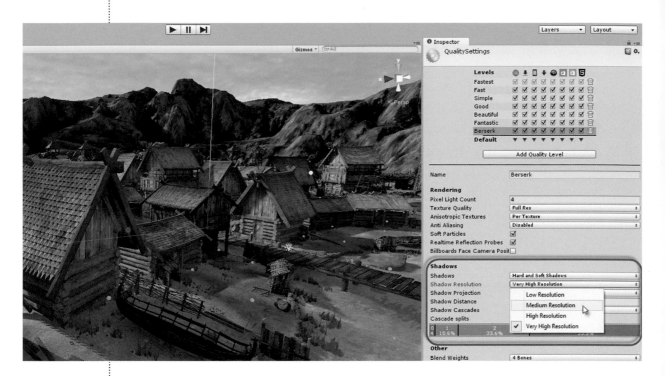

22

8.8 Shader Complexity

Unity ships with a selection of "built-in" or native shaders, many of which will suit your needs for a wide range of projects and assets. Often, the Standard Shader will suit most needs. However, different shaders perform differently, and even across different types of hardware. This section explores some general "dos and don'ts" about the native shaders.

- **Use Unlit Shaders**
  For objects like GUI elements, HUDs or sprites, or for self-illuminated light sources like TV screens and neon signs, you may not need or want your object to be affected by scene lights and shadows. In these cases, prefer the unlit set of materials. ▶23

- **Avoid Transparency**
  Unity supports a range of shaders supporting alpha transparency in textures, such as *Transparent/Diffuse* and *Unlit/Transparent*. Transparency is computationally expensive. Consequently, avoid using transparent shaders unless essential.

- **Shader Stripping**
  When using the Standard Shader, leave all inputs empty wherever you don't need or want effects applied. The Standard Shader will be compiled and effective only for inputs that you actually specify using the texture swatches and sliders. Empty fields will not only be ignored but will simplify the shader complexity.

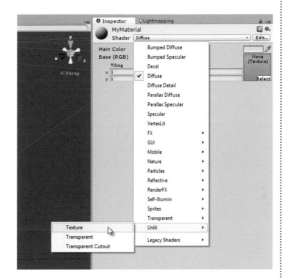

23

8.9 Updates and Coroutines

Event-driven programming can be good for transferring lots of intensive processing away from the frame-based Update event into one-off events, called as and when required. These include events like level changes, damage dealing, health changes, weapon collection, and more. But, sometimes you just need more frequent control and checks, especially for determining collisions (such as when two objects collide) and motion (such as when an object is traveling along a path). In these cases, to achieve smooth and effective results, you need to update often. However, that said, the Update event is not always the best alternative. Sometimes, you can use coroutines instead. There are times when you *do* need frequent updates and checks, *but* not always as frequently as an Update event. Maybe you could get away with updating just once every two or five seconds, for example. While this might seem frequent in itself, it's still much less when compared to the frequency of Update, which can even be 100 times per second. Code Sample 8.4 features a class that runs a specified function on specific intervals.

Code Sample 8.4: DelayedUpdater.cs—Runs a Function on a Specified Interval

```
01  using UnityEngine;
02  using System.Collections;
03  //-------------------—
04  public class DelayedUpdater : MonoBehaviour
05  {
06    //-------------------—
07    //Time to wait between intervals
08    public float Interval = 5.0f;
09    //-------------------—
10    // Use this for initialization
11    void Start ()
12    {
13      //Run delayed update coroutine
14      StartCoroutine(DelayedUpdate());
15    }
16    //-------------------—
17    //Delayed updater
18    public IEnumerator DelayedUpdate()
19    {
20      //Loop forever and perform behaviour
21      while(true)
22      {
23        //Run custom code
24      MyCustomUpdate();
25
26        //Wait for interval
27        yield return new WaitForSeconds(Interval);
28      }
29    }
30    //-------------------—
31    //My custom behaviour
32    public void MyCustomUpdate()
33    {
34      //Do stuff here
35    }
36    //-------------------—
37  }
38  //-------------------—
```

> **T--I--P**
>
> You could use the method *Monobehaviour. InvokeRepeating* to achieve similar results. This function, however, relies on Reflection. More information on *InvokeRepeating* can be found online here: http://docs.unity3d.com/ ScriptReference/MonoBehaviour.Invoke Repeating.html.

8.10 FixedUpdate and Time Steps

If your game is "physics heavy" and relies on frequent physics checks, collision tests, raycasts, and forces, then it's likely you rely on the FixedUpdate function. Like Update, this function is typically called many times per second. But unlike Update, which is called once per frame, FixedUpdate is called at fixed, regular intervals as determined by the internal configuration of the Unity physics engine. Unity, however, offers

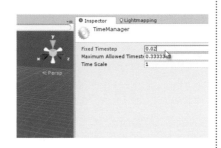

24

you some control over how often FixedUpdate is called, and this gives you some flexibility for quickly and easily improving physics performance. Specifically, you can control how much time (in seconds) should elapse before each FixedUpdate call. Increasing this value therefore results in long intervals between calls and thus fewer FixedUpdate calls. The result is an improvement in performance at a reduction in physics accuracy. Indeed, a reduction in accuracy is not a pleasant prospect, but what matters is whether the physics look "good enough" to be believable. Therefore, you may be able to significantly play around with this Time Step value to improve performance. To achieve this, open the Time Manager by choosing *Edit > Project Settings > Time* from the application menu. Then enter a new value for the Fixed Timestep field in the Object Inspector. ▶24

8.11 Static and Dynamic Arrays

Probably every game needs arrays of some kind. If you need a list of all enemies in the level, or all weapons, or all special moves, and so on, you'll need arrays. Arrays come in two basic forms: static and dynamic. Static arrays are declared in C#, for example, as:

```
//Array of 5 integers
int[] MyNumbers = new int[ 5];
```

Static arrays have their maximum capacity fixed and decided at declaration time, and that capacity never changes. You can add and remove elements to and from the list, but the maximum capacity can never be exceeded. And if you have fewer items than the capacity, you just end up with empty entries in the array because the capacity can never be shrunk. This makes static arrays limiting. An alternative is a dynamic array, such as the List class from the Mono Framework. Unlike static arrays, lists resize themselves to accommodate exactly the number of items required: they can grow and shrink at Run-Time. For example:

```
//Declare empty list
List<int> MyNumbers = new List<int>();

//Add number
MyNumbers.Add(5);
//Add number
MyNumbers.Add(3);
//Add number
MyNumbers.Add(1);

//List has 3 entries. Now remove first one.
MyNumbers.RemoveAt(0);

//List now has two entries
int NumEntries = MyNumbers.Count;
```

Dynamic arrays are elegant and useful, but expensive compared to static arrays. For this reason: always use static arrays unless you really *need* a list of items whose capacity changes over time.

8.12 Audio

25▶

For games that use just a few sound effects and one, short music track, it's unlikely that audio will prove a big problem for performance. But, if you have longer tracks lasting for minutes or even an hour, coupled with voice acting and other looping sound effects, then audio import settings can have a significant impact on Run-Time performance. The following loose "rules" can be helpful. ▶25

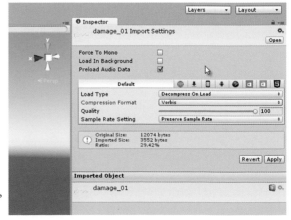

- For best audio quality, always import in a lossless format, such as *WAV* or *AIFF*. Unity may need to recompress the audio to other formats like *MP3*, depending on your target platform.

- For longer background music or ambient tracks that play on a loop or one-off, choose *Compressed in Memory* for the *Load Type*. Doing this prevents long loading times and heavy memory usage, though often results in slightly slower performance. ▶26

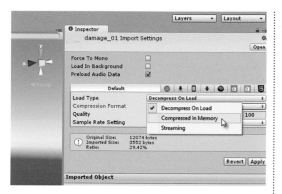

26

- For short sound effects that play repeatedly (like footsteps and gun shots), select *Decompress on Load* for the *Load Type*. This means smaller sounds will be loaded entirely into memory, but will play faster. ▶27

27

- One alternative loading method that's useful for shorter music tracks, such as incidental music and transitional effects, is to use *Compressed* for the *Audio Format* type, and *Decompress on Load* as the *Load Type*. This allows music to have a smaller memory footprint, but requires Unity to decompress the track when the level loads. This can result in slower level loading times, but faster performance for music playback.

NOTE

Audio Importing. More information on audio importing can be found at the online Unity documentation here: http:// docs.unity3d. com/Manual/ AudioFiles. html.

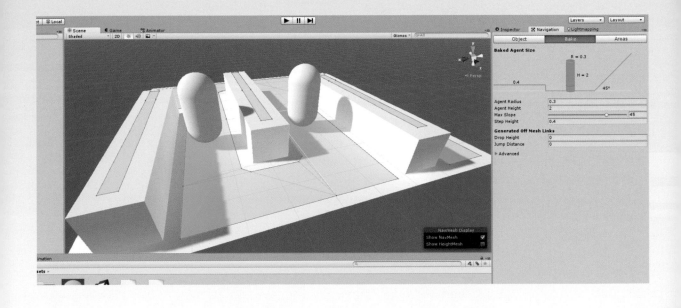

9

Physics, Collisions, and Pathfinding

Games are interactive in an immediate and direct sense: the player provides input, the game responds to input, and the player responds to the game's responses, and so on. Part of this interactivity consists in creating believable experiences. And physics, collision detection, and pathfinding are some ingredients critical to creating believability. "Physics" is a general term, referring to many Unity features for simulating physical forces affecting the motion of GameObjects. "Collision" refers here to a smaller subset of physics features dedicated to detecting when two objects or entities collide. And finally, "pathfinding" means the ability for objects, like enemy characters, to navigate their way around the scene while avoiding tangible obstacles like walls. This chapter explores many tips and tricks relating to this trio of feature sets.

9 Physics, Collisions, Pathfinding

9.1 Building Navigation Meshes

1 There are many ways to achieve pathfinding in Unity—most of them require "manual coding." However, Unity ships with a native or "built-in" pathfinding system that is especially suited for 3D games, called Navigation Meshes. With this mechanism, pathfinding rests on the generation of a *Navigation Mesh*, which is an internal mesh whose faces define the walkable regions of an environment. "Walkable" here refers only to areas

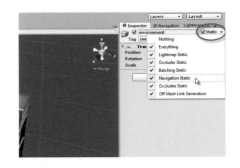

where intelligent characters (**agents**) *could* move, *if* they needed or wanted to. Building a Navigation Mesh is simple, provided you have an environment and level made. To start, make sure your level is marked as *Navigation Static*. To do this, select all environment objects, and then click the *Static* drop-down from the Object Inspector, and choose *Navigation Static*. ▶1

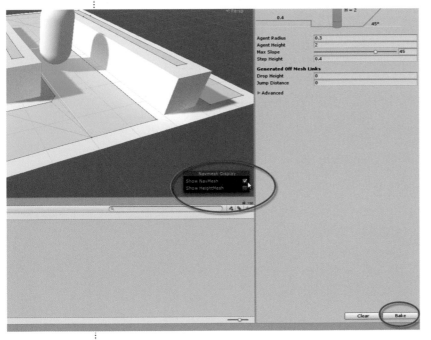

Then open the Navigation window, by choosing *Window > Navigation* from the application menu. Then select the *Bake* tab, and click the *Bake* button to generate the Navigation Mesh. When you do this, Unity projects a ray from the top downward, tracing all intersections with navigation objects to create a horizontally aligned map of the floor, constituting the Navigation Mesh. This appears in blue, inside the Scene Viewport when it's not maximized, provided the *Navmesh Display* is enabled. You can toggle navmesh display using the *Show NavMesh* check box. ▶2

2

After generating the Navigation Mesh and inspecting it in the Scene Viewport, it's likely you'll spot some "problems." Specifically, your mesh will be different from the true floor in two important ways. First, the Navigation Mesh will be "thinned out" or offset from the real walls. And inside thinner regions, like doorways, the mesh may even be broken entirely—disconnecting the outside of rooms from the inside. Disconnections like this are "bad" because agents cannot, by default, cross or travel over areas not covered by the Navigation Mesh. ▶3

3

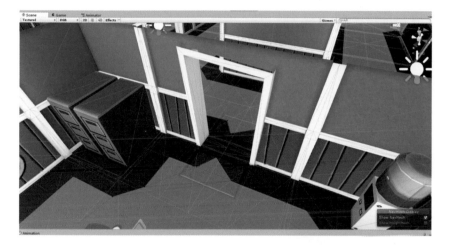

You can fix this problem by reducing the *Agent Radius* setting from the Navigation window. This defines the total radius of an imaginary circle offset against the wall and surrounding the agent. Larger values result in wider gaps between the Navigation Mesh and the wall. This setting is important because it represents how close to a wall an agent can move while traversing the Navigation Mesh.

Note: if this value is "too small," an agent may be able to partially penetrate a wall. For this reason, a balance needs to be reached. An alternative method for correcting the breakages between doorways is to use off-mesh links, as we'll see later in this chapter. ▶4

4

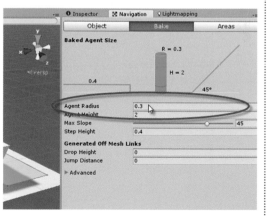

T--I--P

Remember, on changing any Navigation Mesh parameters, you'll need to click the *Bake* button again to generate a new Navigation Mesh.

The second problem is that a Navigation Mesh may appear vertically raised or lowered above or below the true floor. This is problematic because agents will always walk on the Navigation Mesh and not on the floor, and where the elevation of the two differs, agents will appear to hover or sink. ▶5

5

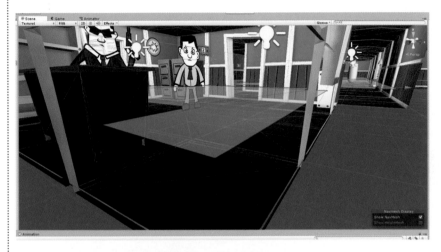

6

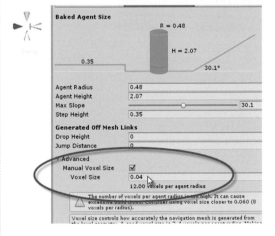

The elevation issue is fixed by expanding the *Advanced* tab in the Navigation window, and by enabling the field Manual Voxel Size. Lower values increase the fidelity of the mesh, moving it closer to the true floor, but increases the calculation time. ▶6

Alternative Applications: Manual Meshes

There're times when your game will need pathfinding abilities but when the standard Navigation Mesh features don't support your needs. For example, if you need characters to walk in the sky or "in the air" or across non-visible regions, or if you need to make certain floor areas un-walkable, or if you need characters to walk across unconventional terrain, then it may be easier and more intuitive to manually create a Navigation Mesh in your 3D modeling software, like 3DS Max or Maya or Blender. To do this, simply model a floor mesh, like a regular mesh. When modeling, though, keep in mind that the mesh will not be visible in game: its purpose is simply to define all walkable regions. For this reason, the object needs no mapping coordinates and its topology need not be optimized for animation. ▶7

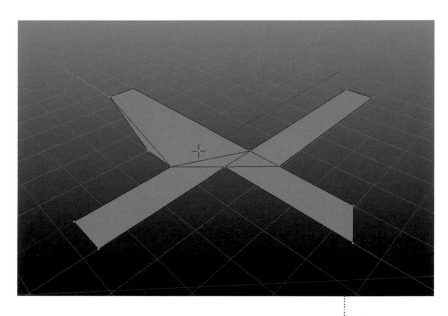

7

Import your floor mesh into Unity as a regular mesh, and add it to the scene, positioning it appropriately to match the floor. Select the mesh and make sure *it's the only object* in the scene to be labelled as *Navigation Static* from the Object Inspector. If it's not, then other meshes will also be included in the navmesh baking process. ▶8

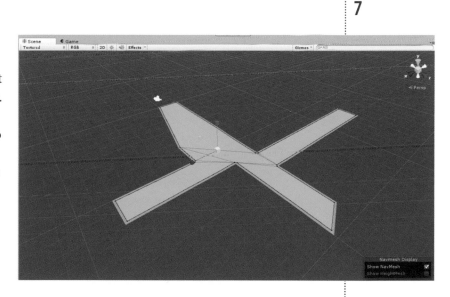

8

After the Navigation Mesh is generated, you can manually hide the floor object in the scene (by disabling it), or you can write a script that will disable the object automatically on start-up, as shown in Code Sample 9.1.

Code Sample 9.1: HideOnStart.cs—Class to Disable Object on Start-Up

```
01  //----------------------------------
02  using UnityEngine;
03  using System.Collections;
04  //----------------------------------
05  public class HideOnStart : MonoBehaviour
06  {
07    //Should we hide on start-up?
08    public bool Hide = true;
09    //------------------------------------
10    // Use this for initialization
11    void Start ()
12    {
13      //If we should hide, then hide
14      if(Hide)
15        gameObject.SetActive(false);
16    }
17    //------------------------------------
18  }
19  //----------------------------------
```

9.2 Off-Mesh Links

Whether you're generating Navigation Meshes directly from scene contents, or from a manually made Navigation Mesh, you'll probably need to work with off-mesh links in some way. If you need stairs to climb, or ledges from which you can fall or jump, or teleporters that zap you from one place to another, then off-mesh links will be critical. Essentially, there're many reasons a break or gap may be created in a Navigation Mesh, such as a narrow doorway or chasm. By default, agents cannot cross gaps. In many cases, this is exactly the behavior you want. But sometimes the gaps need to be cross-able. Thus, off-mesh links are needed to define which gaps can be crossed. ▶9

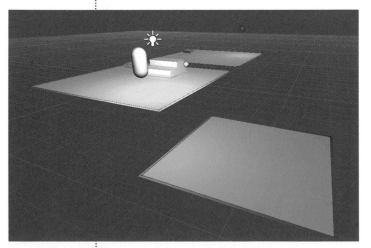

9▼

In the case of stairs and ledges from which you can "fall down" to lower parts of the terrain, you can automatically generate off-mesh links during the baking process. Consider the specific case of an upper and lower ledge from which an agent should be able to fall, when moving from the upper ledge to reach a destination on the lower. By default, the upper and lower ledges will form two disconnected parts of the Navigation Mesh. But in this case, the agent must travel between the two. That is, they should walk over the edge of the higher ledge, falling down onto the lower ledge below where they can resume movement and reach the destination.

NOTE

You can follow along with the off-mesh link pathfinding example used here, by using the book companion files. Consider the folder *Chapter09\OffMeshLinks*.

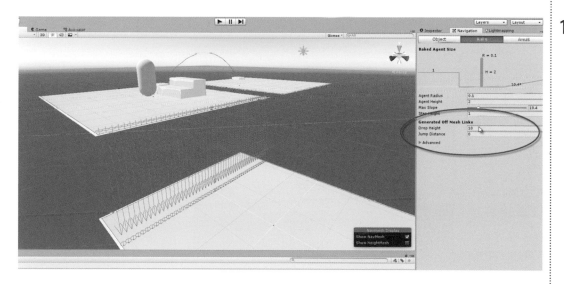

10

To achieve this, you should increase the field *Drop Height*. This defines the total vertical height in the scene (in meters) along which an agent can fall from an upper floor to a floor below. On re-baking the Navigation Mesh, a set of arrows will be drawn between the upper and lower ledges, indicating the connection between them via off-mesh links. This allows an agent to bridge the connection and continue moving. ▶10

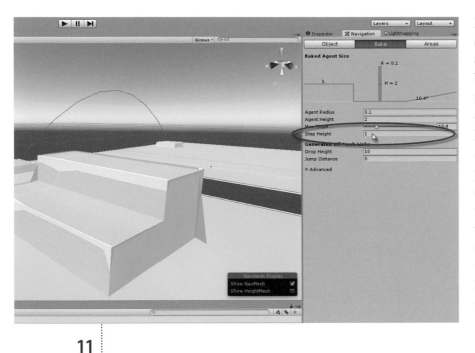

11

In the case of stairs, you can also create automatic off-mesh links through baking. Simply adjust the field *Step Height*. This defines the maximum height of a step in a staircase, along which the player can ascend and descend—allowing a two-way movement. Higher values support steeper steps. Again, on re-baking the Navigation Mesh will be regenerated to support the stair incline. ▶11

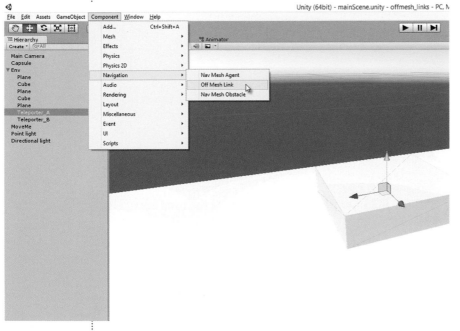

12

However, your needs may be more intricate than just steps and ledges- for example: teleporters. Teleporters "corrupt" Navigation Meshes and traditional pathfinding because they create shortcuts or regions in which agents are immediately transferred to new locations, regardless of any other spatial obstacles or distances between. To create teleporters in Unity, you'll need to create off mesh links manually. To do this, add an Off-Mesh Link Component to each tele porter spot (a location on the teleporter which the player can reach). To add an Off-Mesh Link Component, select *Component > Navigation > Off Mesh Link* from the application menu. ▶12

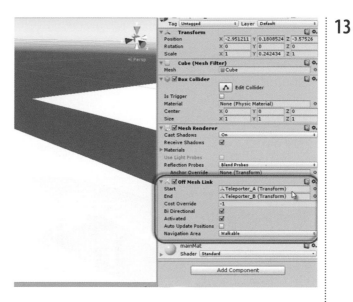

13

Once added, configure the off-mesh link component in the Object Inspector, specifying the transform component for the *current* object for the *Start* field, and then specifying the destination teleporter as the *End* field. Then repeat this process for the destination teleporter. ▶13

Then finally, with manual off-mesh links configured for the scene, re-bake the Navigation Mesh. When you do this, the additional off-mesh links will be shown in the Scene Viewport. ▶14

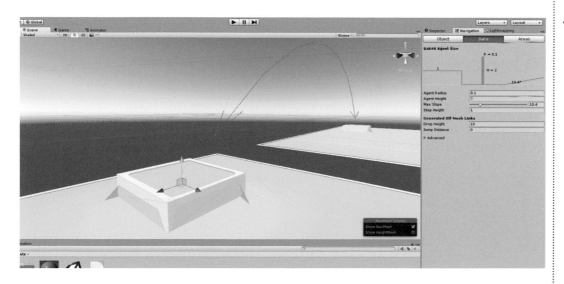

14

9.3 Random Locations, Nearest Locations, and Queries

Given a generated Navigation Mesh with all its off-mesh links, if any, and given a set of agents on the mesh that must move around, there're still many other tasks you'll need to do. Specifically, these relate to the ways agents on the mesh make intelligent decisions about where to move and if they should move at all. Let's explore some of these considerations. ▶15

15

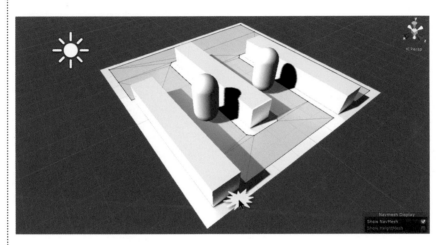

Sometimes, you need the nearest valid point on a Navigation Mesh, in relation to another point. This happens, for example, when the player clicks a location just outside the mesh and you need a character or NPC to walk to the nearest valid location. Code Sample 9.2 demonstrates how to move an agent to the nearest point to any target vector.

Code Sample 9.2: Getting the Nearest Location on a Navigation Mesh

```
01  //Function to move Agent NA to nearest valid location Loc
02  public static Vector3 MoveAgent(NavMeshAgent NA, Vector3 Loc)
03  {
04    //Create tmp dest
05    NavMeshHit Hit;
06
07    //Get nearest location on Navmesh from Loc within 10m
08    if(!NavMesh.SamplePosition(Loc, out Hit, 10f, 1))
09    {
10      //No nearest location found - return start post
```

```
11        return NA.transform.position;
12    }
13
14    //Move agent to position
15    NA.SetDestination(Hit.position);
16
17    //Return the destination position
18    return Hit.position;
19 }
```

NOTE

To see this code in action, as well as more, please see the book companion files. Consider the folder *Chapter09\ navmesh_ queries*.

Another challenge: Given an enemy and a player character on a single Navigation Mesh, you may want to know if the enemy has a direct path, or line of sight, to the player character. If so, the enemy should move toward the player, using the Navigation Mesh, until they reach attacking distance. Conversely, if no direct path exists between the enemy and player, the enemy may need to do nothing, or else should wander until they find the player. Code Sample 9.3 determines whether a direct path exists between two agents A and B.

Code Sample 9.3: Determining if a Direct Path Exists Between Two Agents on a navmesh

```
//Check if direct line of sight exists between two agents
public static bool LineOfSight(NavMeshAgent AgentA, NavMeshAgent
AgentB)
{
    //Create tmp dest
    NavMeshHit Hit;

    //Return whether there was a line of sight
    return !NavMesh.Raycast(AgentA.transform.position,
AgentB.transform.position, out Hit, -1);
}
```

In addition, you'll sometimes need a patrolling character, like a wandering enemy, to pick a random point on the Navigation Mesh as their new destination. Code Sample 9.4 shows you how to do this.

Code Sample 9.4: Move to a Random Position on the NavMesh

```
//Move agent to random destination
public static void MoveToRandom(NavMeshAgent NA, float Radius)
{
    //Get random location
    Vector3 RandomDest = Random.insideUnitSphere * Radius;

    //Create tmp dest
    NavMeshHit Hit;

    //Get nearest point on NavMesh
    if(NavMesh.SamplePosition(RandomDest, out Hit, 10f, 1))
    {
      //Move agent to position
      NA.SetDestination(Hit.position);
    }
}
```

Alternative Applications: Line of Sight and Visibility

Line of sight testing for creating enemy AI, as we've seen here above, is not necessarily enough for our purposes as it stands. The *NavMesh.RayCast* function tells us whether the enemy has an uninterrupted line to the player and whether the player is "near enough" to be seen. But it doesn't actually tell us whether the enemy is oriented toward and is looking at the player. It could still be the case that the enemy was "looking away," in which case they wouldn't see the player, regardless of how close they were. We can fix this by using vector dot product. See Code Sample 9.5.

Code Sample 9.5: Line of Sight

```
//Function to determine if enemy can see player
//Agent = The enemy character
//Target = The player who may be seen
//NearDistance = How close player must be within field of view
//FieldofView = Viewing angle enemy must have to be classified as
facing player
public static void CanSeeAgent(Transform Agent, Transform Target,
float NearDistance, float FieldofView)
{
```

```
//Determine if player is within field of view
Vector3 VecDiff = Target.position - Agent.position;

//Get angle between look at direction and player direction
from enemy
float Dot = Vector3.Dot(Agent.forward.normalized,
VecDiff.normalized);

//If player is behind enemy, then exit
if(Dot < 0) return;

//If player is not within viewing angle then exit
if(FieldofView < (90f - Dot * 90f)) return;

//Enemy is facing player. Is player within range and is there
a direct line?
NavMeshHit Hit;
if(!NavMesh.Raycast(Agent.position, Target.position, out
Hit,-1))
{
  //Has direct line, is within range?
  if((Agent.position - Target.position).sqrMagnitude >
  NearDistance) return;

  //Can be seen (the enemy (Agent) can see the player
  (Target)
  Debug.Log ("I can see you");
}
}
```

NOTE

To see this code in action, see the book
companion files, *Chapter09\LineOfSight*.

9.4 Mouse or Tap Picking

Most gamers on a PC use a mouse, and nearly everybody using a mobile device needs to tap. Both inputs have something in common: specifically, they refer to particular screen positions. A mouse click and a tap both happen at a specific screen coordinate. The question then arises as to how you can retrieve a list of all objects in the scene that overlap the click location, based on the view from a specific camera. This question is important because, when a user clicks on objects in the scene, it's usually to make something happen to them. Code Sample 9.6 will make all clicked objects disappear when attached as a component of a camera object. Notice: this code retrieves a list of all objects intersecting the click location, not simply the nearest object. ▶16

16

Code Sample 9.6: ClickPicker.cs—Code to Pick Objects Based on Mouse Input

```
01  //-----------------------------------
02  using UnityEngine;
03  using System.Collections;
04  //-----------------------------------
05  public class ClickPicker : MonoBehaviour
```

```
06  {
07    //Camera component
08    private Camera ThisCamera = null;
09
10    //-------------------------------------
11    // Use this for initialization
12    void Awake ()
13    {
14      //Get camera
15      ThisCamera = GetComponent<Camera>();
16    }
17    //-------------------------------------
18    // Update is called once per frame
19    void Update ()
20    {
21      //Check mouse input
22      if(Input.GetMouseButtonDown(0))
23      {
24      //Convert screen position into a ray directed into scene
        along camera forward vector
25        Ray ray = ThisCamera.ScreenPointToRay(new Vector3
          (Input.mousePosition.x, Input.mousePosition.y, 0f));
26
27        //Cast ray against scene objects
28        RaycastHit[] Hits = Physics.RaycastAll(ray, Mathf.
          Infinity);
29
30        //Check all hits
31        foreach(RaycastHit Hit in Hits)
32        {
33          //Hide intersected object
34          Hit.collider.gameObject.SetActive(false);
35        }
36      }
37    }
38    //-------------------------------------
39  }
40  //-------------------------------------
```

NOTE

To see this code in action, see the book companion files, *Chapter09\ mouse_picking.*

Physics, Collisions, Pathfinding

9.5 Frustum Checking

Protruding from the camera lens is a trapezoidal volume determining everything the camera can see in the scene, based on its position, orientation, field of view, and clipping planes. This volume is known as the **Frustum**. Visible objects within the frustum may be rendered by the camera, and objects outside will not be rendered (they are said to be **Culled**). Within the frustum, it's still not guaranteed that an object will be visible, because **Occlusion** affects object visibility: that is, nearer objects within the frustum can obscure objects further behind, leaving them partially or even fully hidden. But putting occlusion aside, it's still useful to know whether an object, such as an enemy character or power-up, can currently be seen by the camera. This is useful because, if we can establish that an object is not visible, there are behaviors (like animations) that we can suspend to save computational expense. After all, if behaviors are not visible, then the player will never know when we suspend them. For this reason, it's helpful to have a frustum checker script in your toolbox. See Code Sample 9.7 for code that checks whether an object is within the viewing frustum. ▶17

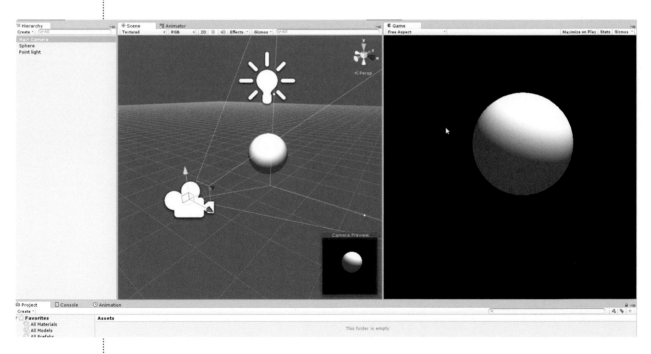

17

Code Sample 9.7: Camera Frustum Check

```
//Function that returns true when meshrenderer is within camera
frustum
public static bool CheckFrustum(Camera Cam, Renderer MeshRender)
{
    //Get frustum planes
    Plane[] planes = GeometryUtility.CalculateFrustumPlanes(Cam);

    //Test if renderer is within planes
    return GeometryUtility.TestPlanesAABB(planes,
MeshRender.bounds);
}
```

9.6 Microgravity: Jumpy Physics

"Jumpy physics" is an affect usually applied to player characters in first-person mode. It's the ability to jump much higher than usual and, after jumping, it takes much longer returning to ground level. The effect of gravity seems much weaker. This effect is easy to create and is useful for many circumstances, including: outer space scenes, underwater scenes, and even "death-match" environments. This section shows you just how easy this is to create. ▶18

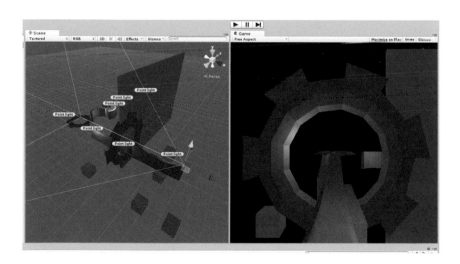

18

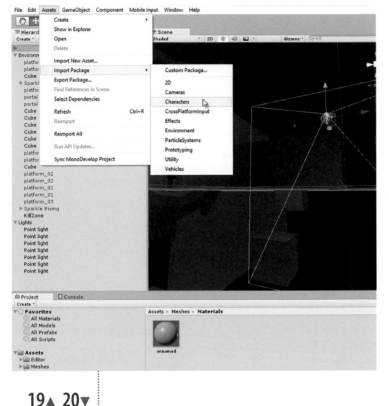

19▲ 20▼

Add a first-person controller to the scene, alongside objects for the level, including a ground plane. The Unity first-person controller can be imported via the standard asset packages, by selecting *Assets > Import Package > Characters* from the application menu. ▶**19**

The first-person controller prefab features a *FirstPersonController* component, offering various properties for controlling the motion and behavior of first-person movement. To create jumpy physics, two properties from the Object Inspector are essential, namely **Gravity Multiplier** and **Jump Speed**. The exact values for these properties will vary depending on your environment. In short, Gravity Multiplier controls how strong gravity is applied to the character: higher values increase gravity, resulting in faster falls after jumping. For this reason, Gravity should be low (such as 0.6 or 0.8). Jump Speed refers effectively to the jump power: higher values increase the jump height. I've used a value of 15. ▶**20**

NOTE

To see jumpy physics in action, see the book companion files, *Chapter09\jumpy_physics*.

9.7 Cloth Simulation

Would you like a pair of curtains that flex, curl, and twist realistically in the wind? I thought so. Unity offers an interactive cloth feature, which accepts a mesh asset and can bend and contort it to simulate cloth and fabric, like leather, silk, cotton, and others.

NOTE

A complete cloth project is included in the book companion files at *Chapter09\ Cloth*.

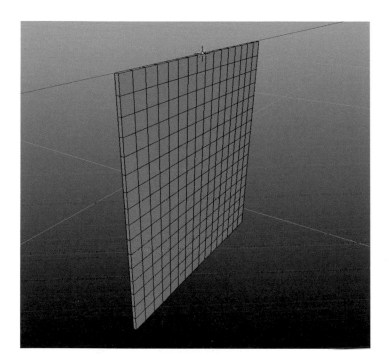

Let's see how to set up a manual cloth mesh in Unity 5. First, create a Plane object or else import a ready mesh from any 3D modeling application, like Maya, 3DS Max, or Blender. ▶21

21

NOTE

When modeling for cloth simulation, be sure to give your model clean, orderly, and evenly spaced edge loops in rows and columns. If you don't, then your model will not deform as anticipated—some parts twisting and curling more than others.

Import your cloth model into Unity and add it to a scene, named *Curtain*. Or else use a Plane mesh. Then remove the mesh renderer component, if it has any, as well as any animator components. To do that, click the *Cog* icon for each component and select *Remove Component* from the context menu. Cloth objects have separate and specialized renderer components, which must be used instead of the regular ones. ▶22

22

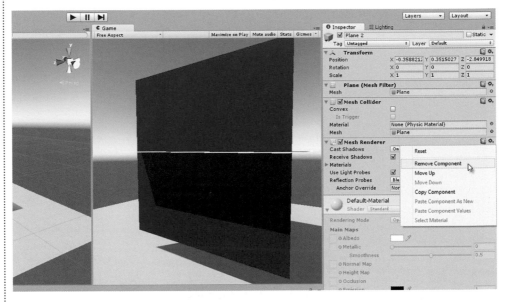

Next, add a Cloth component to the object, using the application menu *Component > Physics > Cloth*. This will also add a Skinned Mesh Renderer to the object. The renderer is responsible for drawing the mesh based on the simulation data. ▶23

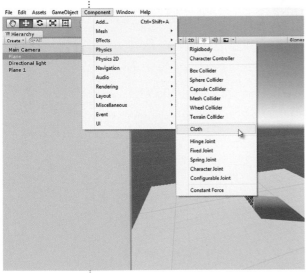

Assign the *Mesh* field of the *Skinned Mesh Renderer* component with the curtain mesh, via the Object Inspector. Simply drag and drop the mesh asset from the Project Panel into the *Mesh* field. After doing this, the cloth mesh should be visible in the Scene Viewport, thanks to the *Skinned Mesh Renderer* component, although the mesh will probably appear textureless. ▶24

Assign a material to the *Material* field of the *ClothRenderer* component to apply a material to the cloth mesh. This can be any appropriate material. ▶25

23

246

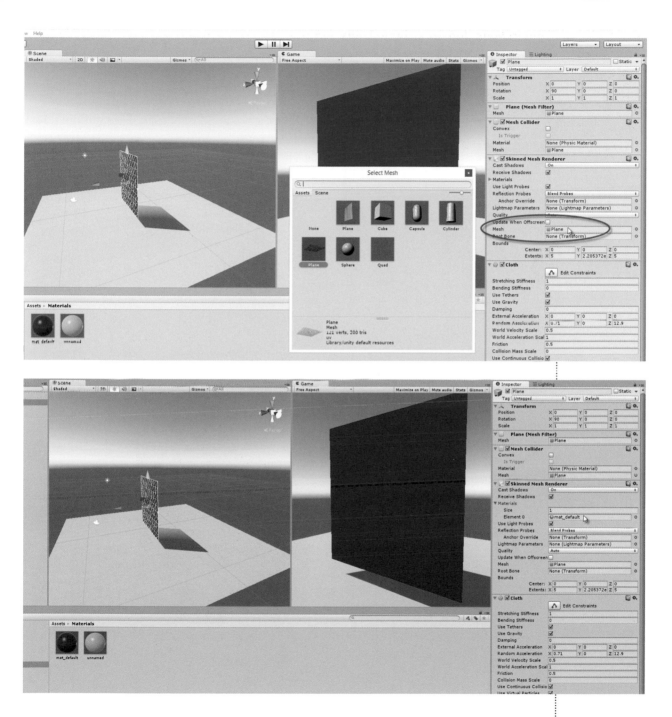

24, 25▲

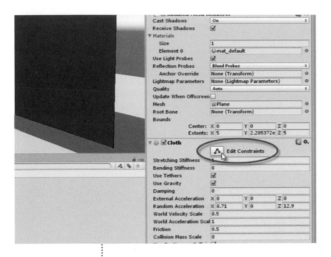

For materials that must hang, like curtains, they'll need a structure to "hang onto." This is achieved using Vertex Weighting. That is, you can choose which vertices should remain in place, holding the structure to a fixed point in the scene. To define this, click the *Edit Constraints* button, from the *Cloth* component in the Object Inspector. ▶26

26

This displays the Cloth Constraints Dialog. Enter *Paint Mode* by clicking the *Paint* button. ▶27

27

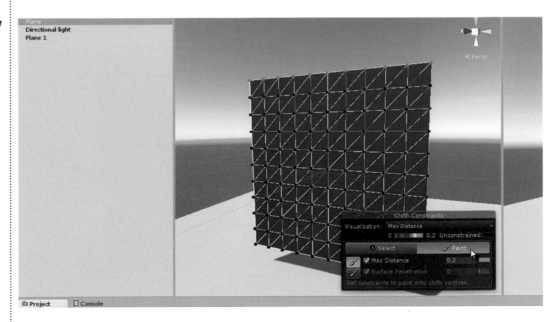

Then click on the top row of vertices in the curtain mesh to paint them Green, locking the vertices in place. This keeps them in position, allowing the curtain to move and sway, as opposed to dropping to the floor from gravity. ►28

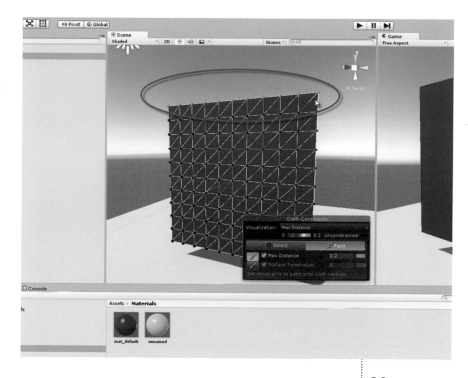

28

Finally, you'll need to apply a physical force (wind) to the curtains for them to move and deform. You can apply either a constant or variable force—these forces are applied in world space and not local space. For this example, a random force will suffice. For *Random Acceleration* in the Object Inspector, I've specified *0.71* for *X* and *12.9* for *Z*. ►29

29

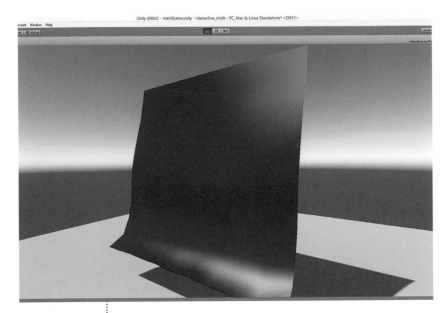

Now, on pressing the *Play* button, you should have a fully working, and very believable, cloth simulation in Unity. ▶30

30

Alternative Applications: Flags
Maybe you didn't want curtains, anyhow? Maybe you'd rather a flag instead? Well, this is easily achievable by just reusing the curtains we've created already. Simply select the curtains and rotate them 90 degrees around the local X axis, orienting them like a flag. Then just change the random acceleration forces for the *Cloth* component. ▶31

31

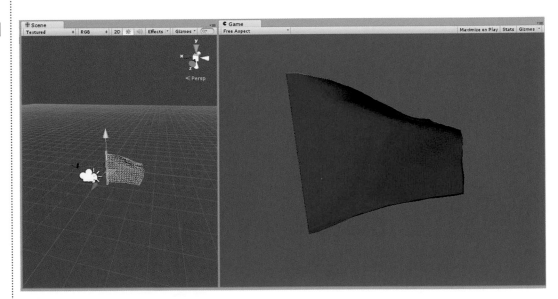

9.8 Triggers and Region Marking

Player movement is critical for video games in many respects, and not just for allowing the player to change their location over time. Video game worlds do, in an important sense, differ from the "real world": specifically, they're "made by" and "exist for" the player. As the player enters a room, a monster may crash through the wall, cause a scene, and launch an attack. Though the gamer may not reflect much on this, it was nonetheless necessary for the player to enter the room and, effectively, make the event happen—simply by moving where they did. The basic point is that the event would not have happened at all, *if* it

32

hadn't been for the player moving into the relevant position. If we reflect on that philosophically, there's something absurd about it. But, what really matters is that it just looks believable to the player. This event, and many others, therefore depend on the player moving around. To create these kinds of behaviors in Unity, we can use triggers. Triggers let us use collider volumes to mark out passable volumes or areas in the level, and we can execute custom behaviors when the player enters, leaves, and stays inside them. Let's see how these work.

To create a trigger, create a new and empty object in the scene. Then attach a box collider to this by selecting *Component > Physics > Box Collider* from the application menu. ▶32

By default, newly created colliders act as impenetrable walls or solid volumes preventing physical bodies, like character controllers, from passing through. In the case of triggers, however, we want to allow the player entry into them so we may detect the intersection and launch relevant events. To achieve this, simply mark the collider as a trigger by enabling the *Is Trigger* checkbox from the Object Inspector. ▶33

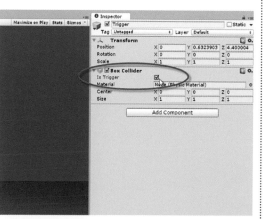

33

To detect player intersections with the trigger, Unity offers a series of *MonoBehaviour* events, specifically *OnTriggerEnter*, *OnTriggerExit*, and *OnTriggerStay*. These events depend on the player, or another colliding object, having a *RigidBody* component attached. *OnTriggerEnter* is called automatically when the player enters the trigger volume, *OnTriggerExit* is called when they leave, and *OnTriggerStay* is invoked continually once per frame for as long as the player remains inside the trigger. Code Sample 9.8 can be used, for example, as a script for a lava pit object, in which the player's health is damaged for as long as they step on the lava. Notice that a GameObject tag check is made when the event is called, to establish the identity of the object that entered the trigger volume. ▶34

Code Sample 9.8: lava_pit.cs—Lava Pit Script Using a Collider Volume Trigger

```
01  using UnityEngine;
02  using System.Collections;
03  //-------------------------------
04  public class lava_pit : MonoBehaviour
05  {
06    //-------------------------------
07    //Amount of health to reduce on player per second while
      standing in lava
08    public float HealthReductionRate = 5.0f;
09    //-------------------------------
10    //Called each frame for object within trigger
11    void OnTriggerStay(Collider Col)
12    {
13      //First check if colliding object is player
14      //Check is important because non-player objects called
        also enter volume
15      if(!Col.gameObject.CompareTag("Player")) return;
16
17      //Is player, now get player component attached to object
18      //Player component contains health variable
19      player PL = Col.GetComponent<player>();
20
21      //Now reduce health at rate
22      PL.Health -= HealthReductionRate * Time.deltaTime;
23    }
24    //-------------------------------
25  }
```

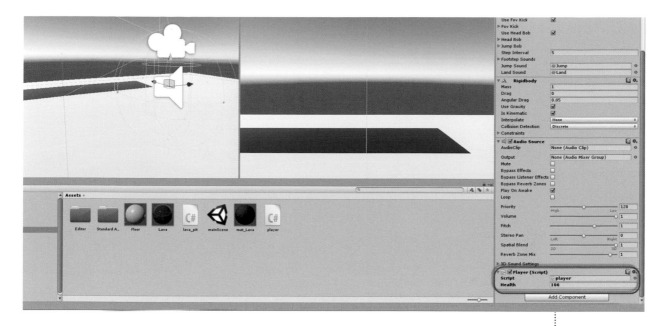

Alternative Applications: Line of Sight

And trigger volumes bring us to the issue of line of sight, which is something we considered earlier in this chapter, in Section 9.3. But triggers offer a possible "line of sight" alternative. Specifically, they can be attached to moving objects, like enemies, too. This means a collider can be attached to an enemy, defining their line of sight and their horizon of vision, and when the player enters (*OnTriggerEnter*), they are classified as "seen."

10

Debugging and Building

When coding Unity games, two main kinds of human-created error arise: these are syntax or "compile time" errors, on the one hand, and Run-Time or logical errors, on the other. Compile time errors, like misspellings and invalid statements, are the easiest to spot and correct because the compiler, at compile-time, simply refuses to compile your code until the errors are corrected. Logical or Run-Time errors, by contrast, cause no compilation errors. Their problematic nature is *not* about incorrectly written statements, which can be easily identified and fixed, provided you know the language rules. But rather, they're about how both correct and valid statements combine together into an overall logic that has unforeseen and troublesome consequences when put into practice. For these latter error types, debugging is required. This is a process of using various development tools to both identify and fix the source of Run-Time errors (errors that happen when the game is running). In an ideal world, the process of debugging would come to an end when all bugs were found and removed, leaving us with a "bug-free" application. But in practice, this aim must be moderated. First, it's not possible to know if all bugs have been removed, simply because (in any software) there may be unidentified bugs that our testing process didn't detect, but which *still exist* and *would* manifest themselves under a different set of testing conditions that we didn't foresee. And second, even among the identified bugs, time and budget may allow only a specific subset of "game-critical bugs" to be corrected. In all cases, however, we'll need to use the Unity debugging tools, and this chapter can help you improve your workflow for using them.

10.1 *Debug.Log* Statements

The most "basic" form of debugging is achieved by the *Debug.Log* statement. In short, any *Debug.Log* statement will print out a string-based message to the Unity console window when executed at Run-Time. *Debug.Log* is not restricted to printing only string literals, such as "Hello World," but also numerical values such as floats and ints and bools, by using their native *ToString* method, which is supported for all C# object types. This member converts an object's internal values into a human-readable string. The primary use of *Debug.Log* is to help a programmer understand program flow, such as whether a specific function is called or whether a specific line is reached, and what variable values are at that time. Consider Code Sample 10.1. ▶1

1

Debug.Log versus Print. Unity supports two functions for printing text to the console, *Debug.Log* and *Print*. The *Print* command, though easier to remember, relies internally on a call to *Debug.Log*, and for this reason is "technically" slower, albeit marginally. In general, then, *Debug.Log* is to be preferred, although ideally all calls to *Debug.Log* and *Print* will be removed from your code for the final build.

Code Sample 10.1: Using *Debug.Log* to Print Console Messages

```
01   // Use this for initialization
02   void Start ()
03   {
04     //Print start function message with current
       system time
05     Debug.Log ("Start function began at:
       " + System.DateTime.Now.ToString
       ("hh:mm:ss"));
06
07     //Enter loop
```

```
08    for(int i=0; i<10; i++)
09    {
10      //Print loop iterator
11      Debug.Log ("For Loop i=" + i.ToString());
12    }
13  }
```

10.2 Overriding *ToString*

The *Debug.Log* statement is especially convenient as a debugging tool. This is because it's easy to use and works for all versions of Unity, in all operating systems, and it doesn't depend on the code editor you use, whether MonoDevelop, Visual Studio, or another. In assembling *Debug.Log* statements, it'd be great, however, to have more control over how a specific object responds to the *ToString* method. When coding your own custom objects, you'll want control over the actual string returned from *ToString*, allowing you to generate more descriptive and meaningful text that's helpful when debugging. Well, you can do this, by simply overriding the *ToString* method in descendant classes! See Code Sample 10.2. ▶2

Code Sample 10.2: Overriding *ToString* to Improve Debugging of Objects

```
01  //Sample Ogre enemy class
02  //This class outputs its member variables to a string from
    the ToString function
03  //-----------------------------------
04  using UnityEngine;
05  using System.Collections;
06  //-----------------------------------
07  public class EnemyOgre : MonoBehaviour
08  {
09    //-----------------------------------
10    //Sample variables for Ogre enemy character
11    //These will be included in the string output from ToString
```

```
12    public int Health = 100;
13    public int Strength = 10;
14    public int Mana = 0;
15    public int Defense = 10;
16    //---------------------------------
17    // Use this for initialization
18    void Start ()
19    {
20      //Print this object to console via the ToString method
21      Debug.Log (this.ToString());
22    }
23    //---------------------------------
24    //Override the ToString method using the 'override' keyword
25    public override string ToString()
26    {
27      //Return your string here
28      return "EnemyOgre Object: " + GetInstanceID().ToString()
      + " Health = " + Health.ToString()
29        + " Strength = " + Strength.ToString() + " Mana = " +
        Mana.ToString() + " Defense = " + Defense.ToString();
30    }
31    //---------------------------------
32 }
33 //---------------------------------
```

10.3 Error Logging

One problem with using *Debug.Log* statements is that you, as a developer, only see and respond to them via the console window, when playing and debugging games from the Unity editor. If you send compiled versions of your game to testers, who could be anywhere worldwide, they won't necessarily have the benefit of viewing any *Debug.Log* statements. They won't be running your game inside the Unity editor. And, in most cases, they won't even have the benefit of detecting or observing errors at all, except those that either crash the game or result in immediate and visible effects in gameplay. In all other cases, errors (or the causes of errors) pass unnoticed, and we want to solve that. Specifically, we can create an error logger feature. This detects errors, as and when they happen, and records them inside a text-based log file, using human-readable statements,

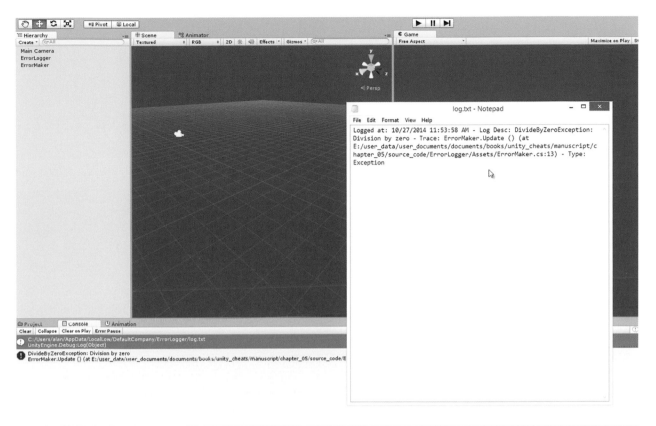

and saved externally to the application. This file can then be sent by testers back to us, the developer, for closer inspection. This helps us see what went wrong for the tester during their play session, and perhaps lets us reproduce the error on our system to begin solving it. The following class in Code Sample 10.3 (ErrorLogger.cs) can be added to an application for recording any errors to a text based log file. ▶3

3

Code Sample 10.3: ExceptionLogger.cs—Logs Errors to a Text-Based File

```
01  //--------------------------
02  using UnityEngine;
03  using System.Collections;
04  using System.IO;
05  //--------------------------
06  public class ExceptionLogger : MonoBehaviour
```

```
07  {
08     //Internal reference to stream writer object
09     private System.IO.StreamWriter SW;
10
11     //Filename to assign log
12     public string LogFileName = "log.txt";
13
14     //---------------------------
15     // Use this for initialization
16     void Start ()
17     {
18       //Make persistent
19       DontDestroyOnLoad(gameObject);
20
21       //Create string writer object
22       SW = new System.IO.StreamWriter(Application.persistent
       DataPath + "/" + LogFileName);
23
24       Debug.Log(Application.persistentDataPath + "/" +
       LogFileName);
25     }
26     //---------------------------
27     //Register for exception listening, and log exceptions
28     void OnEnable()
29     {
30       Application.RegisterLogCallback(HandleLog);
31     }
32     //---------------------------
33     //Unregister for exception listening
34     void OnDisable()
35     {
36       Application.RegisterLogCallback(null);
37     }
38     //---------------------------
39     //Log exception to a text file
40     void HandleLog(string logString, string stackTrace, LogType
       type)
41     {
```

```
42        //If an exception or error, then log to file
43        if(type == LogType.Exception || type == LogType.Error)
44        {
45           SW.WriteLine("Logged at: " + System.DateTime.Now.
             ToString() + " - Log Desc: " + logString + " - Trace:
             " + stackTrace + " - Type: " + type.ToString());
46        }
47     }
48     //---------------------------
49     //Called when object is destroyed
50     void OnDestroy()
51     {
52        //Close file
53        SW.Close();
54     }
55     //---------------------------
56  }
57  //---------------------------
```

10.4 Debugging with MonoDevelop

The two central drawbacks to using *Debug.Log* for debugging is, first, that it requires you to edit the source code itself and, second, it can "spam" the console confusingly when inside loops. Ideally, when debugging, you want to take up a position outside the code, inspecting it from the outside looking in without ever changing it, except to correct a bug once found. *Debug.Log* corrupts this ideal. To resolve this, we can use MonoDevelop's debugging feature set, which consists of many tools. The most critical is the breakpoint. This lets you mark a line in a source file at which execution should pause, or suspend, when it's reached. Here, the developer may inspect the state of the application and its variables, and continue execution on a line-by-line basis, monitoring program flow as it unfolds. This can all be achieved without changing the code. Let's see how. ▶4

NOTE

A sample application using MonoDevelop debugging can be found in the book companion files in *Chapter10\ monodevelop_ debugging*.

10 Debugging and Building

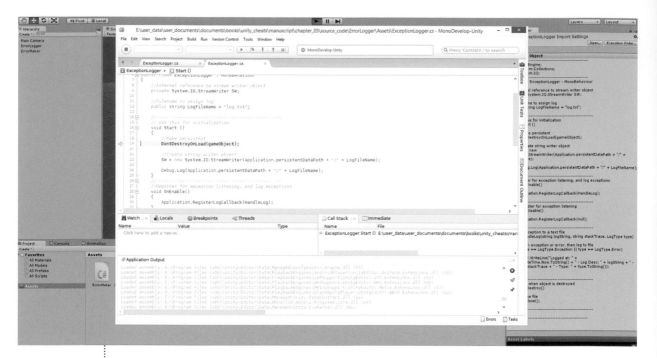

▲4

5

To get started at setting a breakpoint for debugging, choose a line in your source file where execution should pause for inspection, and then choose *Run > Toggle Breakpoint* from the MonoDevelop application menu, or else press the keyboard shortcut F9. After setting the breakpoint, the line turns red and a red circle mark appears in the margin. ▶5

6

Next, you'll need to attach MonoDevelop to the Unity Editor as a connected process, allowing MonoDevelop to detect when Unity enters Play-Mode and when gameplay should be observed. To do this, choose *Run > Attach to Process* from the application menu. ▶6

7

From the *Attach to Process* dialog, choose the Unity Editor from the process list. If you don't see it listed, then make sure the Unity Editor is running, and make sure *Unity Debugger* is selected from the *Debugger* drop-down list. Then choose the *Attach* button. ▶7

Then switch back to Unity and click the *Play* button to run your game inside the *Game* tab. Execution automatically pauses when a breakpoint line is executed, and the Unity Editor is suspended completely, waiting for your input from MonoDevelop.

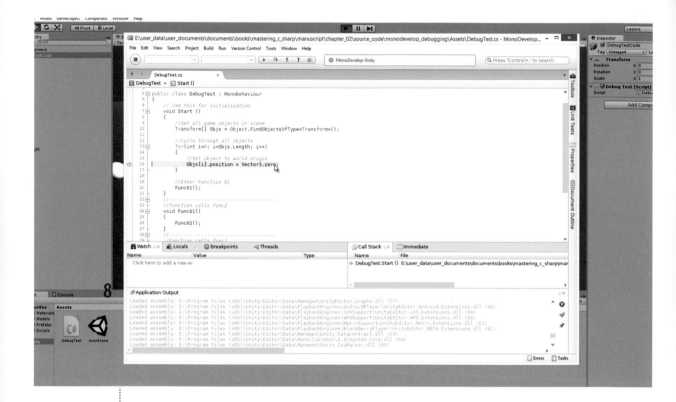

In this mode, you cannot even stop playback of the game from the Unity Editor—you'll need to provide further input via MonoDevelop. ▶8

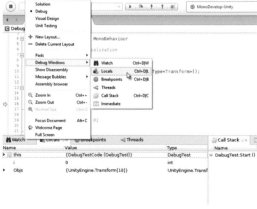

When the breakpoint is hit, the active line highlights inside MonoDevelop. From here, you can use the *Locals* tab to inspect the current state and values of all variables in scope—both local variables of the function as well as class variables. If you don't see the *Locals* tab in the MonoDevelop interface, you can display it by selecting *View > Debug Windows > Locals* from the application menu. ▶9

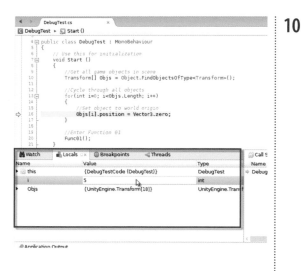

In addition, you can even use the *Locals* tab to *assign* values to the variables, simply by clicking the *Value* field and entering a new value. ▶10

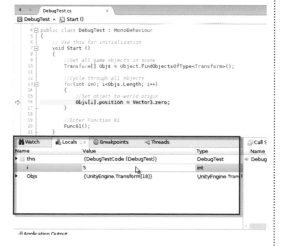

When execution reaches the breakpoint, you'll need to decide how execution should proceed. You can *Step Over*, *Step Into*, *Continue*, or *Stop*. *Step Over* is accessible via the application menu at *Run > Step Over* (or via the F10 keyboard shortcut). This continues execution on a line-by-line basis within the current function, as though a breakpoint were set at each subsequent line. Like *Step Over*, *Step Into* continues execution line by line, but lets you "go inside" any called functions too. *Continue* will resume execution as normal, back in the Unity Editor, unless another break point is encountered. And finally, *Stop* will terminate execution of the game, returning focus back to the Unity Editor. ▶11

10.5 Gizmos

In addition to MonoDevelop debugging, as well as debugging from the Unity Editor through the Object Inspector in Play-Mode, Unity also offers "visual debugging." This refers to a range of methods available from the Gizmos class that can draw wireframe helpers on and around objects to assist in debugging. Or at least, to better help you understand how your program is working. For example, the *Gizmos.DrawWireSphere* function will draw a wireframe sphere of a specified radius around an object, which can be used to graphically illustrate an object's range or line or sight or area of influence. The Gizmos themselves do not change the object's behavior, but simply let us graphically represent concepts and variables inside the viewport to make debugging simpler. ▶12

12

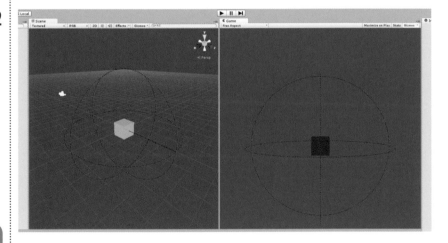

There are two immediately important uses of Gizmos: one is to represent look-at direction, by drawing a line along an object's line of sight. This lets us see which way an object is heading or facing. And the other is to represent area, volume, or a range for an object, such as the attack range of an enemy character. Code Sample 10.4 will draw a look-at direction and spherical radius around an object, using the native Gizmos class and the companion *OnDrawGizmos* event, which is called automatically by Unity on each frame for an object to render any Gizmos.

Code Sample 10.4: GizmoCube.cs—Draw Two Helper Gizmos Around a GameObject ▶13

```
01  using UnityEngine;
02  using System.Collections;
03
04  public class GizmoCube : MonoBehaviour
05  {
06    //Show debugging info?
07    public bool DrawGizmos = true;
08
09    //Called to draw gizmos. Will always draw.
10    //If you want to draw gizmos for only selected object, then
      call
11    //OnDrawGizmos
12    void OnDrawGizmos()
13    {
14      if(!DrawGizmos) return;
15
16      //Set gizmo color
17      Gizmos.color = Color.blue;
18
19      //Draw front vector - show the direction I'm facing
20      Gizmos.DrawRay(transform.position, transform.
      forward.normalized * 4.0f);
21
22      //Set gizmo color
23      //Show proximity radius around cube
24      //If cube were an enemy, they would detect the
      player within this radius
25      Gizmos.color = Color.red;
26      Gizmos.DrawWireSphere(transform.position,
      4.0f);
27
28      //Restore color back to white
29      Gizmos.color = Color.white;
30    }
31  }
```

13▼

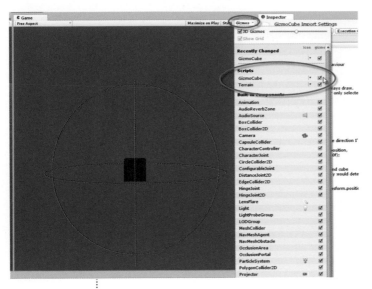

To see Gizmos on an object in either the *Scene* or *Game* tabs, it's important to have Gizmo Drawing enabled. To enable Gizmo Drawing, click the *Gizmos* button from the viewport toolbar, and ensure Gizmo Drawing is enabled for your object in the drop-down list. ▶14

14

10.6 Trace Points in MonoDevelop

Despite all the benefits offered by MonoDevelop with its debugging feature set, it may be that you're only after a substitute for the *Debug.Log* statement, but one that doesn't require us to change the code itself. That is, a means of printing specific messages to the console, but without having to insert *Debug.Log* statements into the code, making them tedious to remove. The debugging feature of "trace points" allows us to do this. They

15

work much like breakpoints, considered earlier, insofar as we mark lines in the code without changing it, but once the lines are executed at Run-Time they don't pause execution, like breakpoints. Instead, they simply print a message to the console—the MonoDevelop console. In addition, they come with some added benefits over *Debug.Log*: specifically, we can add *conditions* to the trace points, allowing them to be invoked only when specific conditions in code apply. Let's see how these work.

To insert a new trace point at a line, select *Run > Add Tracepoint* from the MonoDevelop application menu, or else use the keyboard shortcut *Ctrl + Shift + F9*. For this example, I'll insert a trace point into a for-loop. ▶15

The trace point creation dialog will show, offering two text fields. The top field *Trace Text* defines the text to print to the console when the trace point is encountered at Run-Time. This can be a complete string literal, but can also include the values of variables using the {X} syntax, where X is a variable name. Thus, the string value: *hello {MyName}*, will print the world "hello" followed by the string contained inside the variable *MyName*.

In addition to the *Trace Text* field, there is the *Condition* field. This specifies a condition in code, which must evaluate to true for the trace point to be considered "met." Only when the condition evaluates to true when encountered will the trace point text be printed to the console. Thus, a condition of *i>=3* will only execute the trace point if a variable *i* is greater than or equal to 3. ▶16

16

Once the trace point is added, the associated line will be highlighted in red inside the code editor, and a diamond icon appears in the margin, as opposed to a circle, visually differentiating a trace point from a breakpoint. ▶17

17

Remember, for the trace point to work at all, you'll need to attach MonoDevelop as a running process to the Unity Editor before playing your game. To do that, choose *Run > Attach to Process* from the application menu. ▶18

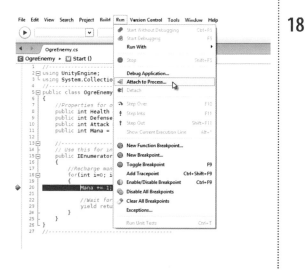

18

19

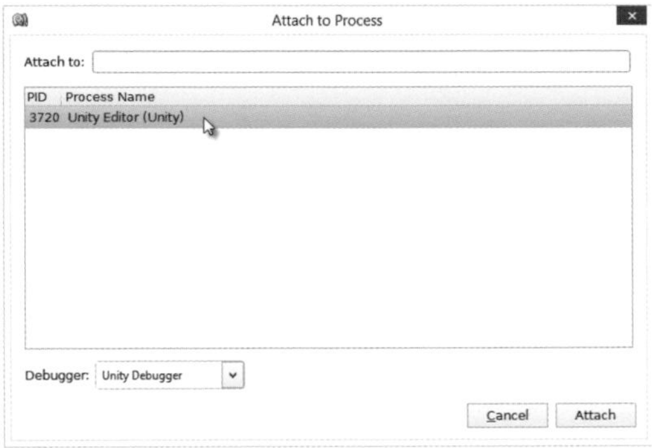

Then select Unity from the process list. If Unity is not listed there, make sure the Unity Editor is running on your system. If it is, then try restarting MonoDevelop. ▶19

20

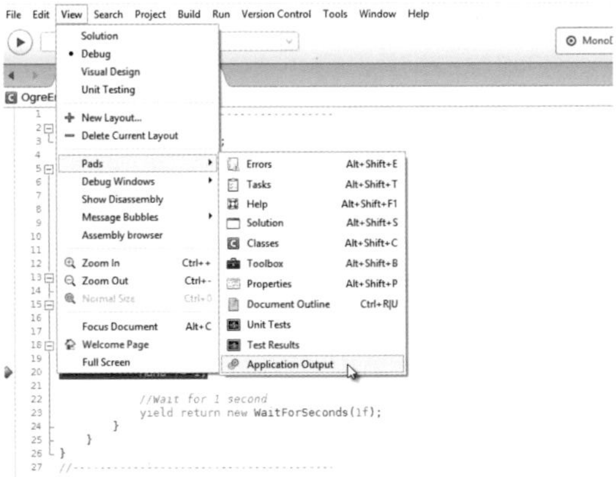

Then run your game in the Unity Editor and the trace point will be executed, as appropriate, if the condition is met. When that happens, the message will be printed to the MonoDevelop console, known as the *application output window*. This can be displayed in the interface by choosing *View > Pads > Application Output*. ▶20

NOTE

Make sure the Unity Editor has focus while running your game, otherwise execution will be automatically suspended and the application output window in MonoDevelop will not be updated.

The application output window is a text-based console in which messages are printed. You can clear the console contents at any time, using the *Clear* button. ▶21

21▼

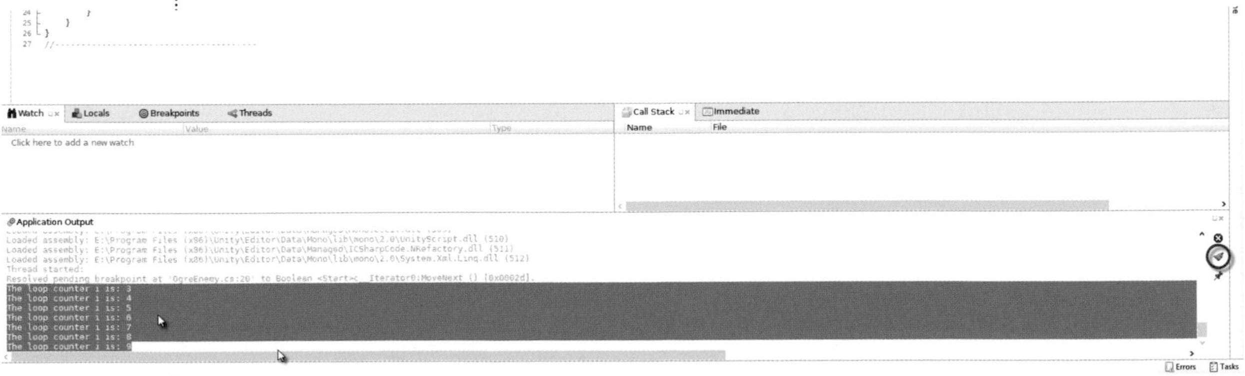

10.7 Debugging the Globals

One lesser-discussed area where "issues" and "quirks" arise has little or nothing to do with your code nor with your scene nor with your assets. You may find your game behaves or looks slightly differently as a build than in the editor, or that your graphics are not looking as good as intended in the final build but you cannot explain why, or there's something just wrong with the game but you cannot describe what, or perhaps you cannot get audio to play at all, or other quirks like these. More often than not, these issues do find their causes in script or with specific assets, but sometimes the cause is elsewhere—specifically, in the global settings of Unity. Let's now look at some of these.

Muted or Distorted Audio

If audio seems muted globally, or if it plays too fast or slow, or if it plays entirely in mono, you may want to check out the global audio settings, known as the audio manager. To access these, choose *Edit > Project Settings > Audio* from the application menu in the Unity Editor. ▶22

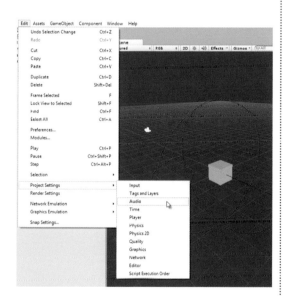

22

The default audio settings should be *Volume*: 1, *Rolloff Scale*: 1, *Speed of Sound*: 347, *Doppler Factor*: 1, *Default Speaker Mode*: Stereo, *DSPBuffer Size*: Default, and *Disable Audio* is not checked. ▶23

23

10 Debugging and Building

24

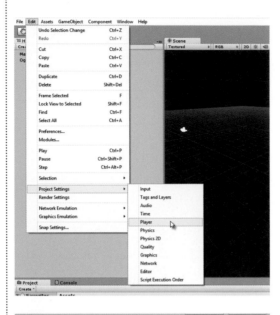

Automatic Pausing

If your game automatically pauses or suspends when the window is deactivated, and if you don't want that, it can be changed easily. The alternative is to have your game continue running, as normal, when the window is in the background. To achieve this, select *Edit > Project Settings > Player* from the application menu. ▶24

25

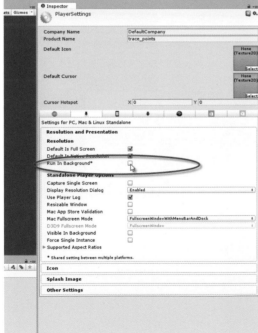

From the Object Inspector, expand the *Resolution and Presentation* tab, and enable the *Run in Background* checkbox. ▶25

Quality Mode

Your game may look great when played in the editor, and perhaps even when run as a standalone build on *your* system. But, as soon as you migrate it to another system for play testing, it looks a lot worse or, at least, decidedly different. This could be caused by application quality settings. To access these, select *Edit > Project Settings > Quality* from the application menu. ▶26

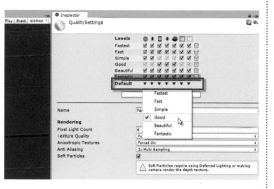

26

Unless the gamer is given the choice of quality settings and resolution for the game, the game will run at its default quality settings and resolution, depending on the features supported by the graphics hardware for the system. These settings may be different from what you intended or expected. You can see and change the default quality settings for your game for any platform, by clicking the downward-pointing arrow at the bottom of each column. For each quality setting, make sure each gives the results you expect, and tweak and amend if necessary. ▶27

27

10 Debugging and Building

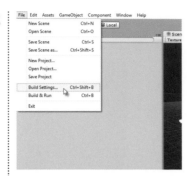

28

29

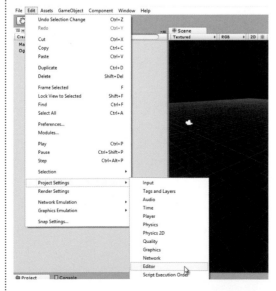

30

Unity Remove Doesn't Work!

You're making a mobile game and want to test it in-editor, using your mobile device as a controller. You can do this using the Unity Remote App, which can be downloaded for free from Android and iOS devices by way of their respective official app stores. Once installed, however, you should just need to connect your device to the computer's USB port and run your game in-editor with the Unity Remote App running on the device, after switching to the Android and iOS target platform inside Unity. To switch platforms, select *File > Build Settings* from the application menu, to display the *Build Settings* dialog. ▶28

From the *Build Settings* dialog, select your target platform and click the *Switch Platform* button to apply the changes and configure the Unity Editor. ▶29

If the Unity Remote App is still not working after this: that is, the Unity Remote App has no affect or connection to the Unity Editor, then make sure Unity Remote is activated in the Editor. To do this, select *Edit > Project Settings > Editor* from the application menu. ▶30

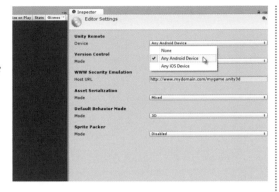

31

From the Object Inspector, check the *Device* field for Unity Remote is set to your mobile device, and not to *None*. ▶31

10.8 Script Execution Order

Each script in Unity is derived from MonoBehaviour, a crucial base class for creating components. This means all Components handle (or implement) a standard set of native events that Unity calls automatically, including *Awake*, *OnEnable*, and *Update*. *Awake* is called when an object is first created in the scene, *OnEnable* is called when an object is activated, and *Update* is called once per frame for as long as the object is active. The technical problem with these events in a scene with many objects is that you simply cannot rely on their call order. You *can* know, for example, that an *Update* function will be called for every object on every frame, but you *cannot* know which object among them will be the first to receive that *Update* call, nor which will be the last, nor any calls between. The order is, by definition, arbitrary—and so, even if there's an order in practice, you shouldn't rely on it as being consistent for all systems or even for play sessions on the same computer. This isn't necessarily a problem, and hopefully is not. Most of the time, you can design your objects and scripts to be independent of this order—and you should strive to do so where feasible. But, maybe the order is important for you in some cases. What happens then?

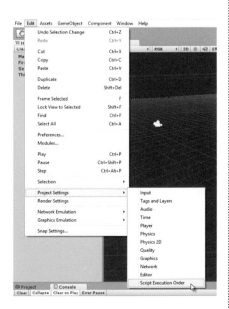

32

Unity offers the *Script Execution Order* manager, letting you stack specific scripts into a sequential list, determining their event order for the *Awake*, *OnEnable*, and *Update* events. To access this feature, select *File > Project Settings > Script Execution Order* from the application menu. ▶32

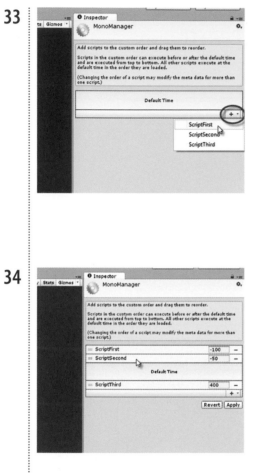

33

34

From the Object Inspector, you can adjust *Script Execution Order*. In this scheme, there are three main forms or time blocks of "order." These are: *Before Default Time*, *Default Time*, and *After Default Time*. *Default Time* refers to the "usual calling order" applied to all scripts that you don't explicitly include in the *Script Execution Order* list: these scripts will continue to be executed in the arbitrary order. Scripts arranged in the *Before* section will *all* be called *before* any other scripts in any later sections, and they'll be called in the specific order you choose. The same logic applies for the later sections. To get started, click the + icon to add all relevant scripts to the order list. It doesn't matter initially where they're added, as the order can be changed. ▶**33**

Next, you can specify the call order of scripts within the list simply by dragging and dropping each script into its appropriate place. Then click the *Apply* button to confirm the changes. ▶**34**

NOTE

A sample application using the Script Execution Order feature can be found in the book companion files in *Chapter10\ script_order*.

Index

Index

Index